Victorian Farm

Alex Langlands, Peter Ginn
and Ruth Goodman

Rediscovering Forgotten Skills

PAVILION

We dedicate this book to all the nameless men, women and children, throughout the British Empire, whose back-breaking labour fed the nation.

This edition published in the United Kingdom in 2009 by Pavilion Books

First published in the United Kingdom in 2008 by Pavilion Books

An imprint of Anova Books Company Ltd
10 Southcombe Street
London W14 0RA

Produced in association with Lion Television Ltd, 26 Paddenswick Road, London W6 0UB

Design and layout © Pavilion Books, 2008
Text and photography © Lion Television Ltd, 2008

Project Editor: Nina Sharman
Designer: Martin Hendry
Cover designer: Georgina Hewitt
Associate Publisher: Anna Cheifetz
Location photographer: Laura Rawlinson

ISBN 978-1-86205-871-2

A CIP catalogue record for this book is available from the British Library.

10 9 8 7 6 5 4 3 2 1

Reproduction by Mission Productions, Hong Kong
Printed and bound by 1010 Printing International Ltd, China
www.anovabooks.com

CONTENTS

INTRODUCTION

VICTORIAN FARM REPRESENTS a unique journey back in time. A specialist team – Ruth Goodman, Peter Ginn and Alex Langlands – have devoted a year of their lives to re-creating life in a 19th-century rural environment. From the warmth of summer to the depths of winter, they have turned the clock back over a hundred years to rediscover a forgotten world from an age gone by.

Their endeavour has been painstaking. They've lived out everything that a Victorian farmer would have undertaken – from planting crops to animal husbandry, from building work to cookery, from tree-felling to operating period machinery. And they've done it all using only the tools and materials that would have been available to them back in 1885.

How It Came to Be

Victorian Farm was undertaken, primarily, as a television project for the BBC. I first worked with Ruth, Alex and Peter back in 2004 when I had the pleasure of producing a series called *Tales from the Green Valley* in which they ran a farm as it would have been in the year 1620 for a full calendar year.

From the warmth of summer to the depths of winter, they have turned the clock back over a hundred years.

Alex and Peter were jobbing archaeologists with a wealth of experience. They proved more than adept at getting their hands dirty – in fact, what impressed me most about them was their enthusiasm for getting stuck in. They seemed to thrive on every task no matter how arduous. What's more they carried with them a wide range of historical knowledge and practical know-how, which they applied to everything. They have the happy knack of being able to use almost any artefact they come across to effortlessly link the past with the present.

Ruth is a historian and a leading authority on Tudor and Stuart period costumes. She was the principal historical advisor to Shakespeare's Globe Theatre. But it soon became evident that there was seemingly no limit to her expertize on social and domestic history. Food was one of her particular enthusiasms – she came equipped with a vast range of recipes and cookbooks and even proved adept at organizing the farm's vegetable garden.

The thing Alex, Peter and Ruth really brought to the screen was a sense of 'have-a-go history'. We're all used to seeing academics trudging around fields and ruins telling us about events from the past, but watching Alex, Peter and Ruth gives you a really vivid sense of what it was actually like to be there. Never mind what it says in books or what theories academics come up with. They roll up their sleeves and actually do it, and very quickly find out what works and what doesn't. While they're doing it, they convey a sense of exactly how it feels to undertake the tasks of the past.

Alex, Peter and Ruth have a natural on-screen chemistry and work exceptionally well together, and when we finished *Tales from the Green Valley*, I was keen to find another vehicle for them. The obvious thing to do was to repeat the farming experiment in a different era where we would learn significantly different things about living in the past. I very quickly settled on the Victorian period. The more I thought about it the more convinced I was. And the more I discussed it with Alex, Peter and Ruth the more enthusiastic they were.

WHY VICTORIAN?

Two things struck me about Victorian Britain. The first was that it was pivotal in connecting the old and new, the traditional and the modern. It's the last period in our history when traditional crafts and ways of doing things existed in daily life before being completely outmoded and replaced by mechanization. The second factor was that many of us are connected to the era having grown up with older relatives who lived through the period.

I thought a lot about my grandmother. When I was a child she would tell me about life on the Victorian farm she grew up on in Sturminster Newton, Dorset. Her father was a former farm labourer who established a successful business as a coal merchant. He acquired land and soon owned a sizeable farm growing crops and raising livestock.

The world my grandmother conveyed seemed to me one of strange contradictions. The motor car had been invented,

THE ERA

Everyone associates the 19th century with the Industrial Revolution. But what's often forgotten is that the Industrial Revolution would have been impossible without the Agricultural Revolution that went with it. The population of Britain nearly tripled in 100 years – from 5.7 million in 1750 to 16.6 million by 1850. And all those extra mouths had to be fed.

A revolution in farming methods – equal to the revolutionary advances in industry – was taking place. It was threefold:

- *New agricultural science – such as four-course 'Norfolk' crop-rotation – which enabled infinitely more efficient use of land for both growing crops and feeding livestock.*
- *New inventions – such as Jethro Tull's famous Seed Drill.*
- *New breeding methods produced more robust and profitable livestock.*

In 1750, three-quarters of Britain's population lived in the country. By 1850, the nation's demographics had been turned upside down – 72 per cent of the population lived in towns/cities. But more efficient farming and new technology enabled a reduced rural population to produce enough food to feed the nation.

Both Shorthorn and Longhorn cattle graze the rich pastures of the Acton Scott estate.

but on the rare occasions that one approached the village, a man with a red flag walked ahead of the vehicle to warn people of its approach. (A tale I never actually believed until, while researching this project, I came across a Victorian photograph of a car being led through a village by a man on foot with a flag.) There were gramophones, but they were so rare that you'd probably have to walk miles to a county fair to see and hear one. Flushing toilets, running water, street lights, gas and electricity, motor vehicles – most of the things we associate with the modern world – all existed, but they were not in common use. And these new marvels tended to exist in cities. It would take a generation or two before they became common in the countryside. In most people's daily lives, oil lamps, candles, coal fires and horse-power persisted.

This was a world that was being transformed by mechanical invention, but was still dependent on traditional practices. It's a tantalizing mixture of old and new. Revolutionary technology sits side by side with centuries-old customs and methods. However, even if there were still many features of life that we'd recognize from the past, this was very much an industrial age. Thanks to the Empire, the range of materials available had massively expanded. Industrial production had increased the range of goods and tools that were available. And thanks to the railways, the movement of resources was far greater than before. All these developments served to influence the way farms were run.

LOCATION

Finding a location for our Victorian Farm project was a big challenge. Even if we'd had the budget to construct a Victorian Farm from scratch (which we didn't!), we did not have the timescale to build one. So we needed somewhere that contained authentic historical buildings in an un-modernized condition. And we needed somewhere that was not open to the public in order to not only run it ourselves but also to have the freedom to film what we needed for a television series.

The vast majority of buildings that date back to Victorian times have been thoroughly modernized and would require major structural work to return them to anything like their original condition. Those that have not been modernized are usually in a desperate state of disrepair, and the few sites that have been preserved or restored are usually open to the public.

For a while it seemed we were going around in circles trying to find the right location. Then we discovered Acton Scott estate in Shropshire. I met Rupert Acton who runs the estate and we quickly identified parts of the estate that would be perfect for our project.

Glebe Farm provided a farmyard area of exactly the size that a small tenant farmer of the period would typically operate. It contained a barn, hayloft,

Acton Scott Hall as it was in 1885, its occupants dressed for a cold winter's day.

cowshed, horse stalls and chicken coop. The farm buildings were not only Victorian but full of period tools and equipment (even including an unopened bottle of 'Horse Tonic' over a hundred years old!). The only modern intrusion in the farmyard was a pebble-dashed shed, which we quickly ear-marked for demolition and conversion into pigsties. The farmyard adjoined a field that would be perfect for grazing. There was also arable land available nearby for growing crops. And best of all there was Henley Cottage, uninhabited since 1945. Although in need of some renovation, it was structurally unchanged since Victorian times and perfect for our needs.

Our main mission before the real work of running the farm could begin would be to restore Glebe Farm and Henley Cottage to their former glory. But we now had exactly the kind of authentic period location we'd been hoping for.

Rupert Acton's family have owned the estate for hundreds of years. His father, Thomas Acton, is a leading authority on Victorian farming. His enthusiasm for the period is evident from the impressive and extensive array of Victorian farm tools and implements he has collected on the estate. In an age when most landowners were busy obliterating all trace of the past to modernize their land and buildings, the Actons lovingly preserved much of the history and heritage of theirs.

So great is Thomas Acton's passion for Victorian farming that he turned part of the estate into a Victorian working farm. Nowadays run by Shropshire County

The Glebe farmyard, complete with pigsties and post-and-rail fence built by the team.

Council, Acton Scott Historic Working Farm operates as a kind of living, working museum. It boasts a plethora of restored buildings housing a range of period breed livestock. Its staff run the farm in costume and they even have their own blacksmith and wheelwright. This wonderful site is open to the public six days a week most of the year. So it's not a site we could have based our project in – but the convenience of having its resources nearby, combined with the generous help of the staff, often lent our project an additional layer of authenticity that would have been hard to establish otherwise.

Alex, Peter and Ruth unloading their worldly possessions at the beginning of the year.

I'm very proud of what has been accomplished on the Victorian Farm project – not only by Ruth, Peter and Alex, but also by the production team on the television series (Stuart Elliott, Naomi Benson, Felicia Rubin, Charlotte Spencer, Rebecca Winch and Donna Poole). This book is a comprehensive chronicle of their achievements. It captures not only the detail of the crafts and techniques that they learned over the course of a year, but also the ups-and-downs of farm life as they struggled to come to terms with its challenges. These pages detail the pleasures and the hardships of life on the Victorian Farm.

DAVID UPSHAL
Executive Producer, Lion Television

Meet The Team

Ruth Goodman

 A project like this yearlong exploration of Victorian farm life opens up so many opportunities and, as a social historian, I find it very exciting. Being involved in something in a physical, practical way makes you think in a very different way. I find it the most wonderful discipline. First you read as much stuff as you can, digging through libraries and archives. You check out the secondary sources – what other modern people have thought about it all – and thoroughly enjoy looking at the original material, written by people at the time. Next you go and do it. Not just once, but really do it – and get fairly good at it. Ideas and problems begin to pop into your head. Ummm, you think, I am not sure about this, and you head back to the books. But now, when you read the very same stuff that you thought you had understood before, you begin to see something different emerging, and you hurry back to the farm to try out your new ideas.

Being involved in something in a physical, practical way makes you think in a very different way.

A couple of years ago, Alex, Peter and I spent a year on a 1620s farm – filming *Tales from the Green Valley* – and that revolutionized my thoughts on early gardening. It got me thinking – and the more I thought, the more I realized we were doing it wrong. When the series finished I plunged myself into the books to try and answer all the niggling doubts which the actual practical experience raised. Whole new questions needed to be asked, let alone answered. This is the best bit about history. New ideas buzzing in your head, new connections being made.

Another daft little 'light bulb' moment came one day when I was mucking out the cowshed. My linen apron was in a terrible state. Cows, like all mammals, have greasy hair and when they rub up against you, you soon know about it. Cow grease, hair and mud stains had turned that apron from snowy white out of yesterday's wash into a filthy rag. My woollen skirts, however, were not too bad. It all just brushed off them. 'Ding' went that light bulb – lots of inventories of that period list aprons, and many of them have woollen ones. Wool is not good apron

OPPOSITE *Picking whinberries (bilberries) on the Long Mynd in the height of summer.*

material for cooking in, but what about for working with animals?. Sure enough, when I later had a trawl through, pretty much all the inventories where woollen aprons are mentioned also make reference to livestock, especially cows and dairy equipment. A simple thing, that perhaps I should have thought of before, but I didn't until the reality was there in front of me.

A year on a Victorian farm gives me a chance to test out so many assumptions, to question so many things that I think I know, to try to get under the skin of ordinary Victorian life.

I hope that some of the things I learn will be things that I can bring forward into my modern-day life. Buried in the past are often really great ideas about how to do things better, greener, cheaper, tastier, and I shall be looking out for them along the way.

Alex Langlands

 When the call came through that the Victorian farm project was on, I could scarcely contain my excitement. What seemed like an age ago, we had spent a year on a small hill farm in South Wales living the lives of early 17th-century farmers. The BBC television series *Tales from the Green Valley* had been something of a surprise success story and, whilst the year had been extremely hard work, it had left me with a feeling of wanting more.

And what better opportunity could you get than to spend a year on a Victorian farm, working and living off the land as people would have done over one hundred years ago. During my first visit to the location for the Victorian farm, I was captivated by the preservation of the buildings, tools and implements. The village of Acton Scott, in south Shropshire, was something of a time capsule where, since the 1970s, all of the accoutrements of 19th-century rural life had been conserved as part of a working farm museum. Mr Thomas Stackhouse Acton, landlord of the Acton Scott estate, was primarily responsible, with a host of other enthusiasts, playing a key role in the preservation of late-19th-century life.

What appealed to me so much was that the late 19th century was a period of such drastic change, and it was going to be so interesting to explore the effects of this change on the rural community. Many of the 'old ways' were in their dying days as new technologies swept all before them. Harvesting by hand, both hay and wheat, had been such laborious and back-breaking processes during the making of *Tales from the Green Valley*. By the late Victorian period, however, machines had taken over much of the hard work and, at Acton Scott, an array of fascinating and ingenious farm implements lay dormant, waiting for us to breathe new life into them.

OPPOSITE 'Punk' duck, so called because of his often-shaved appearance and pest-like nature, was one of our favourite characters on the farm.

As an archaeologist I have always had an obsession with the past, but over recent years I was beginning to refine my area of interest. With one eye on the environmental concerns of today, I had developed the mantra: 'Looking to the past for a greener future', and I was keen to find out whether we could learn anything from our Victorian ancestors that might help us to improve the way we do things today.

I was particularly fascinated to discover and find out more about horse-power. It would be one of my major jobs for the year to acquire and develop a working bond with a horse. All in all, though, there were so many aspects of late-Victorian rural life that I was eager to explore – from agricultural practices, animal husbandry, ancient craft skills and mechanization through to Victorian leisure, pursuits and food and drink – I couldn't wait to get stuck into life on the farm.

PETER GINN

 History is a fluid multifaceted entity that we try to tame often by labelling processes and trying to pigeon-hole events such as the Agricultural Revolution(s) and the Industrial Revolution. However, the smaller the phenomenon the harder it is to quantify. As Orwell recounted in an article he wrote in the *Tribune*: when Walter Raleigh was in the Tower of London writing a history of the world he witnessed an argument between two workmen that resulted in the death of one of them. Raleigh made enquiries as to the subject of the argument but was unable to find out what it was about, so he decided to burn what he had written and give up on the project.

We know about large events in history because they are well documented; they often involve or are witnessed by a lot of people, and subsequently they resonate through time. However, it is the everyday events, the day-to-day living, and the personal lives of everyday folk that usually elude us. This is what the Victorian farm is all about for me. It is an opportunity to undertake a series of tasks (many of which are not well-documented) and through practical experience gain an insight into their true nature. We can then juxtapose this against the wider socioeconomic developments of the Victorian period to try to contextualize them.

One of the reasons why I read archaeology at university was because of the balance between the practical and the theoretical. Therefore, one of the major things that I was looking forward to on this project was that everything that I would read about I would do. One can almost touch the Victorian era, but like a dream in the morning, it slips quickly from our memory only leaving an impression of what it was about. However, on this project I actually did touch the Victorian era (and I've got the scars to prove it).

OPPOSITE *Collecting fleeces after a hard day's sheepshearing.*

CHAPTER ONE

THE GOLDEN AGE

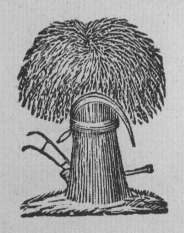

ADVANCES IN AGRICULTURE

GOLDEN AGE TO DEPRESSION

The changes which have been crowded into the last half-century have been so numerous and so important that it would almost seem reasonable to suppose the limit had been reached for the present, and that the next few generations would be sufficiently occupied in assimilating themselves to the new condition of existence.

But so far from this being the case, all the facts of the hour point irresistibly to the conclusion that the era of development has but just commenced.

RICHARD JEFFERIES, 'The Future of Farming', *Fraser's Magazine*, Dec. 1873

Written in 1873, these lines sum up the life that farmers faced as they approached the last quarter of the 19th century. Our vision of rural England as a quintessentially unchanging and timeless pastoral idyll was as much a myth over one hundred years ago as it is today. Indeed, change in the rural economy and the rural way of life could hardly have been more pronounced than in the years 1850–1900. The period in which our project is set was a time during which British agriculture was to experience the highs of a self-proclaimed 'Golden Age' and yet also to plummet into the lows of a

Harvesting wheat in pre-Victorian times with no machinery to help was a very labour-intensive activity.

depression (particularly for those farmers dependent on wheat) from which, it could be argued, it has never really recovered.

In 1846, the repeal of the Corn Laws reduced duties on imports of foreign wheat. Along with the abolition of levies on imports of live animals, meat and dairy products, the British food market was opened up to competition from abroad. Land owners, farmers and agriculturalists were anxious that they would no longer be able to command adequate prices for some of their home-grown goods. However, despite this trepidation there was an undercurrent of confidence in British farming, which was, perhaps, derived from the general mood of self-assurance prevalent throughout the British Empire at the height of its powers.

SCIENCE AND TECHNOLOGY

Advances in the application of science to agriculture, the borrowing of 'factory' processes from industry, huge investments in farm steadings and mechanization were to change the face of rural life irrevocably and to place British farming at the cutting edge of world agriculture. There was increased demand from growing cities, such as Birmingham, Liverpool, Manchester and London, with burgeoning populations whose new, disposable incomes were to stimulate the farmers' market – particularly for meat and dairy products. Finally, the rapid growth of the railways and coastal steamers enabled farmers to reach a much wider market.

Britain was about to enter what many have termed the 'Golden Age' of British agriculture.

Technology alone did not change farming. One of the most significant scientific developments in the fields of England in the mid-19th century was the introduction of chemical fertilizers, which enabled many farmers to break free from the commitments of long-cycled crop rotations.

Sir Humphrey Davy (1778–1829), a British chemist famed for his invention of the 'Davy Lamp' – a miner's safety lamp – had pioneered the chemical analysis of plants and manures and was instrumental in encouraging manufacturers to adopt a scientific approach to production. The German scientist, Justus von Liebig, in *Organic Chemistry in its Applications to Agriculture and Physiology* (1840), proposed applying isolated elements of nitrogen, phosphorus and potassium as the component parts of artificial manures. In particular, he advocated the dissolving of animal bones (hitherto inefficiently either mechanically crushed or burned) in sulphuric acid solution to extract phosphates.

Theory was swiftly put into practice and, after inheriting the estate of Rothamsted (Hertfordshire) in 1834, Sir (then Mr) John Bennett-Lawes founded an experimental station and began to conduct experiments with different chemical manuring substances. So successful were the results that Bennett-Lawes was quick to capitalize on his findings and, by 1842, he was commercially manufacturing Superphosphate manure – a substance derived from adding sulphuric acid to animal bones and mineral phosphate.

With this and many other sources of chemical fertilizer openly available to landowners and tenants of larger farms, productivity soared. By 1870, with over 1,200 artificial manure manufacturers in England and Wales, an average of £3 per acre was being spent on artificial manures. Farmers could now afford to dress their land with the relevant chemicals for whichever crops they wished to grow rather than relying on a crop-rotation system to replenish and restore vitality to the land. Thus farmers could specialize in cash crops, dispense with livestock purely used to generate manure, and more readily respond to market demands.

Similarly, the rise in commercial production of animal feed meant that live-stock farmers could specialize in animal husbandry and were not reliant on home-grown feed. Feed 'cakes' were made from linseed, rapeseed and cottonseed as by-products from other industries, and firms such as Thorley's of Hull and Paul's of Ipswich specialized in their production. In the 1870s over £5 million worth of artificial feed was being sold per year – enough to have fed half of all British cattle.

During the mid-19th century the growing urban population clamoured for more meat, milk and cheese. Farmers responded by developing cattle breeds specifically for either the dairy or meat markets. Sheep, too, were improved to mature earlier and to fatten quicker and, in pursuit of perfection, horse breeders

NATURAL FERTILIZERS

One of the most effective nitrogenous manures was 'guano', from the Peruvian huana meaning 'dung or manure'. To say something of the high esteem in which this manuring substance was held we need look no further than the Peruvian proverb: 'Huano, though no saint, works many miracles'. Guano was sea-fowl droppings that had accumulated over very long periods of time. Many of the soluble ingredients had been preserved due to the hot and dry climate of Peru, and when farmers realized its potency as an artificial manure, demand rose astronomically. Very soon the Peruvian government was handing out contracts to British merchants and as a consequence artificial manures were being shipped half-way

round the world to farms in the homeland. Between 1850 and 1870 the demand grew so high that as many as 200,000 tons (203,200 tonnes) were shipped from Peru in a single season.

Potash, a rich source of potassium found in wood-ash, sea weed and farmyard manure had long been known to be beneficial to crops. Yet it was not widely available to farmers as an industrial manure until the 1860s. In 1859, vast deposits of potash salts had been discovered when the Prussian Government sank an exploratory shaft at Stassfurt in the hope of discovering rock-salt. Consequently, large quantities of potash salts were made available on the British market at prices now affordable to the farming community.

VICTORIAN FARM

NORFOLK FOUR-COURSE ROTATION

 In Europe, from the middle ages up until the beginning of the agricultural revolution in the mid-18th century, the predominant form of farming was by a three-field system in open fields. In each field a crop of wheat would be followed by a crop of barley in the second year and then left fallow in the third year. Then the process would be repeated. However, in the 18th century the open fields increasingly gave way to enclosure (dividing fields up with barriers such as hedges to be farmed by one person). Along with enclosures, certain farming methods began to gain popularity – one of these being the 'Norfolk four-course rotation'.

It is termed 'Norfolk' because it was used and to an extent (often open to debate) pioneered and popularized by Viscount Charles 'Turnip' Townshend and advocated by Thomas Coke, who both had farms in Norfolk. An example of four crops that would be rotated each year is wheat, turnips, barley and clover.

Wheat and barley that survive from the three-field system are known as white crops. They take their nutrients from the soil, which needs to rest to replenish itself. Turnips are a root crop with a long tap root drawing nutrients up from the subsoil. When planted in rows (as they would be because of the machinery used) it was easy to weed between them. In addition, turnips are a fodder crop so they provided a source of food for animals over winter, which otherwise would have had to be culled. The animals such as cattle being sustained by turnips in the winter were, consequently, producing nitrogen-rich manure. White crops such as wheat and barley need nitrogen, and the more they get the greater they yield. Other root crops such as mangelwurzels or fodder beat can be grown instead of turnips.

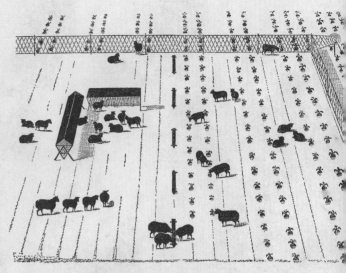

Animals were penned in on a root crop – manuring the field while being fed.

Clover is a green crop and a form of legume, like peas or beans, and is able to extract nitrogen from the air and turn it into protein in their seeds, as well as putting large amounts of nitrogen into the soil (a process known as symbiotic nitrogen fixation). All legumes can do this, but clover is particularly good at it (three times better than the average legume). The types of clover that are usually grown are white or red, and the crop can be ploughed back into the soil as a green manure. Alternatively, sheep can be folded onto the crop and it will act as a fodder crop, while the sheep in turn leave their own special brand of manure on the field. Crops such as mustard or rye grass can be grown instead (as a green manure).

Although four-course rotation was becoming popular in the mid 18th century, it took a while for it to be adopted by farmers, adapted to the local areas and soils, and perfected. There is much evidence to suggest that this development process was continuing well into the 19th century.

Without land drainage, the application of chemical fertilizers would be rendered pointless. This is an example of cutting drainage channels with a horse-powered mole plough.

crossed the strongest and soundest with the best tempered beasts to create the finest draft horses. The very best and magnificent of these new breeds would fascinate audiences at the newly established regional and national shows. Stud books kept records of the most famous breeds and ensured the purity of lineage.

Land Drainage

Another (and much underrated) development was in land drainage. There was little use in investing in large quantities of artificial fertilizers if the land to which they were to be applied was prone to water-logging, thereby rinsing costly nitrates, phosphates and potassium from the soil. The first real breakthrough came in the 1840s with the invention of cylindrical drain-pipe manufacturing machines. Coupled with the Drainage Act of 1845 and the abolition of taxes on clay pipe in 1850, this relatively cheap and efficient method of draining water-logged land was widely adopted. Government ministers recognized the importance of bringing previously untilled land into cultivation, and between 1846 and 1870 some 2 million acres (809,370 hectares) of land were drained at the expense of the public coffers. Private investment on vast drainage schemes by land owners was to surpass even the generosity of cheap government loans.

Mechanization

This Golden Age was also the first major phase in the mechanization of British agriculture. Prior to mechanization, much of the work in the fields and farmsteads of rural England, Wales and Scotland was done by men, women and, in some cases, children. In particular, the harvest would require the whole village community to take to the fields working from dawn till dusk. This practice defined a community and consolidated the bond between landlord, farmer and labourer. Yet, by the end of the 19th century, a wheat harvest could be reaped and bound in the field by machines, mechanically hauled into ricks and then thrashed of its grain by mobile steam-powered threshing machines.

Such mechanization, however, came at a price and for the farm labourer some of his winter earnings came from hand-threshing the heads of wheat with his flail on the barn threshing floor. Mechanization had more of a direct and tangible impact on the lives of the farmers, small tenant farmers and agricultural labourers than any other agricultural advance. In many instances mechanical innovations, be they horse- or steam-powered, were introduced as replacements for human power. Slowly but surely, machines were to take on the bulk of the labour that had previously been undertaken by farm hands who now had little option but to look for work in the factories and industrial complexes of the growing cities. The countryside of late-19th-century England was increasingly depopulated as the general drift to the towns took place.

INFORMATION AND IDEAS

Agricultural developments were discussed in an almost feverish environment of publications, shows, journals and at the newly formed agricultural societies. Information, ideas, new techniques and the most up-to-date advances in scientific application swept the country. In 1844 a landmark publication was to hit the shelves of agricultural literature stockists throughout the United Kingdom. Henry Stephen's *Book of the Farm* was a comprehensive treatise on the practice of farming in Britain. So popular was this seminal work that it was to run to three editions in Stephen's own lifetime and came to be regarded as the standard text on practical agriculture. It was to be one of my first acquisitions as I entered into the business of farming in the Victorian world.

Although the Highland and Agricultural Society had been running since 1784, it wasn't until 9 May 1838 that the Royal Agricultural Society was founded. The first appointed president was the innovator Earl Spencer and the society was to adopt as its motto his favourite saying, 'Practice with Science'. In 1892 the Royal College of Agriculture was founded. Based in Cirencester, the college specialized in educating students on the merits of new farming methods and ran a two-year course costing £60.

James Caird, an agricultural journalist writing in the late 1840s and 1850s, best portrays the vision for British farming during this period of rapid development, improvement and increased productivity. His writing was influential and described this new agriculture as 'High Farming', forcibly arguing that British

Throughout the year, Henry Stephen's Book of the Farm *was always close at hand to offer practical guidance on all things agricultural.*

farmers could overcome the threats of foreign competition by becoming more business-like and progressive.

However, few could foresee the ominous portents that the late 1870s were to bring. High Farming was in essence a finely tuned machine precariously balancing the high levels of capital investment with improved productivity yet increasingly reliant on a population who had become accustomed to cheaper food products. Successively bad wheat harvests in the late 1870s were to drive the prices of some home-grown produce through the roof, and the fears of those who had opposed the Repeal of the Corn Laws some thirty years previously became realized. Cheaper imports flooded the British market place. Grain from the USA, Canada, Ukraine and Russia could be bought at a fraction of the price that British farmers were forced to charge. Cheaper beef from as far away as South America could now be transported directly into the thriving city centres of London, Liverpool, Southampton and Glasgow, thanks to improved reliability in steam shipping. The British sheep-rearing industry was to suffer as a consequence of the developing sheep industries of both Australia and New Zealand, while dairy produce collectives in the Scandinavian nations were able to compete with even the most efficient dairies in the British Isles.

A plethora of Victorian farm implements were lying dormant, waiting for us to breathe new life into them.

For the landed gentry and the capitalist farmers of the Golden Age, bankruptcy was now the popular currency. Funds collapsed and the returns on the massive investments in farm buildings, drainage projects, new machinery and the

other expensive accoutrements of 'High Farming' were never realized. Whilst the towns and cities of the British Isles fed off the fat of the Commonwealth, agriculture and the rural economy had entered the Great Depression.

This, then, is the historical backdrop to the setting of the Victorian Farm. Tenant farmers small and large were staring back at a period of plenty whilst confronted with the uncertainties of the Depression and post-Depression years. The technology that had signalled so much promise during the Golden Age still existed but only what could now be made to pay could be resorted to. Labourers were quick to abandon their hovel-like accommodation in search of better living conditions, wages and security of work in the towns and cities. Farm buildings were altered rather than demolished and rebuilt. In many places a return to 'mixed' farming was the safeguard against the fickle nature of the urban market place. But there was no going back. Mass-produced goods were becoming a feature of town and even village stores. The wheelwright struggled to find

For the landed gentry and the capitalist farmers of the Golden Age, bankruptcy was now the popular currency.

work as American-made wagon wheels could be ordered from catalogues and delivered by rail from London. The bespoke iron-work of the village blacksmith was replaced by standardized fixtures and fittings that could be ordered from catalogues printed as far away as Chicago. Shoemakers no longer serviced the village community in boots, shoes and repairs, as vast factories began to mass-produce and deliver standardized sizes for the nation's feet. The cottage industries that had served the nation so well and for so long were losing the battle against a relentless global market.

VICTORIAN-STYLE FARMING

We were very lucky to take up residence in a farming landscape that had almost stood still for at least 100 years. The history of Acton Scott – both the estate and the historic farm museum – is unique, and an intriguing array of farm buildings, machinery, gardens, orchards, fields, pastures, woods, ponds, tools, animals and people awaited us. Here there was a culture of keeping alive country traditions and a rural way of life now extinct in so many other parts of Britain. The Victorian Farm experience represented an exciting opportunity for us to put ourselves in the situation described by Richard Jefferies, a set of circumstances confronting all rural folk of the late-Victorian period. We had twelve months to immerse ourselves in that world, face up to the challenges that it could throw at us, meet with triumph and disaster in both measure, and bask in a lost rural idyll.

OVERLEAF: Peter on one of his twice-daily rounds, caring for the farm animals.

Renovating the Cottage

Henley Cottage was condemned as 'unfit for habitation' shortly after the Second World War although no one deemed it necessary to tell that to the countless mice, rats, bats and birds that have been residing at number 4 Henley Lane for the past fifty years. 'Filth' is something found in the dark recesses of an average student's bed-sit. We were dealing with mutated über-filth armed only with buckets of cold water, slivers of carbolic soap, brushes, rags and elbow grease. Yes, we were cleaning Victorian style, especially as the Victorians viewed dust and dirt as very unhealthy. Although commercial cleaning products had started to become available, a really efficient cleaning product had yet to be produced – so we had to scrub.

However, Henley Cottage was not just in need of a fifty years overdue bath, we also had to do an awful lot of renovation work. The original staircase needed to be reattached, the gaping hole in the back wall had to be filled (we used some stone and a little window we found on the estate), it was essential to re-lay the stone floor of the kitchen (one tile still has an irritating wobble), and Ruth wanted a nice new range. The existing range, which was a later addition, was extremely corroded and beyond repair but the original fireplace was still intact, although it was bricked up, so we knocked out the stone work of that fireplace and used it to fill in the hole left when we removed the decaying remains of the existing range.

Witches' Marks

Above the blocked fireplace etched into the oak mantel, which was set into the wall, were marks that we first thought to be scratches to give the plaster a key so that it could stick to the wood. However, on closer inspection they appeared to be 'witches' marks'. Basically, where there is an entrance to the dwelling (especially if it has been blocked up) it was customary to make marks to ward off evil spirits and prevent them coming down the disused chimney.

Our New Range

Removing the range was straight forward enough. Although unblocking a fireplace that hadn't been used for well over a hundred years (probably longer) was quite a task – not because it was necessarily hard work, but because of the sheer volume of rubble, soot, dust, organic matter (such as twigs used by birds for nesting in the chimney) and remains of creatures that came out. We started at the top underneath the oak mantel by removing one brick and probing into the chimney with a bar (pretty

scientific stuff). Then we gradually began to remove more and more bricks and, as we did so, more and more debris and detritus came cascading out of the opening until it was difficult to breathe, let alone see. The material was so dry and spewing out of the chimney with such force that it was forming a billowing, rolling cloud of dust that smelt of ash, and the rubble was bouncing on the tiled floor making an incredible racket. Our eyes, ears, noses, mouths and pores were saturated with this sooty material that sucked the moisture out of the air. The whole room was possessed of the centuries-old material that we had freed from its resting place. So, naturally, we left and had a cup of tea while things calmed down.

We all agreed that unblocking old chimneys was one of the most fun jobs we had done in recent times. On our list of items recovered from the chimney were: a piece of stone so big it needed at least two people to lift it; one half of a lower jaw bone of a rat that was as big as my little finger; the remains of a salt pot placed in a little nook up the chimney (in a damp limestone house this is one place that will always be dry and therefore keep the salt from clogging up), and a shoe.

The range fitters, Peter Parker and Steve Powell, proudly surveying their handiwork.

Now that we had unblocked our chimney it was time to fit our range, which I thought would simply be a case of sticking it into the hole. However, like most things on the farm and indeed in life, it was far more complicated than that. Behind the sleek black exterior lay an intricate network of flues and chimneys allowing maximum control of the heat from the fire, and enabling you to use different parts of the range at various temperatures. Essentially, our range had to be 'plumbed in'; it's not just a metal box with a fire in it. Finally, to finish it off we fitted a stone surround and, as stone is porous, we treated it with linseed oil so as to prevent dirt from penetrating the stone.

LIME PLASTERING

However, the major technique that I learnt whilst renovating the cottage was that of plastering – or, more specifically, lime plastering. The bedroom was not too bad and only a few holes in the plaster had to be filled, but most of the downstairs needed to be re-plastered. We started by re-pointing the stone work with a lime mortar in order to make the wall vaguely flat. We were then ready to apply our four coats of lime plaster – two rough undercoats and two fine overcoats. We were

The prospect of cleaning Henley Cottage would wipe the smile off anyone's face.

using lime plaster rather than a modern gypsum plaster because it allows the limestone walls to breathe and therefore does not trap damp, although, unlike a modern plaster, lime plaster takes much longer to dry.

Nothing gets thrown away on the Acton Scott estate and we came across fifteen large bags of plaster fragments that had previously been on the walls of Henley Cottage. We had read that old plaster could be reused. Paul (the stone mason) was dubious that this would work, but we gave it a go and made a fantastic lime plaster for use as an undercoat. The process for making this lime plaster was to smash up the old bits of plaster in a bucket with a posting rod (basically a pole with a weight on the end), then to sift the mix into a container, making sure that the hair has been picked out of the sieve and put back in the mix. When we had three parts of this we added 1–1½ parts of lime putty, one part of red plastering sand, a splash of water and some more horsehair. The hair acts as a bonding material to protect against cracking and to hold the plaster together – in the old plaster we were finding very vibrantly coloured goat hair but we used horse hair as it was available to us (bovine hair is recommended but I felt the local farmers would be angry if I shaved their cows). One mistake I made with the horse hair was to just cut it up. Apparently, one is supposed to beat the hair first to make it lie flat, something that I was told only after the coarse black horse hair started curling out of the distinctly pink plaster. We then mixed this up in a tin bath with a rake until it resembled porridge.

To apply the plaster we used a hawk and a float both made of wood. They are similar to their modern equivalents but due to the grain in the wood they give a coarser finish. The surface to which the plaster is applied needs to be rough and damp but not wet. In addition, the plaster needs to be worked in all directions with the float to get it into all the gaps so that it fully adheres to the wall. I found it almost impossible to plaster ceilings but the walls were fairly straightforward, although it is punishing on the wrists and shoulders. The final coat was a dream to apply; it looked and felt like cream cheese. To finish off the walls we trowelled them up, that is, smoothed the lines and bumps to give a totally flat finish.

During the renovation of the cottage we also reinstated the pantry. We plastered it and tiled the floor and put in a sink, ceiling hooks, wooden shelves, slate shelves and a stone shelf. The purpose of a pantry is for food storage so it needs to be cool – it is, therefore, often situated on the northern side of a house in the shadow of the building and has small windows. A stone shelf is built in primarily for the purpose of reducing the temperature of the room as it absorbs the heat. It also acts as a salting slab.

LIME MORTAR

◉ *This consists of three parts dry lime (or four parts lime putty), five parts sharp river sand, two parts red plastering sand and water*

◉ *Add the water to the mix gradually until the desired texture/consistency is achieved.*

Applying a pale yellow lime wash on the newly plastered walls at Henley Cottage.

THE KITCHEN

The farmhouse kitchen is the powerhouse of both home and farm. Here, everyone comes together, plans are hatched and decisions made. As it was for our Victorian tenant-farming predecessors, Henley's kitchen is a modest workaday space with sturdy and unfussy furnishings, a tough brick floor and plain lime-washed walls. It is the only heated space that we have on the farm and, therefore, it's the place where we spend what little leisure time we have, as well as being the place where we cook, eat, dry the laundry and do the ironing.

When we arrived at the beginning of the year the kitchen was a near derelict shell. Bringing it back into use was a mammoth task. Peter, especially, poured his heart into turning Henley from a building site to a working home and base for the farming year.

Meanwhile, as the agricultural year moved on and our first animals began to arrive, the initial lack of a working kitchen caused a myriad of problems. We found ourselves using a variety of makeshifts, borrowings and favours from our neighbours to get us through. Moving into Henley Cottage was an enormous relief and at last gave us the opportunity to establish some routines.

A TOUR OF HENLEY COTTAGE KITCHEN

CUPBOARD UNDER THE STAIRS Here, all the mops, brushes, buckets and carpet beaters are stored. One hardware catalogue lists 74 different types of brush for use around the home. We have to make do with far fewer than that. But, none the less, you can't use the same brush to black the range and to scrub the table. This is also where we keep the coalscuttle, matches and dry kindling to light the range.

A cinder sifter sits in the corner. Every morning the cinders from under the range are popped in here and sifted. Any intact pieces of coal are then put aside for use in the firebox beneath the copper while the cinders are put in the dustbin. We are saving the cinders in order to surface the garden paths in the spring.

One of the oil lamps in the cottage with a copper disk to reflect the light.

FLOOR A plain, unglazed brick floor is laid directly onto the earth. Middle-class urban homes often had quarry tiles on the floor, but ours is typical of small

Carpet beaters, mop, soap, brushes and buckets are all needed to keep the house clean. The Victorians liked to have a different tool for every job.

farmhouses. I have to sweep it twice a day to control the vast amount of mud that gets walked in. The sweepings are put straight onto the compost heap.

LIGHTING This comprises a number of oil lamps, which have to be regularly filled, the wicks trimmed and the glass chimneys cleaned.

WATER SUPPLY The water has to be fetched from a supply at the side of the cottage. I try to keep a pail of clean water next to the range at all times to save having to nip outside every five minutes.

TABLE A good hardwearing deal table functions both as work surface, dining table and part-time shelf. It gets scrubbed down several times a day with salt and water to keep it clean. I don't like to use soda or borax on surfaces that come into contact with food. I am firmly of the opinion that chemical residues from cleaning products are bound to be harmful to the proper workings of the gut. I have similar worries about the modern cleaning products that are pushed at us all. Both salt and vinegar are good sterilizing agents, as well as being edible.

CLOTHES AIRER Commonly known as a 'Sheila Maid', this is a very handy device (see below) that allows me to get my laundry dry whatever the weather.

RANGE This completely enclosed range dates from the 1890s. The model is 'The Regal' and it was made by Adams & Co. of Shrewsbury. Unfortunately, it doesn't have a built-in water boiler, but I manage by having a large 'fish kettle' full of water always on the go. The shelf acts as a plate warmer, and a handy nail in the over-mantle holds my 'hot-pot' cloth. All the soot that I clean out of the flues is swept into a separate tub and kept for use in the garden.

SWILL PAIL Food scraps and peelings that cannot be turned into another meal are dropped in here ready to be boiled up for the pigs and poultry to eat.

TEA LEAF POT All the used tea and coffee grounds are kept in here ready to be reused for cleaning the floors. When damp tea leaves are scattered on the floors and rugs, the dust sticks to them instead of flying up into the air as you sweep. This makes it much easier to clean a room and saves me from coughing and sneezing as I go.

Doing the ironing in Henley Cottage with the Sheila Maid in action in the background.

Waste Recycling in the Kitchen

Almost nothing went to waste on a Victorian farm. Food scraps, tea leaves, coal dust, rags, sweepings, manure, bones and feathers, all had their uses and were carefully separated and stored. Victorian society in general was keen to recycle absolutely everything. Avoiding waste in the home was presented as a woman's moral duty, not out of environmental concerns but from an economic point of view. Resources in Victorian Britain were scarce, and many people had to do without even the simplest of things. Most people could not afford to waste anything. 'Waste not want not' was a Victorian way of life.

Every last morsel of food in a Victorian farm kitchen was eaten in one form or another, either by people or livestock. The housewife, as a matter of course, was expected to boil up bones to make gelatine, and to render down and save all the fat from whatever meat the family had. One basin for pork fat (lard), one for lamb and mutton fat (tallow) and another for beef fat (suet). Goose and duck fat were especially prized. Stale bread was grated and dried in the oven for later use as breadcrumbs in a variety of dishes.

The Family Save All is a leftovers recipe book. Written in 1861 it typifies the Victorian idea of economy in the kitchen and is full of good ideas about how to turn a bunch of unpromising leftovers into a decent hot meal. Many of these dishes are still firm favourites of traditional British cookery: bubble-and-squeak, corned-beef hash, toad-in-the-hole, pasties, soups and stews.

Anything that people didn't eat became animal food. Some could go straight to the pigs and poultry as it was, and the rest was boiled up with a little water to become swill or 'wash'. In towns you could sell your wash to the 'wash man' who sold it on to pig farmers. On a farm, you cut out the middleman and fed it to your own livestock.

In London, 'wash' from large households, hotels and clubs was often resold for human consumption. There were several shops that specialized in this trade, separating the wash out into: 'meat bones', 'meat pudding', 'sweet pudding', 'pastry' and so forth. Many a poor family managed with the bone out of someone else's ham joint, perhaps with a little meat still clinging to it.

By re-using and recycling as much as possible, a Victorian kitchen could keep people warm and fed with remarkably few resources.

Waste not

As well as foodstuffs, other resources were recycled. Tea leaves and coffee grounds helped to clean floors, whilst cold tea itself was used to wash the windows.

Waste paper was saved to light fires or, if clean enough, was threaded onto string and used as toilet paper.

Feathers were sterilized by being popped in the oven for an hour before filling pillows, mattresses and quilts.

Any piece of clothing or textile that became too worn or stained for further use was cut up to make other clothes. When these were too worn they became rags for use in the kitchen and for cleaning the house. An old flannel petticoat, for example, could have a second life as a vest before becoming a covering for a hot water bottle, a brass polishing cloth and finally a rag for cleaning the range. At the end of its life the rag joins the sweepings from the floor on the compost heap.

Soot and ash were valuable garden commodities as fertilizers, fungicides, pest deterrents and weed suppressants.

Range Cooking

Ranges come in many different shapes and sizes, but are essentially iron boxes that mostly enclose a fire. They are designed to make cooking on coal easier, cleaner and more fuel-efficient. You cook mostly on the hot iron rather than the fire itself.

The simplest and earliest were not really ranges at all but long, thin fire baskets – the shape conveniently contained the coal – with a place for roasting meat, perhaps with bars that could be attached to balance a flat-bottomed pot or kettle on. In many fireplaces it became common to close off the rest of the chimney space around the firebasket. Coal burns best with a good strong draw of air flowing past. The old wide fireplaces were ill-suited to the new fuel, but by simply blocking up most of the space, the airflow was massively improved. As time went by, ranges became more and more enclosed. The chimney became a flue and the whole of the remaining fireplace was covered in iron plates.

One of the first problems people encounter with using a range is the time it takes to get it up to full working heat. You may have a good fire going, but the rest of the range can be stone cold. It feels like an ice age could come and go before an egg will boil. Ranges need to be lit pretty much all of the time. The whole fabric of the range, including the stone and brickwork, needs to be really warm before a cooking heat will develop. A newly installed range may take a week of continuous fire to dry out and warm the walls around it.

Know your Flues

On anything but the tiniest range there will be one or more flues running around the range carrying hot gases and smoke from the fire between and around the cooking spaces before allowing the smoke up the chimney. This is what makes a good range so efficient – all the heat generated by the fire is being put to good use and not just disappearing up the chimney. You need to know where those flues go in order to be able to control

LIGHTING A RANGE

Firstly, clear out the ash from the firebox. Lay the fire using dry paper, straw, twigs and suchlike at the bottom, then a few larger sticks and some small pieces of coal on the top. Open the chimney damper, close all others and light the fire. Once it is burning well, add a couple of larger lumps of coal. Leave for about ten minutes before altering the damper positions. If the fire is glowing or still alight from the previous day, remove any spent ash, and place a couple of dry twigs and some small pieces of coal on the top to get it going.

Blacking the range is one of the dirtiest jobs ever invented.

Henley Cottage's newly installed range. A range doesn't just cook your food and boil your water, it radiates heat from the ironwork and warms your home as well.

the heat. Every range comes with inspection hatches and ways of getting in to clean it, so have a good poke around and work out the path(s) of your hot smoke. There will also be a series of slides, or dampers, which cut off the flow at different points. The dampers allow you to direct the flow of hot gas to where you want it.

Every range behaves differently, even if it is the same model. Therefore, be prepared to play around with different combinations of damper positions, sizes of fire, types of fuel, with and without any removable plates. Feel with your hand where the hotspots are and where the cool areas lie. Once you know the idiosyncrasies of a range you can predict cooking times and control the heat.

THE PANTRY

 A good pantry is both a store cupboard and a fridge all rolled into one. A stone floor and stone shelves, a small window and a north-easterly location means that the temperature remains low without any other help right throughout the year. Even on the hottest of days the butter stays hard and the milk fresh.

A wire mesh across the small window allows air to circulate without letting flies and other pests in. Meat, fish, dairy produce and vegetables all keep very well in the cool and airy environment.

Unfortunately, pantries are not so efficient in centrally heated houses. As our homes have become warmer we have had to find new ways of keeping food cool. There had been iceboxes before in the houses of the rich for help in preparing ice creams and other desserts, but only with central heating did the fridge become more of a necessity and less of a luxury.

Bacteria likes warm, damp conditions in which to grow. When fridges replaced pantries, people encountered a problem. In order to keep the warm atmosphere of the house out and the cold in, fridges are completely sealed boxes. Food inside a sealed box sweats and condensation forms. Fridges, therefore, are not dry environments, but rather damp ones. As bacteria likes the damp, the only way to make a fridge into a safe food storage area is to make it much, much colder – a great deal colder than a nice dry pantry.

Many foods don't do very well in this environment. Cheese, especially, has its flavour spoiled by fridge temperatures, as does fruit. Both cheese and fruit, however, keep well in the cool and well-ventilated atmosphere of a pantry so long as flies and other insects and pests are kept out.

RUTH'S DIARY

Notes on how to use a pantry

Bottom slate shelf: Raw meat only here. This is also the salting slab.
Floor beneath bottom shelf: Space for a dish to catch any drips from the meat above.
Slate space to the side: Useful for beer bottles.
Middle slate shelf: Vegetables keep cool here.
Top slate shelf: For cooked foods and dairy produce.
Bread bin with lid: Prevents bread from drying out too quickly.
Top two wooden shelves: Reserved for pickle and preserves.
Lowest wooden shelf: Ingredients, such as flour and sugar, which need to be kept close to hand.
Hooks: Useful for suspending game, hams and smoked foods away from any animals that may get into the pantry (the cat, for example).
Hanging bags: Loose cotton bags are used to allow airflow but ensure that no flies can get near the hanging meat and fish.
Beaded cloth over jug: A weighted cloth keeps flies out of the milk.
Baskets and barrels under the window and alongside the wall: More vegetables and various grains.

*Detail from the top stone shelf,
where cooked foods and dairy
produce are stored.*

*The pantry at Henley Cottage
provides an excellent cool and
airy storeroom for all types of
food and ingredients.*

Winter Wheat

The first major project on our Victorian farm that I was to get my teeth stuck into was the sowing of a winter wheat – so called because it is sown in late autumn and grown throughout the winter ready for harvest in late summer. I had chosen a long straw variety – Maris Widgeon – as this type was most similar to the types of wheat that were grown back in the late-Victorian period.

Whereas long straw was a commodity back in the 19th century and could be used for anything from thatching to matting and basket making, there is no real call for it in the modern age. Thus, modern strains of wheat have had the stem bred out of the plant so that nowadays the head of wheat develops on a stem that is at best 1–2 ft (30–61 cm) high.

Brian Davis who, like ploughman Jim Elliott, helped us out on the farm. Here, he is with his two grey shire horses, Valiant and Valour, pulling his father's Ransome plough.

PLOUGHING

I was reasonably pleased with the size of the field that we had set aside for arable and I was hoping to use perhaps up to two-thirds for the wheat crop. However, on closer inspection some immediate concerns came to light. The ground had not been worked for arable purposes since the Second World War and consequently a thick grass turf had developed – a sward. This wouldn't normally be a problem as, usually, before ploughing, the grass would be eaten back by livestock – preferably sheep as they nibble the weeds and grasses right back. It was clear that although the field had been reasonably well grazed, there were plants that had since put on a growth spurt in the late summer and they would be difficult to fold in with the plough. Furthermore, there were a number of weeds – dock leaf, hog weed and butter cup – in the mix of grasses and clovers and these were difficult to overcome.

Nonetheless, I was somewhat put at ease by the news that we had acquired the services of champion ploughman Jim Elliott. Jim was a regular at ploughing competitions held throughout the country and was one of the most decorated ploughmen of his generation. He brought with him Prince, a stocky Irish draught horse, and Lion, an enormous black shire horse.

I was itching to get started and to see how the horses would cope with ground that had not been broken up for some sixty-five years, but I would have to put my eagerness aside as we spent the morning 'setting out'. This involved marking out – lightly scuffing a mark with the plough – the centre line of the area to be ploughed to work out from, and the headlands (the part at each end of the field where the horses and plough would turn). This would be ploughed right at the very end. By the time we had finished I realized how important it was to get the 'setting out' just right because the last thing you wanted to have to do was to negotiate a fiddly bit of ploughing at the end of the week when the horses were at their most tired.

The 'setting out' was completed by lunch on day one and finally, after a traditional ploughman's lunch of cheese, bread and an apple, we set about ploughing our field. Regularly, Jim would stop to make ever such fine adjustments to the land and furrow wheels, but towards the end of the day Lion and Prince were happy with what was being asked of them, Jim was happy that the plough was at just the right depth and width, and the sun burst through the clouds promising a good day for ploughing 'on the morrow'.

I awoke early the next day and raced out to meet Jim with the horses in the lane. We tacked up both of them, who, remembering the hard day's work from yesterday, were somewhat reticent to get started. Nonetheless they settled down quickly and, not before too long, Jim had offered me a go of the plough allowing one of my boyhood dreams to come true. For me it was fantastic so soon into the project to undertake one of the oldest farming practices known to man. Kingdoms, nations and empires had been built on this humble and eternal ritual and the inevitable persistence of working the ground to grow food to give life was something that I was thrilled to be a small part of.

Jim Elliot, a champion ploughman helped us to plough the field along with his horses, Prince and Lion.

I very quickly discovered that ploughing wasn't something you picked up in an afternoon, and after a couple of extremely 'wonky' furrows, I handed it back to the master.

SOWING

After a week of light wind and rain, the ploughed soil had settled and was almost ready for sowing. Firstly, to get an even surface and a fine tilth, we would have to drag a set of spike harrows over the field a few times. A horse-drawn seed drill would then be used to sow the seed into rows of wheat. The final stage was then to run over the ground with a heavy Cambridge roller to close the drills up and to press the seed snugly into the seed bed.

I had spent the previous fortnight in search of a Victorian seed drill that we could use but had not had much luck. Mr Acton recalled that he had used one some forty years ago and took us on a rambling walk across fields and marsh to an old disused cow barn where he recalled he had last seen it. When we found it we were dismayed to see that, although it still seemed to have all its working parts,

THE SEED DRILL

Sowing seed with a seed drill represents one of the key developments in the history of farming and allowed a significant rise in yields. It is Jethro Tull, one of the leaders in a movement that has come to be known as the English Agricultural Revolution, who we have to thank for this innovation. The Tull drill for wheat, described and illustrated in the first edition of his seminal work *Horse Hoeing Husbandry* (1733), may be considered typical of his machines but, despite the huge benefits demonstrated from using this new technology, drills were slow to take off. Indeed, in the early 19th century, they were so scarce that travelling drills went from Suffolk to as far afield as Oxfordshire.

Traditionally, broadcast sowing had been used to scatter the seed on to the ground. This involved men pacing up and down the field flinging arced handfuls of grain evenly across the surface. A degree of rhythmic accuracy was called for and a steady hand to distribute evenly. However, it exposed much of the grain to the hungry eyes of pigeons, crows and other pests.

The seed drill cuts a thin groove – a drill – into the surface of the soil with a coulter or 'tongue'. It then mechanically delivers the seed via iron tubes from a wooden hopper box into the bottom of the drill. Rolling the ground afterwards closes the drills on top

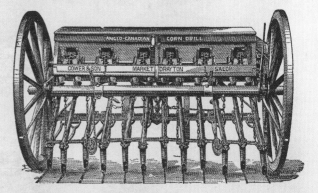

Gower and Son's two-horse Anglo-Canadian seed drill from Market Drayton, Shropshire, is identical to the one we used.

of the seed and presses the earth down around it to create the contact required for successful germination.

The uniform depth and thickness with which the grain is deposited is one benefit of using a seed drill but perhaps the main advantage is that the rows between the young wheat plants can be hoed using a horse-drawn hoe. Weeds had always been the farmer's perennial enemy and the only method to eradicate them had been to use labourers to hand-hoe the field. With a horse-drawn hoe, so much more acreage could be covered, many of the larger weeds knocked back and the yields drastically increased.

By the mid-19th century, drills were gradually beginning to become a regular feature of arable farming and at the 1843 exhibition of the Royal Agricultural Society held in Derby, sixty-one drills, pressers and seed-sowing barrows were shown. Our drill dated from the early 20th century but was a model that was first manufactured in the early 1890s. It had twelve drills to drag through the ground and could be pulled by, depending on the amount of work to be done, up to three horses. The Industrial Revolution and the growth of urban populations lent its encouragement to more efficient methods of agricultural production.

A four-wheel 'Drill Plough' with a seed and manure hopper (1745).

they were heavily corroded, riddled with wood worm, or completely seized up. Peter and I scratched our heads, realizing that we had a major restoration project on our hands if we were to use this 100-year-old seed drill.

I ws beginning to doubt that we would be able to get a crop in the field before the winter set in, but mercifully help was soon at hand. In a conversation with Brian Davis, a local horseman, I mentioned our seed drill woes. Brian had worked horses from a very young age behind a wide range of farming and tillage implements. He had built up a collection of ploughs, harrows, reapers, rollers and, as it happened, a Victorian seed drill.

Illustration from the Book of the Farm *of someone using a hand broadcast sower or 'seed fiddle' (see page 60).*

With the barometer at Acton Scott Hall suggesting a fine stretch of weather, Brian and his team of impressive shire horses, Valiant and Valour, arrived to help us with our next round of field work. Very soon the horses took to the work ahead of them and, after making light work of the harrowing, it was time to fill up the seed drill hopper and hitch it up.

It was vital to make sure that we didn't under sow the field. We also had to ensure that we didn't over sow. The danger in this is running out of grain before the field is finished and sowing it so thick that it competes against itself and does not grow as well as it should. There is an ancient rhyme that is often quoted when sowing seed (see right).

Brian offered me the reins but I knew this task required a steady hand and highly skilled horsemanship. My job was to watch the grain dropping in to the drill and to make sure none of the coulters or 'tongues' got blocked with clods of earth.

After only a short strip we decided to increase the volume of grain sown and steadily set off to complete the field. With that done, I was allowed to drive Valiant and Valour around the field towing a large Cambridge roller. This was exciting as, although the two horses had worked alongside each other many times before, they had never worked in tandem.

One for the rook,
One for the crow,
One to let rot,
One to let grow.

At first it was a tricky task to keep them on the straight and narrow, but gradually they got the jist of what I was asking them to do and by the time the sun was beginning to hang in the sky the first step in our arable project was well underway. Sure enough, we would have more to do in the spring, but with the winter wheat in the ground I could rest easy.

Brian had been a great help and it had been really useful to get a master class in horsemanship and horse-drawn agriculture. I had had a taste of working with horses and was keen to acquire my own draught beast. As I expressed my new-found interest, Brian mentioned he had a certain someone in mind … and a month later Clumper arrived on the farm.

THE WALLED GARDEN

When I first came to visit Acton Scott, one of the features of the estate I was most excited about was the walled garden that sat hidden behind a belt of tall pine trees a short distance to the south-east of Acton Scott Hall. Like most country houses of its time, Acton Scott had a walled kitchen garden, which would have supplied all-year-round fresh fruit and vegetables for the occupants of the Hall, its staff, perhaps some of the estate staff and, on some occasions, for local markets.

By the Victorian period, the walled kitchen garden had reached its zenith and was capable of such sophisticated productivity that it could provide all but the most exotic fruits throughout the year. In many ways, the walled garden was to become one of the grandest status symbols of the country estate, and few places on an estate reflected better the aspirations of the Victorian landed gentry. For in such gardens we not only bear witness to the inventiveness and creativeness of the Victorian ideal but also the adherence to a strict social hierarchy that is evident in the relationship between head gardeners, gardeners and their young apprentices.

ORIGINS

It is difficult to determine the exact origins of the modern walled garden, but its history would appear to be a long one. Depictions of gardens similar in design to those found in late-19th-century Europe can be seen in Egyptian paintings, and classical scholars, such as Theophrastus and Pliny, wrote extensive treatises on plant husbandry, botany and medicine. Such works would have been studied and copied by medieval scholars – particularly those from monasteries. It is perhaps to the English monastic garden and herb garden that we should look to for a more direct ancestor to the late-Victorian and Edwardian walled garden. The skills for tending these gardens would have been passed down from generation to generation with new techniques being periodically introduced from abroad.

The result of what is clearly a long tradition of gardening in the temperate climate of Great Britain was the walled garden of the late 18th and early 19th century. By this period, so wide was the range of fruits, vegetables and herbs grown that gardens became compartmentalized. Those gardens that had no room to cater

One of the first crops we planted in the walled garden were leeks, which proved to be successful.

There is always plenty of work to be done in the walled garden, including ridging the potatoes.

for new interesting plants and innovative techniques were moved to more suitable locations and often set a distance away from the country house so that their increasingly industrial character did not offend its residents. Two key developments in the Victorian period, the repeal of both the Brick Tax in 1855 and the Glass Tax in 1845, allowed for some monumental changes to the design of walled gardens. Most significantly, greenhouses became a standard feature and in many cases different designs were used for different purposes.

Walled gardens were at their peak during the period from the early 19th century through to the early 20th century. Large teams of gardeners would have been responsible for ensuring that fresh fruit and vegetables, along with flowers and herbs, would be available the whole year round in some measure.

It is not hard to understand why walled kitchen gardens fell into decline. With a rapidly depopulating rural work force, exacerbated by the losses of the First World War, the cost of labour soared. Consequently, operations would have needed to have been scaled back and the cost of heating the various glasshouses, conservatories and greenhouses would have been prohibitive to most landowners

Chard and onions left to go to seed for sowing next year.

THE GOLDEN AGE 49

during and beyond the Second World War. It was against an ever-more-global food market that the walled garden was competing, and with improvements in shipping, the prices of imports dropped. The availability of cheap foreign foods on the market meant that it was poor economy to meet the cost of a full team of gardeners and the exorbitant fuel costs of the greenhouse heating system.

DESIGN, LAYOUT AND ASPECT

The unspoilt Shropshire countryside provides the backdrop for Acton Scott's classically designed, tranquil walled garden.

Acton Scott's walled garden conforms to many of the standard conventions for walled gardens of the period. It is a modest example but has many of the features one would expect from a garden of its size. The first thing that struck me was the walls. These were made of brick which was by far and away the best material to use for garden walls. Unlike stone, they had a wonderful habit of absorbing the

sun's rays and trapping the warmth of the day. Stone walls would often remain cold and damp and the many nooks and crannies that are a feature of stone-built walls served as ideal nesting places for pesky insects and rodents. Even where stone was the cheaper option (and especially before the repeal of the Brick Tax), the inner face of a stone-walled enclosed garden would be faced in bricks. In fact, stone was a far cheaper material to source than brick in Shropshire – although the garden walls at Acton Scott are built in brick, the 'back rooms', the storage rooms, potting shed, tool shed and mushroom house are all built up against the brick walls in stone.

Stephen Switzer, in *The Practical Fruit-Gardener* of 1724, recommended that a south wall declining about 20 degrees to the east was best for gardens so that they might make the most of the 'pure' morning air rather than absorb more of the 'languid and unhealthy' heat of the afternoon sun. This orientation seems to be the case at Acton Scott although, because of its positioning on the south-facing slope of a low rise, instead of a south wall, the ground drops away forming a natural boundary across which a thick holly hedge has been grown.

It was traditional to plant fruit trees against the internal walls, and the micro-climate offered by the shelter and sun trap of the walls allowed various varieties of exotic fruit to be grown. It was against the south-facing walls that the most exotic outdoor fruits, such as nectarines, peaches and apricots, would be planted out while the east- and west-facing walls were often home to greengages, pears, sweet cherries, early plums, apples and figs.

The arrangement of the internal beds is very much to the design of the classical model: the 'four-square' pattern whereby four squares, or rectangles in this case, are divided by broad gravel paths wide enough to accommodate two people – possibly even two crinolined ladies – walking side-by-side. A key aspect of the Victorian walled garden was its ornamental and immaculate appearance. Chimneys, coal stores and composts had to be kept well out of sight. The garden had to be somewhere that the owners could bring their friends, family and associates to and impress them with.

Thus the borders of the beds would need to be clear and well defined, and a favoured method for this in the Victorian period was growing a 'live' edge. Perennial herbs, low flowers or plants were popular, but by far and away the most prestigious method was a dwarf box hedge repeatedly clipped in such a way as to

HOTBEDS AND PITS

A 'hotbed' was one method of raising the ambient temperature to aid or 'bring on' the growing of fruit and vegetables out of season using farmyard manure. A thick bed of manure (tilted towards the sun) was overlain with a rich garden soil into which seeds could be sown directly. The fermenting warmth of the organic matter beneath the soil created a micro-climate that helped early cultivation.

Various developments were made to this practice – cloth canopies or straw mats were used to retain heat – but gradually more advanced methods were employed. Wooden frames with sash windows were placed over the hotbed and allowed the heat from the sun and the dung below to be retained. Hotbed design peaked in the late-Victorian period when permanent brick-built structures were built with manure pits, like moats around a central 'house' or frame within which the plants were grown. This was a popular way to grow melons and pineapples.

Greenhouses

The term 'greenhouse' is used today because, traditionally, these were simply houses with large south-facing windows where wealthy families of the 17th and 18th centuries would keep 'green' plants – jasmines, bays, myrtles, dates, pomegranates, oleanders and orange trees. These rooms would be heated with stoves to provide a temperature in which rare and exotic fruits could be grown.

Gradually, however, gardeners realized the merits of sunlight and good ventilation, and more and more glass was used in the construction of green houses. They become a standard feature of all walled gardens by the mid-19th century due to the Repeal of the Glass Tax in 1845. It became much cheaper to build greenhouses on a large scale, and to have them built up against the south-facing walls of the walled garden. The money saved in glass, however, was very soon being invested in heating sources – the initial outlay for boilers, flues, pipes and the continual cost of fuel.

The earliest methods of heating greenhouses in walled gardens were basic and time-consuming. Fires lit in hearths on the outside of the north wall would be stoked and the hot air and smoke would pass through flues that passed horizontally through the walls to a chimney at the top. This method would heat the wall against which the greenhouse was situated but often proved smoky and required constant attention. Boilers that heated steam which in turn passed through cast iron pipes were a cleaner and more direct method of heating, but, again, they needed constant attendance and steam is liable to cool quickly.

Evidence for the most effective method of heating water and passing it through a series of pipes around the internal edges of the greenhouse, can be found in the greenhouses at Acton Scott. Unlike steam, water would retain the heat throughout the night and, as such, wouldn't require a team of gardeners to stoke fires throughout the night on the coldest days of the year. Sadly, the heating system at Acton Scott has long since fallen in to disrepair and, unless we could find alternative methods, the extent to which we could truly replicate the tropical conditions of some late-Victorian greenhouses was limited.

Greenhouses could be purpose-built for different types of plants grown under different conditions. In larger walled gardens there would be specific designs of greenhouses such as conservatories, lean-tos, free-standing for different fruits, flowers, ornamental orangeries, palm houses, even aquatic houses. The modest lean-to greenhouse in the walled garden at Acton Scott is divided into three for the practical purposes of early, mid-season and late productions.

Acton Scott's lean-to greenhouse, which is currently being restored to something of its former glory.

make it narrow and low. The cost of their thrice-yearly clipping would have impressed, but for lesser garden borders of stone, brick, tile, or, as is presently the case at Acton Scott, a wooden shuttering would have sufficed. Again, in the interests of immaculacy, boot scrapers would have been located at the corner of each bed so that gardeners wouldn't traipse soil onto the spotless paths.

The beds surrounding the walled garden were called the slip gardens and were usually dedicated to growing more robust vegetables, such as cabbages, potatoes and onions. They might also contain the 'frame-yard', tree nurseries, manure dumps, compost heaps and nutteries. Acton Scott's walled garden seems only to have a slip garden to the exterior of its west wall with belts of pine trees, ash, oak and beech to the north and west providing shelter from the cold winds.

Like most examples, Acton Scott's walled garden has a range of buildings built against the north-face of the northernmost wall. These buildings are referred to as the 'back sheds' and would have had a range of functions. Most importantly there would have been a boiler house, tool shed, potting shed and store room, but many larger walled gardens found room for a separate office for the head gardener, mushroom houses, pot-washing rooms and bothies for some of the younger gardeners to sleep overnight in as they tended the stoke holes of the boilers and made adjustments to the greenhouse ventilation throughout the day.

Potting up chilli plants in the greenhouse.

ACTON SCOTT'S WALLED GARDEN

Walled gardens were very much the preserve of the country squire, and at their peak they would have provided an extra source of income for the owners of the best-run gardens. So important was the produce of a walled garden that even when certain landed families were on holiday, the daily produce would be washed, packed and sent down to them by train or even horse-drawn coach.

Although, as with so many walled gardens in the British Isles, Acton Scott's has experienced a significant period of neglect, a dedicated team has set about reinstating it to something of its former glory. Peter and I were keen to offer our services to the project. Although not really gardening 'experts', we had both dabbled and we knew one end of our spade from the other and were happy to spend time undertaking some of the more laborious tasks such as digging, weeding and muckspreading. A garden of this size would have commanded a considerable work force in its heyday and we saw this very much as an opportunity to supplement our role at Acton Scott. As tenant farmers on the estate, people in our situation would have been grateful for the extra income some labouring tasks in the walled garden would have offered, and if we were successful in Victorian gardening, we may even get to try some of the produce later in the year!

THE PIGSTIES

Over the six weeks it took us to construct our porcine palace we had six types of weather: wind, rain, frost, sleet, snow and hail. These are the worst conditions for tackling this kind of project, but then that is what you get if you start in the middle of November. Why? Well, apart from it being so cold that your hands stick to the rocks, which in turn are stuck to the ground, lime mortar only 'goes off' if the temperature is 5°C (41°F) or above (modern cement needs 1°C/34°F to 'go off'). In addition, rain will turn perfectly mixed mortar into thin soup.

However, we soldiered on and devised ways to combat the weather. We erected a makeshift tent from ropes, poles, beams and a canvas sheet to keep the rain off. We lit fires during the day and employed the Victorian technique of laying sheep fleeces over the newly laid stone at night to protect against the frost. We warmed the water that we added to the mortar mix (or 'muck' as it is affectionately known), we kept the stone and the sand covered at all times, and we plied ourselves with regular mugs of hot tea.

Practising our stonework by laying the foundations of the pigsties.

Although we have only just finished the pigsties, the whole process seems unreal, and looking at them I think they have the appearance of contemporary longevity in comparison to the other Glebe farmyard buildings. This is in part due to the fact that, about 20 years ago, Mr Acton employed Mr J. E. C. Peters, an architect, who specializes in farm structures, and who is the author of *Traditional Farm Buildings*. We used his plans as a guide, making inevitable alterations.

These plans enabled us to estimate the materials that we would need. Our list (excluding timber, door fastenings, and mortar) comprised of 1,600 (9 x 6 in/ 23 x 15 cm) roof tiles, 20 (1 in/2.5 cm) ridge tiles, 20 ton of stone, 750 bricks and 450 bottles. Over the years on the Acton Scott estate a number of buildings have been dismantled and the materials have been kept, so we were able to easily source some tiles for the roof. The stone, however, was buried under a sizeable amount of soil and building detritus so we had to manually dig it out. I say 'we', Tom Pinfold, a friend of mine, dug the stone out while Alex and I discussed architectural form and function. We thought about making the corners or 'quoins' out of brick which would save time, although having spent a couple of days reclaiming bricks for the pantry we decided to tell Tom to dig harder and use stone. We needed the bottles to lie in the floor to form an air gap and insulate the sties and their occupants from the cold coming up from the ground. This building technique was often applied in the 19th century. It was unrealistic to use Victorian bottles so we used modern wine bottles. Working for a West London television production company made laying our hands on 450 wine bottles easier than finding sand on a beach.

Alex demonstrating his skill with a trowel as he lays a stone in the wall.

Drilling a rafter to the wall plate while Tom's foot holds it in place.

Fixing batons to the roof, while maintaining our balance, was and tricky and tiring work.

BUILDING WORK BEGINS

We broke ground on 14 November, cutting a lattice work of foundation trenches orientated to the existing walls that we were going to incorporate into our pigsties. They were 2 x 18 in (5 x 46 cm) and needed to support our 16 in (41 cm) walls (building stone walls narrower than 16 in/41 cm is difficult). We built our foundations out of stone and mortar in an 'if it fits it goes in' approach. However, when stonemason Paul Arrowsmith visited he decided that we needed his expert tutelage.

He set us up using string lines fastened between temporary wooden crossbars, set just outside the external perimeter of the sties, and nails tapped into the existing walls. He then showed us how to work the stone, which needs to be clean and dry and not too cold. For this we used chisels, club hammers, bolsters (like a wide-bladed chisel), brick hammers and sledge hammers. Often the stone would have a face on it that just needed a couple of chips taken off, other times you had to crack a stone open to create two stones, or a pile of gravel, if you were unlucky.

Once a stone had a face it was ready to be used – a stone should be laid with any stratagraphic layers horizontal to prevent cracking. The best way to describe a stone wall is two walls built side-by-side each hiding the other's unsightly features. You start building one side by placing each stone (with a bit of muck) so that it touches its neighbours with the worked face on the external side and the rough side facing inwards. You then go round to the other side and do the same thing. It is bad form to build over hand – that is, don't lean over and build the other face as it will look unsightly. As you build the two sides a cavity will form which you fill with muck and the pieces of stone you have chipped off from your main building blocks or indeed the numerous pieces of gravel you have created when hitting your well-worked prized lithic one too many times. Every so often you must place a tie stone that spans both sides of the wall and secures them together. As our walls were 16 in (41 cm) wide the tie stones needed to be 16 in (41 cm) wide. Like a dry stone wall our pigsties are structurally stable by themselves and the muck (although it binds it all together) is primarily there to keep the wind out.

Paul said that the hardest part of the process was building off of our foundations. However, once we had established a couple of courses in our walls we concentrated on building quoins up to the finished height to give ourselves two points to build between. A quoin (corner stone) has two main faces at right angles to one another – making one is a time-consuming process. Once the walls were built we scraped out the joints and pointed them with mortar using a hawk and a finger trowel. We also used the mortar as coping to cap the top of the wall and protect it from the elements.

For the floors in the back enclosed sties we laid sand and ash followed by the bottles as insulation and then concrete, which we sloped to give a run-off for liquid, in both the back and front sties. The Romans' knowledge of concrete and cement was immense including having hydraulic concrete (sets underwater) and adding blood to make it air-entrained to protect against frost. However, it wasn't until the 19th century when this technology started to be rapidly redeveloped.

The timber work included putting on wall plates, tie beams, door frames, rafters and tiling batons. We made sure the bottom baton was level and used a couple of homemade wooden spacers to ensure an equal distance between subsequent batons. We then mortared the tiles to these batons with the help of Alex's brother, Tom. On the inside we 'torched' between the batons with mortar, to help fix the tile on and add a degree of insulation. The doors were hung on pintles, although the top pintle needed to be inverted to stop the pigs levering the door off of its hinges. Finally, we placed a beautifully carved (by Paul) date stone above the door. It reads 'T S A [Tom Stackhouse Acton] MMVII' – only 106 years too late.

Friday 21 December

I was an extremely proud man when Mr Acton, the landlord, came to inspect the pigsties this morning. At one point it had looked unlikely that we would finish our porcine palace at all. The weather had set us back, we were behind on the tight schedule we had set ourselves and there still seemed an enormous amount to do. However, we had battled through, gritted our teeth and were now staring at what we felt to be a monumental achievement.

Pig ownership was definitely a status thing in the late-Victorian period and marked out the not-so-poor farmer from his labouring friends. We felt very strongly, in our position as tenant farmers that we simply had to have a pigsty, and we wanted to build something that was in-keeping with the surrounding farm buildings and something that even the Victorians would have been proud of.

Over the course of the next few weeks, I found myself wandering into the farmyard and simply standing and staring at our monumental achievement.

Mr Acton to my right, Paul Arrowsmith on my left, with the Langlands boys in front - all very pleased with the end result.

THE CLOVER CROP

Early spring and it was time to think about what crop I was going to sow in the field. I already had half of the field turned over to a winter wheat which was doing reasonably well but, clearly, there wasn't as much nitrogen in the soil as I had expected. The wheat of the neighbouring farms, which had already been given a top dressing of nitrogenous fertilizer, was fairing much better. Thus I decided on a two-pronged attack. Firstly I would consult the experts at Rothamsted, an experimental station still in operation but set up in the late 1830s to test certain fertilizers, and see if I could acquire something that I could improve the yield of my wheat crop with.

The second thing I planned to do with the other side of the field was to sow a clover-heavy grass crop. Clover, being a leguminous crop, is a very good nitrogen 'fixer'. Essentially, it traps atmospheric nitrogen and stores it in small nodules on its root system. These can greatly enrich the soil when ploughed back in. There are other benefits to sowing clover, however, and these centre around its use as a nutritious fodder crop which can be either cut like hay once a year or left in the field and grazed on by livestock.

Now it may seem weird having taken the time to plough over a grassy sward only to re-sow with a grass mix, but this was commonly practiced in the late-Victorian period. Essentially, it is worth going to the effort because it can refresh pasture with species better suited to both grazing and cutting as a hay crop. Pastures can become tired. Weeds can invade and take much of the goodness from the soil, replacing valuable meadow grasses and herbs.

Sowing grass crops was really something I hadn't properly conceived of, but by the Victorian period it was a common practice. During the years of depression in the late 1870s and 1880s, many fields that were traditionally used for arable crops were turned back to permanent pasture but over the ensuing decades the practice of sowing short term 'leys' – species of clover and grass crops that were particularly high-yielding in their first two years – became increasingly popular. They would provide valuable fodder for livestock as both a cut crop and as pasture. However, by virtue of their nitrogen-fixing properties they could also be ploughed in and followed by a wheat crop in their third year.

Clover and grass mixes were often used in Victorian times.

The Acton Scott Special Grass Mix

Mr Acton and I set about choosing a selection of grasses that would give the flexibility of both a short-term and long-term pasture. In the short term, the Italian Rye Grass and Red Clover would be high-yielding and could provide a number of bulky hay crops in the first few years.

MEADOW CAT'S-TAIL This is a fairly widespread grass found on pastures and roadsides, and one relished by all kinds of livestock. It is an important fodder crop that is widely planted for both hay and grazing. It is also known as 'Timothy grass', after Timothy Hanson the 18th-century agriculturalist who introduced it to the USA where it became extremely popular.

FOX-TAIL A good grass for both long- and short-term pastures, Fox-Tail is a species with very early growth and found throughout Britain on damp meadows and grassland. The leaves are broad and dark-green in colour and are eagerly eaten by all kinds of stock.

CRESTED DOG'S-TAIL This is a native perennial that forms in tight clumps found throughout Britain and grows late on into the year. It is drought-resistant and, therefore, useful for seeding permanent hill pastures for sheep. Generally, sheep fed on pastures with a high proportion of Dog's-Tail are less susceptible to foot-rot.

MEADOW FESCUE One of the most productive of the native British grasses, Meadow Fescue is a species that grows early in the year. It is better adapted for moister soils but has the excellent quality of fattening up both cows and horses whether as a green pasture or as a dried hay.

SHEEP'S FESCUE This is a fescue grass that is famously popular with sheep and is most keenly sown on upland pastures used for sheep grazing. Although the plants are smaller and the foliage finer, this is amply made up for by its excellent nutritive qualities.

WHITE CLOVER A species of clover native to the British Isles, White Clover is an herbaceous perennial plant that makes for an excellent forage crop, being both widespread and high in protein. For permanent pasture, its ability to fix nitrogen reduces leaching from the soil and can reduce the incidence of diseases that affect meadow grasses. Unlike Red Clover, it is low-growing with creeping stems and can tolerate close mowing.

ITALIAN RYE-GRASS It was contentious back in the late-19th century as to whether Rye-grasses should be used in meadows for pasture as they have a tendency to die back quickly. However, there can be little doubt that in their first year they are particularly high yielding. Italian Rye-Grass was introduced into this country in 1831 and is most famous for its rapid growth and succulent herbage.

RED CLOVER Imported into Britain during the late-19th century, Red Clover – or Broad-leaved Clover – can make for an excellent and bulky herbage crop when grown in conditions that are neither too dry nor too wet. Unlike White Clover it grows upright with a stem of up to 80 cm (31 in). It is less resistant to repeated mowing and will tend to die back after the first few years. Its nitrogen fixing properties are famous and wheat crops grown on the same ground two to three years later will benefit enormously from its inclusion.

IMPLEMENTS FOR SOWING CLOVER

SPIKE HARROW The operation undertaken by the harrows is vital to all forms of arable. In the instance of our grass and clover crop, it was necessary first to harrow the land to create a fine tilth on which to sow and secondly, after sowing, to create that intimate contact between seed and soil to aid in germination.

Tasker's celebrated drag harrows, with handles.

BROADCAST SOWING BOX This horse-drawn implement has its origins in the mid-19th century and consisted of a large box, some 16 ft (4.9 m) long that contained the seed. Through the length of the box ran a spindle rotated by mitred gearing from the ground wheels. At intervals along the spindle a series of radial pinions scoop the seed up and drop it over outlets equally spaced along the box. Over the outlets a shutter system operated by a handle can determine the size of the hole through which the seed passes and thus the thickness with which it is sown.

Henry Stephens described the broadcast sower in 'the most perfect form' and the type he describes is remarkably similar to the implement that Mr Acton

had dug out for me to use. The sowing-chest, the large 16 ft box from which the grass seed is sown, is so constructed that it can be divided into sections and folded upon the barrow making transportation between field gates trouble free.

SEED FIDDLE The seed 'fiddle' – a hand broadcast sower – was invented in the USA where it was termed the 'Little Wonder'; it was introduced to Britain by Mr J. H. Newton, West Derby, Liverpool. A light box of plywood is carried under the left arm with a strap over the shoulder. Into this box is attached a canvas sack for the seed. On the front below the box is fixed a tinned iron wheel that revolves on a spindle around which is passed a leather thong. The ends of the thong are fastened to each end of a bow which, when drawn back and forward by the operative, spins the wheel. There is an adjustment on the hopper that allows the seed to drop onto the wheel which, when spinning, scatters the seed evenly for a width of some 16 ft (4.9 m). (See illustration on page 47.)

ROLLER The final job is to press down the seed bed to create a really snug connection between soil and seed. To do this a large and heavy roller is required. Unfortunately the heavy roller that we had access to was for use with two horses and I felt that this might prove a little too much for Clumper. Therefore, I had to settle for using a small wooden roller and perching precariously on top to add the weight!

William Elder's broadcast sowing machine.

Perkins's double cylinder land roller.

Mr Acton was by now becoming more and more interested in what we were doing on our Victorian farm and was fast becoming an indispensable source of knowledge. It was for this reason that I decided to consult him on the make-up of the clover and grass mix. He took up the task with his usual ageless enthusiasm and looked up a publication entitled *Gramina Britannicus* (*British Grasses*). This was a beautiful book dated to 1804 with hand-painted illustrations of all of the meadow grasses prevalent in Britain. Interestingly, between each page a specimen of each grass had been collected by the book's original owner, Frances Stackhouse Acton – Mr Acton's great-grandmother.

Prior to sowing the clover, I took advice from Dr John Jenkins on what fertilizer to use on the winter wheat. Here, we are using a horse-drawn fertilizer box.

So, together we made a selection of the grasses that we wanted to sow in the field and, as has been the case with so many things that I'd undertaken so far, I decided to go with something of the old and something of the new.

For the old I was to use a selection of grasses recommended by Mr Acton from his book of 1804. The grasses and clover sown would provide a long-term pasture and it is likely that a mix like this hasn't been sown on a working farm in Britain for well over 100 years.

For the new I was to use the advice of Stephen's *Book of the Farm* and would opt to add to the mix the latest innovations: perennial Rye-grass and Red Clover. These were high yielding in the first two years and would be ideal to cut for winter fodder but would begin to die back and allow the older traditional meadow species to take over.

PICKLING

A selection of fruit and vegetables ready for pickling.

Pickling is one of the simplest jobs in the kitchen. There is no mystery to it, you simply immerse food in either an acid or a saline solution. Of course, making it taste good requires slightly more care.

All vegetables can be pickled. Green vegetables need to be blanched first (dropped into rapidly boiling water for two or three minutes and then drained). Clean prepared vegetables are packed tightly into a clean jar. Vinegar and spices are brought to the boil in a pan and then allowed to cool. Once cool, the vinegar and flavourings are poured over the vegetables. Done.

The Victorians were very fond of using combinations of salt, black pepper, cayenne, mace, allspice and ginger in their pickles, but were also willing to use soy sauce, sherry and lemon peel to flavour the vinegar.

Pickled Beetroot

INGREDIENTS

2 lb (1kg) whole fresh beetroots
2 pints (1 litre) white malt
 vinegar
1 tbsp whole black peppercorns
1 tbsp allspice

MAKES 3 LARGE JARS

Here is a simple recipe, taken from Mrs Beeton's cookbook, to get you started.

METHOD

Trim off the leaves and carefully wash the beetroots, taking care not to damage the skin. Place the whole beetroots in a saucepan of lightly salted water and simmer for about 1½ hours, until tender. Drain and allow to cool. Put the vinegar and spices into a pan and bring to the boil. Simmer for ten minutes and then allow to cool. Peel the beetroots and cut into thick slices. Lay the cool slices of beetroot into clean, dry jars. Pour the cold vinegar and spices over the beetroot and seal the jars.

A Bengal Receipt

Indian food has long been popular in Britain. Indeed, as early as 1694, Mrs Anne Blencowe records a recipe entitled 'To Pickle Lilla – an Indian Pickle', which she acquired from Lord Kilmory.

Ketchup or catsup was common by the mid-18th century and chutney soon followed. Many people were so used to eating these Indian sauces that they were unaware of their origin. Eliza Acton, who was very well informed about food, believed that ketchup in particular was entirely and peculiarly English, never having encountered it in continental cuisine. Ketchups 'belong exclusively to English cookery, they are altogether opposed to the practice of the French cuisine, as well as to that of other foreign countries'. She did however recognize other chutneys as Indian, entitling this one 'A Bengal Receipt'.

Method

'Stone the raisins, and chop them small, with the crab appless, sour apples, unripe bullaces, or any other hard acid fruit. Take the coarse brown sugar, powdered ginger, salt and cayenne pepper and grind these ingredients separately in a mortar, as fine as possible. Pound the fruits well, and mix the spices with them, one by one; beat them together until they are perfectly blended, and gradually add as much vinegar as will make the sauce of the consistance of thick cream. Put it into bottles with an ounce of garlic, divided into cloves, and cork it tightly.'

'This favourite oriental sauce is compounded in a great variety of ways; but some kind of acid fruit is essential to it. The mango is used in India; here gooseberries, while still hard and green, are sometimes used for it; and ripe red chillies and tomatoes are mixed with the other ingredients. The sauce keeps better if it be exposed to a gentle degree of heat for a week or two, either by the side of the fire, or in the full southern aspect of the sun.'

An Excellent Pickle

This recipe comes from a reader's letter to the *Englishwoman's Domestic Magazine*, which was published by the Beeton's. However, it is much the same as a modern piccalilli recipe, especially if you add cauliflower.

Method

'Slice sufficient cucumbers, onions, and apples to fill a pint stone jar, taking care to cut the slices very thinly; arrange them in alternate layers, shaking in as you proceed salt and cayenne in the proportions opposite; pour in the soy and wine, and fill up with vinegar.'

Victorian wine glasses are much smaller than modern ones so a wine glass would equate to a couple of tablespoons of soy and sherry per large jar of pickle. This pickle is best eaten within six months.

INGREDIENTS

4 oz (113 g) stoned raisins

8 oz (226 g) crab appless or other
    acid fruit

4 oz (113 g) coarse brown sugar

2 oz (56 g) powdered ginger

2 oz (56 g) salt

2 oz (56 g) cayenne pepper

1 oz garlic

vinegar, enough to dilute

MAKES 2 LARGE JARS

INGREDIENTS

Equal quantities of medium
    sized onions, cucumbers, and
    sauce apples

1½ tsp of salt

¾ tsp of cayenne

1 wine glass of soy

1 wine glass of sherry vinegar

MAKES 1 LARGE JAR

Preserves

Jams, jellies, marmalades and preserves were the pride of many a woman's pantry, as well as a staple of many a family's diet. In Victorian Britain, sugar was cheap and for many people a spoonful of jam made a diet of bread and more bread that bit more appetizing. But, while bread and jam were many a poor child's only meal, good jams and jellies also graced the tables of the more wealthy.

Fruits preserved in sugar in a myriad of ways formed the base of many cakes and desserts. Rhubarb, gooseberry, cherries, strawberries, raspberries, redcurrants, whitecurrants, blackcurrants, pineapples, oranges, greengages, plums, apricots, peaches, nectarines, damsons, red grapes, apples, quinces, crab apples and barberries all appear in Eliza Acton's section on preserves in her cookery book, and a similarly comprehensive list can be found in other cookery books, such as Mrs Rundell's and Ann Cobbett's.

Some preserves were served alongside cold meats and game – redcurrant jelly was one of the most frequently mentioned accompaniments to game. Blackcurrant jam and jelly was thought to be medicinal, and many households kept a pot or two for dosing headcolds. Fruit compotes and bottled fruit served with cream were desserts in themselves or used to garnish other dishes. Damson cheeses were often served alongside dairy cheese as an aid to digestion.

The range is perfect for slow cooking, which is needed for preserving damsons.

Fruit Harvest

DAMSONS are a much-underrated fruit in modern Britain. Victorian Britain was much more aware of their delights. With a stronger, richer flavour than plums, damsons lend themselves to a whole host of uses. Perhaps a little tart for most people when eaten raw, cooked damsons combined with a range of hearty toppings make fantastic puddings. Damsons with suet crust, damsons with a sponge on top, crumbles and so on, all work superbly well. Light creams, mousses and syllabubs also suit damsons well. The finished deserts are less tart than when something like blackcurrants are used in this way. They give a full round finish, but with more punch than strawberries. Damson jams and jellies, and damson wine, all have an honourable place in the Victorian kitchen. I also like damsons served with beef.

ROSEHIPS were highly prized during the Victorian period for their medicinal qualities. Rosehip syrup was a standard medicine for sore throats, coughs and colds. It was believed to be especially good for children. The fact that it could be produced at home with very little cost added to its popularity. Wild or dog roses make the best syrup. Garden roses, though their hips may look large and juicy, don't work so well.

SLOES are best known for their affinity with gin. A good couple of handfuls of well-ripened sloes in a bottle of gin, along with a large tablespoon of sugar, make for a superb Christmas tipple. It takes a few months for the gin and sloes to do their magic, so make it when the berries are ripe and it will be ready for Christmas.

BLACKBERRIES are the quintessential hedgerow fruit. Some of my most carefree childhood memories are from pootling along the hedges eating nearly as many as I took home.

ELDERBERRIES make very good wine, but are usually best in combination with other fruit. If you don't have quite enough blackberries for your blackberry and apple pie, then a handful of easy-to-pick elderberries is just the thing. Elderberry jelly can be good, too, especially if you add a splash of whisky.

CRAB APPLES Pale pink crab apple jelly glistening on the plate is one of the prettiest and deliciouse of things that you can have with a 'cold collation' of ham and cheeses.

Damson preserve is delicious served with yoghurt, fresh cream or ice cream.

Preserved Damsons

This is a simple preserving recipe: damsons are packed into a jar with some sugar and very slowly cooked in a *bain marie* or left on the back of the range for a few days. They provide an instant dessert and are absolutely fantastic served warm with a little double cream. Fruit preserved in this manner will keep for several months.

METHOD

Wash the damsons and wipe dry with a clean cloth. Prick each damson once with a pin and pack the fruit into a large clean jar. Pour in the sugar, giving the jar a little shake to help the sugar get between the fruit. Put the lid on the jar, but make sure that it is not tightly sealed (you could use a small saucer a this stage). It is essential that air and steam can escape when the jars are heated.

Fill a large saucepan with cold water and stand the jar up to its neck in the water. Turn on the heat at the lowest temperature possible. You want to bring the water up to the boil very slowly – the slower the better. The sugar will melt into the fruit as the fruit begins to cook. As soon as you can see that the level of juice produced has risen above the whole fruit, turn off the heat and leave to stand until cold. Lastly, secure the lid of the jar tightly.

YOU WILL NEED

1 kg (2¼ lb) whole damsons
100 g (3½ oz) sugar
1 kg jar

MAKES 1 KG JAR

CHAPTER TWO

VICTORIANS MAKING MERRY

Leisure Activities

The rural population of Victorian Britain, while missing out on some of the leisure activities of towns, had a range of pastimes and pleasures of their own that were quite distinct. Other leisure activities such as reading and music crossed all boundaries of geography and class.

Fairs and travelling shows formed the only professional entertainment available to most people outside the towns. Most villages received at least the occasional travelling one-man show, and people made the most of the opportunity. Many rural schools record large truancy rates when any such entertainment turned up. Nor was it just the children who were drawn to the show. Puppet shows went down well with children, whilst a few magic tricks appealed to young men and women. A travelling musician could usually be sure of a warm welcome so long as he didn't step on the toes of any local musician.

A large number of small fairs also travelled the country, usually following a regular circuit, and were timed to coincide with market days so as to draw in extra people. Fairground rides, such as swing boats and roundabouts, were common at these events, along with coconut shies, fortune tellers and freak shows. Trials of strength and skill drew in the men keen to show off to their friends and any potential sweethearts.

The pub

It was mainly men who enjoyed having a drink in the local pub.

Village pubs are a long-standing part of our heritage, and most villages had several. The Victorian village pub was usually small, with room for only a dozen or so (male) customers who enjoyed the warmth, beer and company they offered. The pub also provided men with a place to be out of the weather and out from under the feet of their women folk when work was slack. While a woman's work is never done, the agricultural calendar has a rhythm of its own that is always subject to the vagaries of the weather.

Pubs in towns and cities did a roaring trade in gin, but rural pubs largely stuck to beer. Many a landlord brewed his own but even in the countryside large breweries were making their mark, offering a cheap and reasonably consistent mass-produced product.

COUNTRY PURSUITS AND PASTIMES

Officially, all game and freshwater fish belonged to the landlord rather than the tenant – a source of much resentment when that same game was getting fat eating the tenant's crops. The landed gentry controlled the hunting, shooting and fishing that went on in the countryside. However, there were some opportunities for this sort of leisure for poorer people. As Charles Francatelli points out in his book, *A Plain Cookery Book for the Working Classes,* 'industrious and intelligent boys who live in the country, are mostly well up in the cunning art of catching small birds at odd times during the winter months'. While not strictly a leisure activity – since they got paid for it – acting as a beater for the local pheasant shoot could also form part of a rural man's enjoyment of the countryside.

The first fox hunts took place over 300 years ago, and continued throughout the Victorian period.

The collecting of wild flowers, ferns, mosses, bugs and bird eggs also provided a free hobby for many people. All were popular in the Victorian period. For some people, the selling on of spares to other collectors could be a valuable sideline. Something of a two-edged sword, these pastimes both greatly broadened our understanding of the natural world and collected it to extinction at times.

Picking wild flowers (buttercups and red clover) growing on the edge of the wheat field.

Sport

Among working people in the towns football soon became the king of sports, but among the rural population it had less appeal. In the countryside, horse racing and blood sports, including bare-knuckle boxing, remained firm favourites.

Horseracing was the grandest spectacle. Most men working on the land worked with horses day in and day out. It is no surprise, therefore, that they considered themselves as good a judge of horseflesh as any gentlemen. Huge crowds of people of all social classes attended race meetings and the bookies were keen to take money from them all.

Bare-knuckle fights drew smaller crowds, but were far more common, taking place up and down the country in pub yards and on village greens. They needed few facilities and less equipment but the gambling was just as fierce. Local champions were feted and boasted of throughout the county. Some of them even went on extended tours.

The old animal blood sports of cock fighting, and badger, rat and dog baiting went on largely unheeding of upper class disapproval.

One rural sport that the upper classes did approve of was cricket. Village cricket teams were usually run and sponsored by the village elite, and the squire and parson often played. While many ordinary countrymen played alongside the wealthier members of the community, cricket was the most genteel of sports.

Magazines

A newly accessible form of entertainment could be found in the popular magazines of the period. Print had long been a luxury, but by the mid-19th century inexpensive printing and distribution systems led to an explosion in the number of magazines produced and sold. Publishers competed for a share of the market and were quick to exploit any interest area that appeared. There were magazines aimed at men, married women, single girls, a few for children and some for all the family. Gardening, farming, fashion, satirical and political magazines, the list goes on and on.

Low prices meant that magazines were an affordable pleasure for even the lowest middle classes. They offered a similar mix of interest and escapism to that of today's magazines. Among my personal favourites are: *The English Woman's Domestic Magazine* for its wonderful needlework and clothing patterns, and the *Young Ladies' Journal* for its excruciatingly sentimental fiction and specially written piano music. While perhaps my least favourite is *The Quiver* for Sunday reading, which sums up all that is most life-crushing about a Victorian sense of religion.

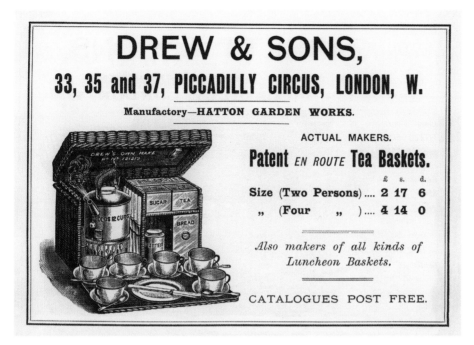

The Sunday magazine called *Good Words*, however, offers a more upbeat Victorian Sunday with articles on subjects as varied and outward looking as modern steam laundries, a journey across Africa and textile recycling.

Among the special interest magazines, gardening makes a big showing. My favourite of these is *Gardening Illustrated*, which does exactly what it says on the cover. As well as being a highly useful and informative gardening text, it is exquisitely illustrated with engravings of all the most fashionable and interesting gardens and plants of its day. A real pleasure.

Mail order catalogues were popular in the mid-19th century, offering rural communities a wide range of products.

CATALOGUE SHOPPING

Shopping was well established as a leisure activity in many towns and cities by the beginning of the 19th century, but for those living in the countryside such shopping centres were remote and expensive. Rural shopping gave little choice and little opportunity for browsing. By the mid-century, however, mail order catalogues were beginning to offer these opportunities to the farmer and his family. Soon there were clothing, seed and farm machinery catalogues. Others contained home furnishings, hats, boots and furniture. Almost all consumer goods were paraded before the eyes of the keen customer, wherever they lived. Many a half-hour in potting sheds, barns and kitchens was now whiled away flicking through catalogues of the latest things.

MUSIC

Our nation is one that has always had a robust tradition of popular music. Whilst Mendleson was the darling of the classical concert hall, popular commercial music flourished. Sheet music publishers were churning out every possible style, be it scurrilous political ballads, sentimental piano music, trades union rallying cries, suggestive music hall songs, new carol collections, patriotic ooompah tunes, dance music or tragic tales of woe, an eager audience snapped it up. By the end of the century, the Folk Song Society were bemoaning the decline of 'traditional' folk music in the countryside, but they couldn't deny the vigour and gusto with which rural people had taken to 'modern' music. Popular music constantly changes, so too did the tastes of the Victorians. But music itself remained a major part of life. Some held on to older forms, some blended them with the new, some looked only to new forms, but every village had a few people who could play an instrument and many more that could sing. Music in church, music at home, music in the pub, music at weddings and celebrations were all a part of village life. It was also a leisure activity in which women could participate, sometimes equally with men.

John Kirkpatrick visited the farm and brought with him songs and music from Victorian rural Shropshire for our May Day celebrations.

Seasonal Leisure Opportunities

Whilst some forms of leisure were available all year round, others were part of the annual cycle. Here, as in so many things, the country differed from the town.

For rural children the highlight of the year was often May Day. In many parts of the country children were spared from school and work for the day to celebrate. They spent the morning gathering flowers and branches from the hedgerows and making garlands out of them. Early in the afternoon they got together and paraded around the village showing off their handiwork to everyone and collecting money. The money paid for a 'tea' of cakes and party food – a really slap-up tea that was remembered for months among children who often knew hunger.

The agricultural year both began and ended at harvest, and this had long been a time of celebration. Farmers were expected to provide a good spread for all those who had worked for them during the year. Food, alcohol, music and dance were all provided and such gatherings could be very raucous. Extending this celebration into the church was a new thing, perhaps introduced to quieten and 'civilize' the customary harvest home.

May Day was a memorable experience for Victorian children (and Edwardian, as here) and is still celebrated in certain parts of the country to this day.

THE RISE OF CHRISTMAS

The one seasonal holiday that the Victorians made their own, above all others, however, was that of Christmas. At the beginning of the 19th century Christmas was something of a dead duck amongst the fashionable classes. It was outdated, dull and tedious and could safely be ignored. Many businesses took no holiday at all. Easter, May day, Lady day and Michaelmas all got more mention than Christmas day. By the end of the century however Christmas had become the biggest annual feast and holiday, eclipsing all others.

The change happened fast and came from several directions all at once. Writers, clergymen, royalty and, lastly, salesmen began to join the rush. The mood of the time simply changed. Tradition became a good thing to be embraced and celebrated and Christmas became the time to do it. 'Keep up all the old seasonable observances that time has hallowed, which create good feeling and fellowship' instructs the author of *The Domestic World – A Practical Guide* (1878).

Both Prince Albert and Charles Dickens were important in furthering the spreading popularity of the Victorian Christmas, but they didn't start it by any

VICTORIAN CHRISTMAS INNOVATIONS

Tom Smith invented Christmas crackers in 1848 as a way of selling more sweets at Christmas – he was a confectioner by trade. Fairly early on, the sweet was replaced with a small gift and paper hats were added around 1870.

Christmas carols were not new as such, but the Victorians overhauled the old tradition out of all recognition. A series of antiquarians and folklorists made several attempts to record, publish and promote the old Christmas songs, which they felt were fast disappearing. In 1871, Christmas Carols Old and New *was published. The word 'old', however, was rather misleading, as the carols were almost all 'new' or at least old words to brand new tunes. Most of the Christmas carols that we are so familiar with today are these new Victorian songs.*

Christmas presents were not so much new as different. New Year's Day had been the traditional time for giving gifts, but the custom shifted to Christmas Day as it became more important in people's minds. The old tradition called for seasonal food treats such as an orange or some nuts plus a trinket – hair ribbons or a

whistle. For those who could afford it, shop-bought toys were taking over and a slightly competitive edge had taken hold with presents being displayed either on or beneath the Christmas tree. Once again, the rural population and the poor in general were much slower to change their ways. Lack of resources meant few presents, and those mostly still given at new year.

Christmas in Britain had long been personified as old Father Christmas, a character fond of good food and drink, but that is all he was. The idea of a jovial chap who delivers presents in a sleigh pulled by reindeer was entirely new and, in fact, American. In 1822, New York professor Clement Clark Moore made up a fanciful poem for his children. Some of the elements came from Dutch stories of Saint Nicholas, but more sprang from his own imagination. The poem was published, without his permission, in the local newspaper and became an immediate hit. The story reached Britain in 1854 as part of Susan and Ann Warner's The Christmas Stocking, *and by the 1870s had become the Father Christmas we know today.*

means. Twenty years before either of these two men entered the Christmas fray, a string of pieces by journalists and writers of fiction were holding up the traditional celebration of Christmas as a model of family warmth, charity, and good times. Prince Albert's publication of an image of the royal family at Christmas in 1841 lent those stories a gloss of royal approval, and two years later Dickens' *Christmas Carol* summed the whole mood up in a book that sold like hot cakes.

A Victorian Christmas in its early days consisted of a family gathering, with perhaps a token present to each child and a large dinner including mince pies and a Christmas pudding, parlour games, a kiss beneath the mistletoe, a forgiveness of past wrongs, and some small acts of charity. In its 25 December 1841 issue, *Punch* has a story entitled, 'How Mr Chokepear keeps a merry Christmas', which mentions going to church, decorating the house with holly, a dinner of turkey, goose, pheasants, brawn, pudding, custards, mince pies and port, followed by card games … and other country dances. All these things remained, but by the end of Victoria's reign they had been joined by Christmas trees, more presents, crackers, cards, carols, pantomimes and Father Christmas.

Christmas trees arrived from Germany with immigrant German families. The custom gradually spread out among their British neighbours, until Prince Albert's famous adoption of them in the royal family speeded them into middle class homes the length and breadth of the country. Generally, rural families and the working classes were a little more conservative and mostly stuck to the use of holly and ivy to decorate their homes. For those who did have trees, the fashion was to attach candles and small toys or gifts to brighten them.

Victorian Christmas cards are surprisingly secular – very few carry any overtly Christian images. The cards themselves are like postcards; the address was written on the back and any message written on the front around the printed design.

CHRISTMAS CARDS

Christmas cards appeared slightly later than trees. In 1843 Henry Cole (the first Director of the Victoria & Albert Museum) commissioned J. C. Callcott to design a card. One thousand cards were printed. The design showed a merry group of people around a table eating and drinking with two smaller pictures of people dispensing charity to the poor. These cards were costly at one shilling each and the idea didn't catch on. Goodalls, the stationers, had another go in 1862 with some cheaper plain greeting cards; then a few years later, with a leap in printing technology, the price of coloured picture cards dropped significantly. These cheaper cards coincided with a new halfpenny postage rate for postcards. Suddenly Christmas cards were popular and, by 1878, four-and-a-half million cards were sent.

Cider Making

Making cider has to be one of the simplest processes: take some apples, crush and press them to extract their juice, put this in a container, wait a while and drink it. Despite a recent commercial revival of more upmarket cider, local production of farm ciders seems to be minimal. But not at Acton Scott, where Mr and Mrs Acton have kept alive the production of farm cider and have a small glass each day with their lunch.

The Acton's have one of the only working, horse-operated stone apple mills in the country. They also have a mobile wooden cider press, as well as a more common stone press. The mobile press was used in this area from the mid-19th century and went from farm to farm making cider. Farmers often relied on cider (and beer) as a form of payment and it certainly flowed liberally at hay and cereal harvest times. A farm with no cider would have found it hard to attract a casual workforce at this crucial time in the agrarian calendar. Cider was also safer to drink than water from unreliable sources.

Our first step was to collect cider apples from the orchard. Cider apples are smaller and harder than cooking and dessert apples with an astringency that dries

The mobile wooden cider press that would have gone from farm to farm.

the mouth when one bites them, rather like crab apples. They have a high concentration of sugars and tannins – sugar ferments into alcohol and tannins give cider its characteristic flavour. We took a wicker basket about 3 ft (90 cm) deep, some hessian sacks, and a panking pole (about 7 ft/ 2 m long with a hook on the end) used to tug on the branches of the trees to encourage the apples to fall. However, most of the apples were already on the ground, courtesy of the wind. It was believed that the fall (often resulting in bruising) was good for the apples. In addition, because the apples were going to be crushed, little care was taken in the orchards. One of the few things that the farmer might do was to limewash the base of the trunk of the tree to discourage insects.

It didn't take long for us to fill our sacks and our basket and we soon had enough for an initial press. At the mill the apples get placed on the raised centre and the horse pushes the stone around – someone then follows behind pushing the apples into the trough of the mill. The Acton's mill has a slightly misshapen wheel which is due (Mr Acton thinks) to people sharpening their tools on it when it stood idle. Many wheels had a circular rack and a pinion cog attached to the axle to stop them skidding on the crushed apples. It was also common practice to add a bucket or two of water to the mix of crushed apples (or pomace) to stop them adhering to the stone wheel.

Once we had milled our apples we took them to the press and placed them into our hairs – a large mat about 5 ft (1.5 m) square made out of coconut hair, but which would have originally been made out of horsehair. As each hair became full, the sides and corners were folded in and a new hair was placed on top. Multiple hairs form a cheese. We had six hairs in our cheese but a cheese may consist of any number of hairs. In order to get the hairs in line there is a wooden frame – simply a square box with no lid or base – with two poles that go through it so it can rest on the previous hair. Once all the hairs are full with the crushed apples a final hair is laid on top to complete the cheese and then the pressing can begin.

We started the press by placing a heavy wooden board called a shooter, which resembled a cut-out piece of a medieval castle gateway door, on top of the cheese. The weight of this alone began to squeeze the liquid out of the cheese. We then put two short oak beams between the shooter and the cross bar of the press.

Cider making: 29 October

... Peter and I started to crank down the pressure. All of a sudden, a torrent of apple juice gushed, waterfall-like, down the sides of the hairs, into a drip tray and from there into a bucket waiting beneath.

The next steps were very simple – the juice was poured into a barrel, sealed and taken away to the hall. Again, a deal had been struck between us and the Actons that if we helped with the cider making, we would be able to claim our share in late spring – early summer.

Peter and I were invited by Mrs Acton to inspect the fermenting cider at around Christmas time, and as she opened the door to the cider room in the cellar of Acton Scott Hall, a strong smell of alcohol filled our nostrils. The barrels of cider had been laid on their side and a tower of froth spewed forth from the central bung holes. This was a good sign. The natural yeasts in the apples were working to ferment the sugars to alcohol. It would seem we were in for many a flagon of cider come the hay harvest in July.

A traditional stone flagon used to store cider.

After a busy period working on the farm (in this case after the sheep shearing), it was customary to partake of some cider or beer.

Our press had twin screws, which is a style of press that came into use during the 1830s – prior to that, presses had a single screw. The first cast iron screws were made in Coalbrookdale, Shropshire, in the 1780s. Initially, we wound the screws down by hand and then we used long pole levers to tighten them further, always in unison. As the cheese was compressed, the brown oxidized liquid poured out and was caught in a drip tray that channelled it to the front of the press and into a vessel known as a cooler. From here we poured the liquid into a tunpail (essentially a wooden funnel), which in turn directed the liquid into our casks.

Traditionally, nothing is added to the cider, one just watches the cask and tops it up to stop air getting in. After a while froth appears at the bung hole as the cider ferments, and after that the cask is sealed and left while secondary fermentations take place inside. Sometimes things were added to the cask to aid the fermentation, such as meat or soil, but little was understood about the process. The pumice could be re-hydrated for a secondary press but this does produce an inferior diluted cider, although it is still around 4.5–5.5 per cent (rather than 8.5–9.5 per cent). However, in the morning the liquid found in the cooler (having seeped out of the cheese overnight) is a truly delightful clear drink called moonshine.

Beer Making

As we approached the end of the year we decided that it would be a good idea to make a couple of beers: a small ginger beer for the hay harvest and a big beer for our Harvest Festival. Beers drunk during harvest were small beers, which were safer, tastier and more nutritious to drink than the water but had negligible alcohol content. Although, for our Harvest Festival, we decided to make a big beer. Initially we had delusions of grandeur deciding that we would make a barrel full of beer. However, to make this much beer (36 gal/164 litres) one either needs containers big enough to boil and mash it in one go, or enough containers to hold the liquid in its various stages as one boils and mashes it bit by bit. We could not fill either of these criteria. In addition, our barrel that we had been soaking for the past week to swell the wood and make it water-tight was still leaking. Therefore, we decided to go for a more manageable amount.

The basic steps of making beer are: boil, cool, mash, strain, boil with hops, cool, add yeast, pray. So step one is to boil up some water, which we did in a cauldron over some hot coals. You then pop this water into your kive or mash tun (we used a tin bath) and let it cool to 155°F (68°C). You then add malted barley (moist barley allowed to sprout then dried in an oven),

A different sort of back-breaking farm work – wringing out the bag that contains the hops prior to adding the yeast.

until the mix resembles a thin oatmeal, and stir. The key to this stage is temperature control. If the temperature is lower than 145°F (62°C) then the enzymes in the barley, which release the sugars, will not be activated. If the temperature is higher than 155°F (68°C) then the enzymes will be killed. We managed the heat by placing hot coals around our mash tun, covering and stirring for two hours.

The resultant mixture is known as a wort (sugar water), which we strained into the cauldron (easier said than done). We sparged the leftover barley (sprinkled it with hot water) until we had the same amount of liquid out of our mash tun as we'd put in. We put the hops in with the wort and boiled the mix for one hour adding honey and elderflower for flavour. We then cooled the liquid, activated the yeast by putting it into a saucepan of warm wort, and added it to the remainder of the cooled wort. The yeast feeds off of the wort and the result is beer. After three days we skimmed the yeast off the top, which seems to brings out any impurities that may have come from the coal, and after eight days we popped it into a cask to mature until harvest (about five weeks).

The yeast becoming active in a saucepan of warm wort.

WEATHER LORE

One of the single most important influences on the success of a farming year is the weather. A farmer can get every other aspect of his job right and yet, if the weather decides to take a funny turn, he can loose everything. Thus, since the dawn of time, it has been the objective of farming folk to predict the weather and to foresee the seasons. Signs in the sky, in animals, plants and trees have all been used. A rich body of weather lore has developed over time and this has been handed down from generation to generation.

In much of this weather lore there is some sense to be had, although a great deal is nonsensical and says more about the superstitions and beliefs of the people than it does of meteorological phenomena. A good example of the former is the oft-quoted phrase: 'Red sky at night, shepherds delight.' With a prevailing wind to the south west, a red sky at night is evidence that there are clear skies to come. The sun, at its lowest in the sky to the west, passes through a great thickness of atmosphere filtering the violets, blues and greens of the visible spectrum. Unbroken by cloud cover to the west, the remaining light from the red end of the spectrum shines on any cloud cover overhead, giving the appearance of a red sky.

Bad weather for ducks – the pond is frozen so they are having to take a walk.

An example of weather lore nonsense is the well known saying: 'St Swithun's day if thou dost rain, For forty days it will remain, St Swithun's day if thou be fair, For forty days 'twill rain na mair.' The feast day of St Swithun, the 9th century Bishop of Winchester, is on 15 July – the height of summer. It is difficult to imagine anyone taking this proverb seriously, even in the context of the somewhat irrational belief systems of the medieval period.

Although the Victorians had developed means by which they could measure and gauge heat, pressure, rain, wind and moisture, as Richard Inwards in his 1893 collection of weather lore informs us, 'Meteorology itself, especially as regards English weather, is very far from having reached the phase of an exact science.'

Arguably this is a situation that continues to this day, and I confess that during my first few months on the farm I often canvassed various people on the weather reports they had heard and what the predictions were according to the 'Met Office'. Suffice to say the predictions were invariably wrong and I often found myself cursing the forecasts of radio and internet and wishing I had had the instinct to try to read the weather myself.

An atmospheric photograph of
Acton Scott's walled garden as
the sun is setting (left).
Unusually clement weather
in February meant that the
daffodils arrived early (below).

The modern age of weather forecasting was heralded by the development of
the telegraph in 1837. Previously, it had been impossible to move information
quickly enough to have been of any use to people down-wind. However, by the late
1840s a system was in place whereby telegraphs describing the weather up-wind
could be sent to large areas of the country. Two men can be credited with the
development of forecasting: Francis Beaufort (he of the Beaufort Scale method of
measuring wind speed) and Robert Fitzroy (whose innovative barometer combined
the mercury barometer with a thermometer). Initially, they were mocked by the
press but gradually their approach was accepted, significantly by the British Navy,
and their ground-breaking work provided the foundation for today's forecasting.

In fact, our most reliable source of weather forecasting was Mr Acton. It
turned out that Mr Acton had, since the 1950s, kept detailed records of the
weather. This, coupled with the careful observation one might expect of a landowner farmer who had lived off and worked this land for over 60 years, lead to him
developing something of an expertise in the weather of Acton Scott.

We had a particularly warm and bright spell in early February and I naively
quipped to Mr Acton as we set out for work that I thought spring might be just
around the corner and that perhaps an early hay crop could be had. To my somewhat school-boy remark Mr Acton responded with a well-known piece of weather
lore: 'If Candlemas day be dry and fair, The half of the winter's to come and mair
('more'), If Candlemas day be wet and foul, The half of the winter's gone at Yule.'

Looking back, Mr Acton was right. The second half of the winter was yet to
come and throughout March and into April we had some of the worst weather of
the year. Late winters are always a problem but, most of all, it is the shepherd who
suffers: 'The shepherd would rather see the wolf enter his fold on candlemas day
than the sun.'

OVERLEAF *There are many old*
terms used to describe cloud
patterns: wool sack clouds,
mackerel sky and mares' tails.

Gamekeeping and Poaching

During a hot July night in 1891, seven of the Duke of Devonshire's gamekeepers stumbled across a band of eight poachers armed with snares, nets and some makeshift weapons. A frightful struggle took place between the two groups whereby one keeper was 'fearfully battered around the head', two were left with serious injuries and one of the poachers was left 'insensible on the field'.

Between the years marked by the first Game Act of 1831 and that of 1870, affrays such as these were not uncommon in rural England. Desperately hungry men and boys, with families to feed, would be driven to trespass on the land of the local gentry and catch, by net, snare, traps or dogs whatever game they could. As the popularity of game hunting and shooting increased in Britain during the reign of Queen Victoria, spurred on by the enthusiasm of Prince Albert, Game Laws became ever more stringent, game 'reserves' ever more a feature of the country estate and game-keepers more guarded, vigilant and violent in their attempts to thwart poachers.

Desperately hungry men and boys, with families to feed, would be driven to trespass …

Game laws caused possibly the greatest friction between well-to-do members of rural society and their poorer counterparts in the villages. By far the most hated law passed was the Poaching Prevention Act of 1862. Under the terms of this act, the police had the right to stop and search any individual who they suspected of poaching. This represented, in the eyes of Joseph Arch, an agricultural trade union leader giving evidence to a select committee on the Game Laws in 1873, a 'black day for the labourer' and an infringement of the basic liberty afforded to people of the labouring classes.

Poaching was a risky business, not least because, if caught, the poacher would invariably find himself sat in front of a magistrate who was likely to be the very landowner on whose land and game the poacher had originally encroached! Rarely could the convicted poacher afford the fines meted out by the courts and often a jail sentence, hard labour and perhaps even transportation awaited the guilty party.

Yet, poaching continued throughout the Victorian age and well into the 20th century. In view of the somewhat harsh penalties doled out to the casual poacher it is hard to understand the continual abuses of the Game Laws, although it is equally difficult to comprehend the extremes to which hunger can drive individuals. A creeping perception of the lack of fairness over the game laws created what might be termed a 'cult of poaching' whereby successful poachers were celebrated and honoured as local heroes. James Hawker (1836–1921), a poacher from Oadby in Leicestershire, famous for combining sport with social protest, wrote in his book, *A Victorian Poacher*: 'If I had been born an idiot and unfit to carry a gun – though with plenty of cash – they would have called me a Grand Sportsman. Being born poor, I am called a Poacher.'

Rabbiting with Ferrets

A relaxing of the Game Laws in 1880 meant that rabbits and other low-level vermin were considered fair game for the labourer and tenant farmer. Landlords of the period, however, were guarded about allowing any forms of hunting on their land, despite the damage an unchecked rabbit population might do to the crops of the farming community. Trapping and snaring animals was an indiscriminate method of hunting and/or pest control and allowing the common man to set such devices might result in a woodcock, partridge or pheasant getting caught.

In truth, rabbits had become something of a pest by the late 19th century. The ever-stricter game laws – including the one in 1862 that gave police some of their first powers to stop and search – were harshly enforced over increasingly

One of the most important rules of rabbiting is to carefully cover every hole with a net.

larger parts of parishes and estates as field sports became ever more popular amongst the upper classes. Areas of pasture, meadow and hedge banks became infested as the potential poacher weighed up the risk of free food against a stretch on the treadmill at the workhouse.

'Rabbiting' with ferrets is probably one of the most effective and discriminate ways to clear out a warren, and it was for this purpose that ferrets have been used since ancient times. The lithe frame and aggressive nature of the animal makes it ideal for shoving down a rabbit hole to flush out the occupants. The Romans were known to have supplemented their rations with rabbits caught in this fashion and perhaps were even responsible for bringing the rabbit to these shores.

By the medieval period, when the practice is attested to in a number of laws and decrees, the keeping of ferrets was a privilege extended only to those of wealthy means. That they became a fashionable accessory is evident in paintings of Queen Elizabeth I, adorned with her pet ferret. The royal connection continued with the ceremonial presentation of albino ferrets, by Queen Victoria, to visiting heads of state.

By the late 19th century, however, ferrets and the practice of rabbiting was more widespread and considered less of an infringement of the game laws. Indeed, with cheaper food in the emerging village stores, rabbiting was less a means of feeding starving children and more a method of pest control.

A Day Rabbiting

Whichever period, the rules of rabbiting remain the same. There are certain dos and don'ts and two generations of rabbiters, Bob and Doug Jones, had invited me to spend a morning up on the hills above Acton Scott to teach me the basics.

Bob was retired from farming but still enjoyed a spot of rabbiting for the purposes of both the cooking pot and a £1-per-rabbit reward at the local game-dealer. He had learnt everything from his father Doug who remembers rabbiting on these very hills back in the 1940s. What was most fascinating to me was that Doug, too, had been taught by his father who had rabbited the same stretches of hillside nearly 100 years ago – my rabbiting guides clearly had some pedigree.

Rule 1 was to choose the right ferret. Don't go for an enormous aggressive male. Choose a nice young female that is less likely to kill its prey in the burrow. Rule 2 is to make sure you get the season right. Too late in the year and there is a greater chance of young in the burrow, and a ferret, irrespective of its temperament, is likely to make a kill, gorge itself and spend a good while sleeping off its meal. Getting ferrets stuck in the burrows can result in having to dig them out. Not only is a good ferret valuable and worth this effort, it is extremely irresponsible

The young female ferret is about to be put in the warren to chase the rabbits out.

After about two hours we had caught six rabbits, which we hung by their legs from an old blackthorn tree.

to leave a ferret in a warren. They can cause considerable damage to the local wildlife and, as a consequence, are banned in many countries.

The final rule is to make sure you've covered every hole with a net and if there are too many holes, block up the others. I was charged with skirting around the very extremities of the warren and looking out for any 'pop' holes – small rabbit escape routes – and ensuring they were carefully netted.

With the ferrets in the hole it is a case of playing the waiting game. Bob advised me to listen closely to the ground because it was possible to hear the backside of the rabbit thumping against the roof of the burrow as it bolted from the ferret. There was an anxious moment as our first warren – or 'berry' as Bob and Doug referred to them – proved non-productive. The ferret returned to the surface empty handed but with clear signs of fur on its claws. Bob suggested that a rabbit might have got 'arsed-up' in a burrow, a term he went on to explain as meaning stuck in a dead end. Pretty soon, though, as we worked our way up the hillside, rabbits started shooting out of holes and the kill-count rose.

Bob and Doug were quick to pounce on any rabbit that became trapped and in a flowing movement unfurled them from the net, broke their neck and stuffed them into a bag. After two hours we had six rabbits hanging by their legs from an old blackthorn tree. Doug had 'legged' them – slitting between the sinew and bone on one back leg and passing the other through the gap – and had dug a tidy little hole within which to bury the guts. We split the proceeds evenly.

Whilst I'm no great fan of hunting as a sport, I had been keen to try working with ferrets because, unlike trapping, poisoning and baiting, it is targeting the problem directly not indiscriminately. It is a lively pursuit and is a fantastic method for keeping populations of rabbits at a manageable and disease-free level.

SHOOTING

The shooting of ground and winged birds was a popular sport in Victorian times, and when the offer came to attend a shoot at Acton Scott I jumped at the opportunity to help rid the local area of some of the pesky pheasants that had done so much damage to our crops. We had been invited to 'beat' on the day – that is to drive the birds through the undergrowth and up into the air from where they could be picked off by the waiting guns.

It was an unfortunate reality for the tenant farmer that under the arrangements of the tenancy, the game that resided on the land still belonged to the landlord. In this instance, one man's 'game' is very much another man's pest. Many farmers would have been forced to watch on as pheasants, partridges, rabbits and hares all helped themselves to their hard work without themselves being able to act directly in reducing their numbers. Shooting rights were strictly guarded by the upper classes and, like all forms of hunting, shooting was reserved for the higher echelons of society and those in their favour.

Prince Albert played a vital role in the evolution of the shotgun and, as a keen field sportsman, commissioned a number of London gun-makers to provide him with guns and rifles for his famous shooting parties. The cult of the shooting party was to really take off under the auspices of his son Bertie (later Edward VII), who after the death of his father was denied any meaningful role in the affairs of state by Victoria, and so spent much of his time indulging his passion for shooting.

There is a fantastic, late-18th century print in Acton Scott Hall that depicts a country squire and his retinue out shooting the partridge in the harvested wheat fields. The wheat is still stooked in the field, a covey of partridges is greedily feeding on the freshly dropped grain, and the hunters are firing off their muzzle-loaded shotguns as their dogs flush the birds in to the air.

This type of shooting was known as 'rough' shooting and might consist of a small party following hedgerows and flushing covered areas and woodlands in the hope of startling a bird into the air from where it could be safely

Peter's Diary

The Pheasant Shoot

I had never been on a shoot before and I was slightly apprehensive that I myself might get shot. However, it was very well organized with the guns in the open ground and us, the beaters, driving through a safe, pre-arranged path.

As we set off I felt a little foolish squawking like a bird and bashing the surrounding trees with sticks but I soon found my stride and, anyway, I was not alone, everyone else was doing the same.

Our task was to scare the pheasants into taking to the skies and flying over the guns who would then take their best shot and hopefully bag a few for the pot. As we made our way noisily through the dense undergrowth to the continual shout of 'hold the line', other beaters stood on the outside of the copse with flags to make sure the birds came out of the correct side of the woods.

Having been apprehensive at the start of the day, I was pleasantly surprised by how much I enjoyed beating, and I'm looking forward to eating our share of the quarry.

dispatched. Gradually, however, the 'sporting' element of shooting began to gain popularity with the lay-about loafing classes and shooting became very much a 'game' and less a means of vermin control.

The Game Preserve

Thus we bare witness to the beginnings of the Game Preserve. Vast areas of estates and parishes would be set aside for the purposes of preserving certain species and breeding and raising imported species. Anything from deer to hare would be considered fair game with grouse, pheasant, partridge and duck being popular.

During the latter part of the 19th century when arable produce struggled to fetch a decent price, shooting became an attractive alternative for the landed gentry. In many areas it was to take precedence over other industries. Excessive preservation of game birds would impact upon the harvest of cereal crops as pheasant, partridge and other game had their share. The already fragile woodland industries were to suffer also. Unchecked populations of Roe, Red and Fallow deer would often graze on the fresh shoots of coppiced trees, ruining the chances of good-quality coppiced wood. The systematic planting of ivy by gamekeepers in a bid to protect tree-roosting birds from poachers led in places to the degeneration of good timber stocks.

Steadily, the status of gamekeepers on rural estates grew in importance and influence as an increasing amount of income for country houses was to come through shooting and other field sports.

After a long day's beating, armed with flags and sticks, we take home our share of the spoils (four pheasants).

Our Victorian shooting party – the local gentry never turn down the opportunity to 'drop' a brace of pheasants.

THE KITCHEN GARDEN

Commercial market gardening in Britain was in the early days of development in Victorian Britain, and transport links had not yet made the mass importation of foreign vegetables economically viable. As a result, vegetables were not cheap to buy. The wealthy had the most wonderful supplies all year round from their professionally staffed walled gardens. Those of them who also had houses in London ordered produce to be sent to them daily from their country gardens.

However, most of the less-blessed urban dwellers had to make do with very few vegetables, with the exception of potatoes. The cheap foods were the starchy ones. So recipes for feeding the poor economically, either in institutions or from charity, focus on gruel, porridge, sago pudding and the like.

Our cottage had a reasonably good-sized garden at the front. We, therefore, decided to make the most of the plot and to grow as many of our own vegetables as possible. There is a huge body of information surviving about the gardens of the upper classes in Victorian Britain – both pleasure gardens and walled kitchen gardens have received a great deal of attention in recent years. It is also possible to be fairly certain about the prosperous town gardens of the period, thanks to the wealth of gardening magazines aimed at the new middle-class amateur gardening market. But the humdrum gardens of the countryside are a much more elusive flower. Winkling out information about what we should grow and how we should do it has been a voyage of horticultural discovery.

The Victorian allotment movement proved to be an invaluable source of information. They were eager that landless labourers should have some stake in the status quo, and the means to feed their families without recourse to poor relief or higher wages. Their pamphlets and tracts set out just what they thought a man could achieve in a perfect gardening world and just what they thought he should grow. Farmers, rather than landless labourers, were expected to grow a rather more refined set of vegetables.

Potatoes, cabbage, onions, carrots, parsnip, broad beans and scarlet runners were all thought to be the mainstay. Peas, however 'require more space than their produce is worth'. Rhubarb came highly recommended as the only fruit a cottager should find room for, while a corner for pot herbs was also thought essential.

A few flowers were planted in the garden to give a little bit of colour, including a rose.

THE GARDEN PLAN

After much thought, we decided to have defined beds in our garden with path-ways between them. It seems that some farmers still used this old system while others took it for granted that the whole area would be dug over each year – dug by hand in the smaller plots and ploughed on larger ones.

Our plot is not very large and we have little spare time to devote to it. Consequently, we decided that the bed system would suit us best. We had a few timbers left over from the pigsty roof to edge them with, and the range produces plenty of cinder to make permanent paths.

After pouring over period seed catalogues, Victorian gardening magazines and manuals, we planned to grow: cabbage, kale, scarlet runners, beetroot, rhubarb, carrots, parsnips, potatoes, onions, gooseberries, red currants, white currants, radishes, parsley, sage, thyme, fennel and winter savory. And for a little bit of colour: a rose, a few pinks and some marigolds. I would have liked to grow

Some of the defined beds outside Henley Cottage, edged with leftover timbers.

broad beans and garlic but, as there were so many jobs to do, the garden got neglected right from the start and I missed the earliest sowings.

Cabbage and kale had long been the most important vegetables of common gardens, long before the introduction of the potato. They provide desperately needed vitamins as well as bulk all through the winter and for much of the summer, too, if the plantings are carefully planned.

Gooseberries made it into our list because of the popularity of this fruit among ordinary people. The plant requires very little attention or care to fruit prodigiously. It also fruits early, a little after the rhubarb but well before any other fruit is available. Competition among working people to grow the largest possible gooseberry bush was very fierce in some quarters.

Scarlet runner beans were a must. Although a fairly new vegetable in British gardens, they had taken off amongst the gardening population very quickly. As long as you plant them out after the last danger of frost has passed, they are an easy plant to grow. They need something to climb up, but are not fussy what that something is. They do equally well tied to the side of a drainpipe as scrambling over a hedge. Their bright cheerful flowers make them attractive as well as delicious. When cropping, they go on and on producing more and more beans right until the first hard frost kills them off.

All the sand left over from repairing Henley Cottage has been dug into the soil in one area of the garden, so we hope that this will give us a good area to grow

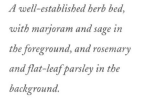

A well-established herb bed, with marjoram and sage in the foreground, and rosemary and flat-leaf parsley in the background.

carrots and parsnips. The ability to store throughout the winter is what makes these vegetables so desirable. Getting enough healthy fresh fruit and vegetables in the spring and summer is not that difficult but the winter months can be very challenging, especially with no imported vegetables to supplement what we grow. Vegetables that keep well, therefore, have to be our priority. For instance, onions, once pulled and allowed to dry, can be hung in the pantry all year. A bit of onion livens up the farmer's bread and cheese lunch no end and added flavour to many of those cheap starchy dishes that people relied on when money was scarce.

Radishes are quick to grow and little rows of them can be popped in whenever there is an empty bit of ground. They can be harvested at almost any size and so whipped out again if the next crop needs the space.

Potatoes, of course, could not be forgotten. They produce a higher calorie yield per patch of ground than anything else that grows comfortably in our climate. This is why the poor across Europe – and especially Ireland - became so reliant on them. With potatoes you can feed more people on less land that the traditional grain crops. When the blight destroyed potato crops there was simply no way that other foodstuffs could fill the gap. Blight-resistant varieties were being trialled all the time by seed merchants in the second half of the 19th century, who were in search of the food stability that could bring a degree of security to the poor, and a very profitable line for them.

Beetroot in the foreground, a large fennel bush in the centre and rhubarb in the background.

Beetroot is something of a favourite of mine. Usually thought of as more of a farmer's vegetable than a staple of the poorest, it is nonetheless easy to grow and high-yielding. Pickled, it enlivens meals throughout the year. A few left in the ground over the winter will provide a fresh handful of vegetables whenever the weather turns mild for a few days.

Currant bushes are slightly more of a luxury – food for pleasure, rather than necessity, and perhaps a little one-upmanship over poorer neighbours.

We decided to put the herbs and flowers near to the house where they could lighten our spirits as we go in and out, and be close at hand for popping into the cooking.

We put the herbs and flowers near to the house where they could lighten our spirits as we go in and out.

Sourcing seed and plants proved relatively straightforward. *Gardening Illustrated* carried numerous advertisements from seed companies listing the names of varieties. Some of these companies still exist and a few of those original varieties are still on their books. The heritage seed library of the charity Garden Organic has a few more, and scattered around the country a number of specialist nurseries nurture a handful of the old fruit bush varieties.

SMOKING

Setting up

You need a large barrel, a metal dustbin, a large wooden box or tea chest. In short, anything that can contain both your food and a good dose of smoke moving freely around it.

Next, you need to suspend your food within the container so that the smoke can get all around. No two pieces of food should be touching each other. In a barrel it is easy to drill a few holes and push a strong stick or piece of dowel through. Hey presto, a bar to hang things from. If you were really clever you would knock both ends of the barrel out and then knock up a removable lid with several hooks on the underside. This would make getting your food in and out of the barrel very easy. A wire rack would also do a good job if you can rig one up inside your container. Be ingenious. It doesn't have to look pretty, or be permanent. Pretty much anything will do. The aim is delicious food, not great DIY.

Now find some bricks or stones to prop your barrel up on. One brick high is about perfect. Form your stones or bricks into three-quarters of a circle up against a wall with the open side of the circle furthest from the wall, and balance your barrel on top.

I like to get the food in place at this stage, while there is still no fire to worry about. Now assemble your fuel. You need it all at hand before you light anything. It would also be very sensible to have a bucket of water on hand before you light the fire, just in case you need to put it out suddenly.

Two sides of salmon and a jointed duck ready for smoking.

Eight holes drilled in the barrel and four long sticks provide a frame on which to hang the food from within the barrel.

The Smoking

The trick is to get the smoke from the fire but not the heat. Heat would just cook the food rather than preserve it. Make your fire slightly in front of the barrel, not under it, and if you have sited your barrel up against a wall, a natural gentle updraft will usually direct the smoke inside for you.

The fire itself should be cool and smoky, which is why it is best to use wood shavings and sawdust. You could, however, use anything woody that will smoke. Autumn leaves will do quite a good job. Straw can also be coaxed into use.

Light a small twig fire as usual, feed it for five or ten minutes with some more twigs until you have a hot little centre going, and then smother it with shavings. It will soon smoke nicely and you should feel very little heat coming off it. Every time a flame breaks through into the open, chuck another handful of shavings on to smother it.

After a while you will become confident enough to leave it smouldering by itself and just pop back and glance at it every half-hour or so, adding shavings when you think it needs them.

Smoke itself tastes good and it is a simple matter to play around with the flavours of the food by altering the fuel. Oak has long been the preferred wood, but fruitwoods are also good. Pine is not that great – too resinous, but can be improved with a few fresh rosemary twigs. There are a huge number of herb flavours that you can experiment with. Another really delicious smoke is that made by shavings and chippings of old whisky barrels.

A whole side of salmon takes around six hours, depending on how thick the fillet. Mackerel and herrings can be smoked whole in four or five hours, sardines and sprats rather less.

Mrs Beeton suggests forty hours for an entire ham, which sounds about right to me. (Large pieces of meat should be salted first, before smoking.)

Anything with plenty of natural oils or fats can be easily and successfully smoked. Pork, goose and duck are very good.

Wood not Coal

Setting up the smoking barrel was so simple, everyone should have a go. If you burn wood on your fire, then smoking meat and fish in the chimney space is both easy and extremely effective. But smoking over coal just does not work. Not only does coal smoke tastes terrible, but also it does not contain the right chemicals to do the job.

Loading up the smoking barrel with salmon fillets.

Adding the first wood shavings to the small hot fire of twigs.

CHRISTMAS PREPARATION

Christmas is coming. I had a good look at the turkeys this morning, checking them over. Lillian has perked up. The bald patch on the back of her neck where Ena was pecking her has gone now. Changing where we put the feed seems to have helped. The two females are now much the same size. With the weather getting so much colder and the grubs and insects, which they were supplementing their diet with, in shorter supply, we have been giving them a little extra corn. Just a scattering out in the field. It will be Ena for Christmas dinner.

Alex cut down a tree and brought it into the cottage. Christmas trees were becoming very popular by 1880, especially among the urban middle classes (see page 75). Among the working classes it was adopted much more slowly, and it was not until the 1950s that the Christmas tree fully replaced the older tradition of hanging up holly to decorate the house. We decided to have both, a Christmas tree and holly, combining the new and the old traditions.

Food preparations for Christmas included making the stuffing for the turkey as well as a jelly and blancmange. Cold jellies and creams were an important part of Victorian entertaining; all of the recipe books devote large sections to them. Almost every junk and antique shop in the country still has a few jelly moulds on the shelves. I am particularly fond of a rabbit-shaped mould and decided to use it for the blancmange. The recipe suggested flavouring the blancmange with apricot preserve, but since I didn't have any I substituted some of the damson preserve that I made back in September. Of course, this resulted in a pale pink rabbit.

The high point of the build-up to Christmas was the carol service. Alex and Peter hitched up the market cart, I dug out my new smart cape, and off we went to church. (I really love these cart rides, they are so exhilarating, so much so I have asked the boys if they would give me a lesson on driving the cart with Clumper.)

It was just getting dark as we reached the church. The candles were already alight and the church looked gorgeous. People soon started arriving, and to the accompaniment of Mr Acton on the organ, we belted out those most Victorian of songs – Christmas carols. The thing I like about this sort of singing is that it is doing the singing that matters, not the listening. It doesn't matter what it sounds like or how good you are, it's the taking part, the joining in, the togetherness.

THE FARM

—◆—

CHRISTMAS
BOOK

INTRODUCTION

Christmas Eve.

This year, when we returned to the Victorian farm, we were asked to help provide a Christmas party for Mr Acton's neighbours and tenants. It was to be a far fancier affair than last year's more humble farm celebration. This time we would have the opportunity to recreate the new style of Christmas that was developing among the urban middle classes. More presents, grander food, elaborate decorations, Christmas cards and Christmas crackers.

Wondering quite what we should do, I dug out my ever-increasing collection of Victorian magazines. Articles on how to do Christmas properly abound in the latter part of Victoria's reign. Everyone wanted to be part of this new tradition and was eager for help in achieving the perfect Christmas. It was no good asking your parents how to make the decorations or what to serve at dinner, they hadn't done it when they were young. This was a new experience and people were anxious to get it right – more right, hopefully than their neighbours.

So for anyone wanting to re-create a Victorian Christmas, there is luckily no shortage of evidence, and we have been able to follow all that wonderful magazine article advice ourselves. Some of it is detailed in the following pages if you would also like to have a go. I particularly enjoyed making ivy ribbon and eating too much pudding. I would also recommend storytelling if you are lucky enough to have the right raucous bunch of people around.

DECORATING THE HOME

Decorating the home for Christmas took on a new significance for the Victorian family. For hundreds of years, country people had brought boughs of holly and ivy into their homes to brighten up the place and celebrate the feast of Christmas. As the Victorian period progressed, however, people were looking for increasingly elaborate decorations – no longer a few sprigs and boughs made into wreaths and garlands. The well-decorated home now also had table centrepieces and wall treatments. Lamps, picture frames and banisters were all to be decorated, and a fashionable home would also contain a beautifully presented tree.

Magazines and household books all carried instructions on how to make these new, more orderly decorations. In addition to the evergreens themselves, the writers of *Gardening Illustrated* recommended perforated zinc sheets for 'ornamental devises', brown paper to back letters formed of evergreens, laths and hazel rods for upright wreaths, and decorative panels and wire for smaller wreaths. In the towns, where holly and ivy were harder to come by, evergreens from the suburban garden such as laurel, bay, cypress, juniper, yew and spruce were supplemented by artificial flowers, berries and coloured paper.

WAX HOLLY BERRIES

Where holly berries were in short supply books recommended rose hips, arbutus berries, Gladwin pods and artificial wax berries. The designs could be very intricate, requiring a great deal of time and skill to produce. A fiddly job, but the finished berries do look good and are easy to use in a wreath or any other decoration. Put simply, they are dried peas coated in red wax on a thin wire!

How to make them

First, you need to gently melt a good, strong red wax over a low heat. I used sealing wax, but a red candle would work equally well. It is best to work in very small batches, so one stick of sealing wax or half a usual sized candle at a time. This will be plenty for thirty or forty berries.

Next, prepare a stand for the dipped 'berries' to cool on. I found an apple to be ideal for this. You can stick the unwaxed end of the wire into the apple very easily, which allows the 'berry' to dry in a good round shape. When I just laid them down in a saucer to cool I ended up with very one-sided berries.

Take a piece of the wire, florists fine green wire is ideal, and dip it in your melted wax. Whilst the wax is still hot and liquid, pop a pea onto the wire and allow to cool for a moment or two until the pea is well stuck to the wire. Now, quickly dip the pea with its attached wire into the wax to coat the pea with the red wax and stand the whole thing upright (using the apple stand) to cool and set.

Once thoroughly set, the 'berries' will keep for ages and can be twisted into any evergreen arrangement to add a bit of colour. They look best if they are used in little bunches.

IVY RIBBON

This is the most typically Victorian form of decoration that I have come across. It is mentioned in just about every Victorian article on Christmas decorations. Rather than using the natural, untidy tendrils of ivy, the leaves were stripped and re-arranged in a symmetrical and regimented fashion which could then be used in ordered geometric designs.

Lattice patterns of ivy ribbon were especially popular. They were used pinned on the long hanging sides of tablecloths at buffet suppers or to cover large areas of bare wall. Sometimes a lattice of ivy ribbon was used to decorate a coloured calico panel hung rather like a picture. Lengths of the ribbon were used to border mirrors and mantlepieces and sometimes even decorated dresses. As well as being used alone, ivy ribbon was often combined with coloured ribbons and artificial flowers for even more elaborate designs.

How to make them

The base for your ivy ribbon can either be strips of newspaper glued together to the required length – use three or four thicknesses so that it doesn't tear – or you can use a strip of fabric or ribbon.

Next, gather lots and lots of ivy and strip off all the leaves. Ideally you should also sort them into different sizes so that your ribbons will be even. The leaves are sewn onto the base one by one. I have found that with small leaves you only need one stitch per leaf but larger leaves need two or they flap around too much. Use a fairly big needle and reasonably thick thread as very fine thread tends to cut the leaves. A simple running stitch is quite good enough.

Each leaf should be sewn on slightly overlapping the previous leaf, so that you get a continuous green ribbon without the backing material showing. Once sewn they last surprisingly well for three or four weeks and are robust and flexible enough to make into pretty much any shape you desire.

HOLLY ROPE

Like the ivy ribbon, a holly rope was a Victorian improvement upon the natural form of the evergreen. Holly leaves were stripped from the branch and then a piece of strong cord was measured off to the required length. The cord was threaded onto a large packing thread needle. Each leaf was pierced in the centre and threaded onto the cord until the entire length was full.

This makes an even, flexible and lush-looking rope which can be used as a garland. You can wire some bunches of artificial wax berries on at intervals if you wish.

Some sources advise painting your evergreens with a thin wash of gum water (a dilute solution of gum arabic) when you have finished, both as a preservative and to make them shine slightly in the gas light.

ABOVE *A design for a Christmas garland with decorative cross in the centre.*

DYED RIBBONS

The *Housewife's Friend*, along with several other cheaper household books, has a whole section devoted to home dyeing. The vast majority of textiles were, of course, dyed commercially in factories, but small-scale home dyeing could be a valuable economy. When clothing began to look shabby and worn, a dip in a good strong dye could give it a new lease of life. Stains could be hidden by an over-dye and there was the frequent need to turn one's wardrobe black for mourning.

A spot of home dyeing also allowed people to have a bit of cheap, cheerful colour in their lives. Making bright, cheerful ribbons out of old scraps of fabric or plain cotton tape is mentioned in several of the books and is especially useful at Christmas.

ABOVE *Walnuts carefully wrapped in festive ribbon make for instant Christmas cheer.*

Debbie helped me through the process of turning some very dull cotton tape into a whole range of attractive colours which I used everywhere. I tied crackers and gift boxes up with it; I brightened up presents with it and added it to garlands, walnuts and table decorations.

We used madder, weld and indigo to dye our ribbons, but Debbie also brought along the original sample of the first chemical dye which came to be called mauvaline. It was the most violent eyeful of colour, so different from the soft natural colours we had been using; it was easy to see why the Victorians went mad for this new vibrancy.

CHRISTMAS CRACKERS

Tom Smith was a Victorian confectioner with a very sound business head. He sold a large range of sweets and knickknacks, some of his own manufacture and some bought in. In 1848, he came up with a new way of packaging and selling his produce – the Christmas Cracker – complete with mini explosion when pulled. They quickly proved popular and his business went from strength to strength. After a while he replaced the sweets inside the crackers with novelty gifts and mottoes, and by the end of the 1870s the paper hat began to appear.

Made in his own factory, the trade catalogues of Tom Smith's Crackers include a vast array of beautifully made designs. Many were themed to reflect popular theatre productions, songs or notorious characters. Some reflected Arts and Crafts tastes, some were mock historical. There were boxes of crackers aimed at adult dinner parties and others intended for wealthy children. There were also humorous boxes such as those for spinsters and bachelors whose gifts included hair restorer, anti-wrinkle cream and unpaid laundry bills. Crackers were such a big hit that a music-hall act employed a giant cracker on stage, which, when pulled, yielded not just paper hats but complete paper outfits for the two performers!

The crackers themselves were a shop-bought product, one of the most obvious aspects of a new commercialized Christmas. Their price put them way out of the reach of such a small farm as ours. But an upper middle-class family like the Actons would have been spoiled for choice. Some of Tom Smith's catalogues were brought along to the farm for me to look at, along with some materials so I could have a go at assembling my own crackers for the Christmas party that Mr Acton was giving for his neighbours. The women and children employed in the factories turned out thousands of neat, perfectly assembled crackers a day. Mine came out a bit lumpy, but none the less they did brighten up the table enormously and I was able to pop some of my home-made sweets into them instead of gifts.

SAVOURY CHRISTMAS PIE

For the pastry
1 lb (0.5 kg) plain flour
4 oz (113 g) butter
2 egg yolks
Water to mix

For the filling
1 whole chicken
1 small wild duck
1 whole pheasant
2 pigeons
8 oz (227 g) veal
8 oz (227 g) pork
8 oz (227 g) suet
Large handful of fresh herbs (I used thyme, parsley and sage)
Black pepper and salt to taste

Along with plum pudding, roast meat and mince pies, a large game pie was a staple of wealthy Victorian tables at Christmas. All game was the property of those who owned the land upon which the beast was caught. Tenant farmers could not legally kill the wild game that wandered over their rented fields or ate their crops. This, of course, gave all game a certain social cachet. A present of game from the landlord was much prized – far more than its mere financial value – for it spoke of good relations with one's social superiors and a taste of privilege.

This Christmas we were given a couple of game birds to prepare for the Christmas meal. A couple of birds don't go far with twenty or thirty people to feed, so I was glad to find a recipe which also used a good fat chicken and lots of pork and veal forcemeat. Ivan Daye popped along to give me a hand with producing food to a quality seen in the grand houses of the day, transforming my humble food presentation skills with his wonderfully fancy Victorian moulds and tips from Victorian professional chefs.

The pastry recipe came from a small book aimed at professional bakers rather than the domestic market and the pastry itself behaved quite differently to the hot-water crust or shortcrust pastry that one would expect to find in something like Mrs Beeton's book. Hot-water paste would have been strong but rather heavy eating and shortcrust pastry, though nice to eat, would probably have collapsed once the mould was removed. This recipe for lining paste was both good to eat and strong enough to hold a large deep game pie.

METHOD

First, the butter was rubbed into the flour and then the egg yolks and water were mixed in. The paste was then worked rather more firmly than I am used to doing with a shortcrust pastry. Using the heel of the hand, Ivan showed me how to shear and stretch the paste, almost as if kneading though not quite as heavy handed as for bread dough. The pastry was then left to rest in a cool place for a few hours.

For the filling, we began by making the forcemeat. The pork, veal and suet were first chopped and then pounded together to a fairly smooth paste. The herbs and a little of the pepper and salt were then worked through the forcemeat and that, too, was put to stand in the cool of the pantry.

Next, the birds had to be boned out. You can get your butcher to do this for you if you are nervous, but in truth it's not that hard – just slow. Taking a small sharp knife, the aim is to work it between the bones and the meat. Make an initial cut in the skin of the bird on its back – i.e. the opposite side to the breast – and when your knife touches bone, which it should do straight away, start to follow the bone. As long as you keep your knife next to the bones and don't pierce the skin again anywhere else you won't go wrong. As I said, not complicated just slow and painstaking.

Now we were ready to start assembling our pie. Ivan had an amazing original mould to shape our pie, but any tin will of course do perfectly well. Once we had lined the tin with the pastry, we made a second lining with the forcemeat. Next we wrapped the pigeons inside the pheasant, the pheasant inside the duck, and then the whole thing inside the chicken, and pressed that inside our forcemeat-lined pastry case. A lid of forcemeat, a lid of pastry and some decorative pastry leaves later, the pie was nearly ready for the oven. Before the pie was popped into the oven, paper was wrapped around the whole thing to prevent it from over-browning.

A pie like this needs to go into a hot oven to begin with, about 425°F (220°C) for twenty minutes, and then the heat should be lowered to around 350°F (180°C) for around another hour and a half. Test that the pie is cooked by pushing a skewer right into its centre. If any blood runs out, the pie must be returned immediately to the oven and given a bit longer to cook right through.

SWEET MAKING

Sweets were a Christmas treat for many a child, whether bought from a shop or made at home. Many were popped into pretty home-made gift boxes and hung on the Christmas tree.

VICTORIAN LOVE HEARTS

Ingredients
1 tsp powdered gum
tragacanth – available
from cake icing specialists
Juice of one lemon or
1 tbsp rosewater
2 lb (1kg) icing sugar
(this is a very
approximate amount as
each batch varies quite
considerably)
A few drops of food
colouring

These are the simplest of sweets to make at home. Begin by mixing the gum tragacanth with the lemon juice or rosewater and allow it to stand for twenty minutes for the gum to swell. You should end up with a gloopy mixture. This is the moment to add some food colouring. It may be a good idea to divide your gloopy mix into several tiny batches so that you can have each one a different colour. Be sparing with the food colouring – one or two drops will be enough for each batch.

Now begin to add in the icing sugar. Keep working in more icing sugar until you achieve a ball with a texture like Plasticine. You will be amazed at how much sugar it takes with such a tiny amount of liquid. If you can bear to wait, the paste is much easier to mould if you pop it in the fridge wrapped in Clingfilm overnight. But you can go ahead straight away if you are the impatient type – like me.

Now you are ready to roll it out very thinly, cut it into little rounds and press in a pattern. If you have some small shaped cutters, use those. If not, you can just cut shapes with a knife. There are lots of rubber stamps available in craft and cake icing shops if you wish to use those, or you can use whatever is

at hand to press decorative patterns into the surface of your sweets. Even a few pricks from a fork can look good. A sieve makes a good 'basketweave' impression.

You will need to be fairly quick in making your shapes and designs once you have rolled out your paste as it will begin to dry in a couple of minutes. Let the sweets dry out completely on a wooden board before boxing them up.

HOME-MADE TOFFEE

This recipe comes from Mrs Beeton's *Modern Household Cookery*. First, butter a tin to put the toffee in. Next pop all the ingredients into a heavy bottomed pan over a gentle heat and stir until the butter has all melted into the sugar. Now stop stirring. Mrs Beeton is not very helpful at this point, just telling us to keep going until 'it sets when a little is poured on to a buttered dish.' If you have a sugar thermometer, keep gently heating until the mixture reaches 300°F (149°C).

If you don't have a sugar thermometer then you should heat the mixture until you reach hard crack stage. The easy way of telling this is to have a glass of cold water handy. At intervals put a drop of the mixture into the glass of water and watch what happens. At first it will immediately dissolve, but when a certain temperature is reached – about 270°F (132°C) – it will stay as a ball. If you fish this ball out you will find that it is soft and squashy. This is the soft crack stage. You haven't got where you want to be yet but are well on the way, so be encouraged. A few moments later, when the heat has risen further, a new drop will not only remain solid in the glass of water but when fished out will be hard. This is the hard crack stage and your toffee is now done.

Pour your hot toffee out into the buttered dish and allow it to cool. Once cold, turn the toffee out of the tin onto a wooden board and break it up into lumps by hitting it with a clean hammer or rolling pin, then box it up.

Ingredients
1 lb (0.5 kg) white sugar
1 teacup of water
4 oz (125 g) butter
6 drops of lemon essence

FESTIVE GIFT BOXES

Small gift boxes containing mini presents, sweets, dried fruit or nuts were seen on most Victorian Christmas trees. Most were made at home out of odds and ends. Whilst the more valuable presents would have a little label with someone's name upon it, the less expensive or personal gifts were often raffled for or handed out as prizes for parlour games.

The cornucopia or cone design is the simplest of the lot. Begin with a square of card; fold it diagonally into a triangle and round off the top edge as shown below.

This can then be rolled into a cone and glued in place. Sew a loop of ribbon through both sides to hang it up.

The cones can be as plain or fancy as you like. Decorate your card whilst it is still flat with whatever you have to hand. Coloured paper, strips of foil, feathers, buttons, fabric cut-outs, pictures cut from old Christmas cards, ribbons, shells, dried flowers – whatever you can dream up. The Victorians liked such little boxes to be bright and pretty and often spent hours on them.

STORYTELLING

Sitting around the fire telling stories is a long-neglected pleasure. Some people still make up bedtime stories for their children, and great fun it is too, both for the people listening and those making it up as they go along. Some of my best childhood memories are of such evenings; my Dad in particular has a wonderful imagination. Cecil the pig who lived down by the railway embankment enthralled my younger brothers for months as Dad came up with adventure after adventure. Amongst adults, however, we are all too embarrassed these days and boy do we miss out. The Victorians had a lively storytelling tradition, and not just for children. Ghost stories, especially, enlivened many an evening and at Christmas, when many people were gathered together at home, they were just the thing. For those with less active imaginations there were stories to be read aloud to the family. Many of our best-loved stories and books began their life as stories told to family and friends.

For the last twenty years of his life, a sizeable portion of Charles Dickens's income came from public readings of his stories. The halls up and down the country were packed out as he read excerpts – with all the voices – of many of his works. The most popular were *The Pickwick Papers* and *A Christmas Carol*. If you try reading *A Christmas Carol* aloud you will soon discover how wonderfully it works. It actually feels better spoken aloud than read silently; the rhythms and repetitions are glorious when spoken.

"A Right Merrie Christmas and Happy New Year."

1. A right mer-rie Christ-mas and hap-py new year, To the friends that are far! To the friends that are near, Here's

2. And oh! when we drink to the friends that are met, To the ab-sent and far, Whom we wish had been here, Here's a

wish - ing them health! here's wish - ing them wealth, And a right mer -rie Christ - mas and hap-py new year.

cup to that man who for -gives and for-gets, And our hand, and our heart, and a hap-py new year.

Here's a health, drink it deep, to the bon - ni - est lass, Her name, by my troth, there is no need to spare, We

All hail! with a song, to the year at its birth; A - dieu, with a sigh, to the one on its bier; Oh with

all know full well who is best worth the glass, Our loves and good wish-es— a hap-py new year.

this may a mourn-ing be changed in - to mirth, A right mer - rie Christmas and hap-py new year.

* After each verse play first symphony.

CHRISTMAS MUSIC

The Christmas Number One is a tradition that can be traced back to Victorian times. It wasn't record sales that counted but copies of the sheet music sold. There was plenty of competition. The most popular had good, easy-to-sing tunes and rousing words. 'A Merrie Christmas and a Happy New Year' was the offering from the *Young Ladies' Journal* Christmas issue for 1869. Being published in a regular magazine guaranteed a certain circulation, but the publishers would have been hoping that the tune would catch on and that people would be writing off for further copies for their friends and family. A popular Christmas hit could run for years.

Amongst those for whom sheet music was a luxury too far, new words often got applied to well-known tunes. In churches up and down the country local musicians used the tunes they knew already for Christmas carols, playing local folk tunes on a motley collection of instruments. Such town bands, formed of everyone and anyone who could play an instrument, were beginning to be looked on with disapproval in some quarters. It was, after all, the same motley crew who played together in the village pub and were called in for every village celebration. They had a reputation for irreligiosity and sometimes drunkenness. In wealthier parishes, which were able to install an organ, the new sheet music versions were dominating, spreading the same new tunes across the country.

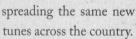

OPPOSITE PAGE *This music was originally produced in* The Young Ladies' Journal.

CHRISTMAS FOOD

Food at a Victorian family Christmas gathering was a mixture of tradition, innovation and plenty. From at least the Middle Ages, Christmas was a time of feasting in Britain. The Church deemed that advent, the four weeks running up to Christmas, was a time for fasting – like lent, although not so rigorous. Christmas Day was a feast, a celebration, when for the first time in weeks diet was totally unrestricted.

Throughout the Medieval and Tudor period, Christmas food was about eating as much of the good things as you could – the time when you not only made the most of the Church's permission to eat meat, but also had those luxuries that you couldn't usually afford. This meant as much dried fruit, sugar and spices as you could get hold of and afford.

Victorian and indeed modern Christmas fayre brings us strong memories of this time. Christmas puddings, Christmas cake and mince pies celebrate our enjoyment of dried fruit, sugar and spices, while a huge bird accompanied by lots of meat trimmings, such as chipolata sausages and forcemeat stuffing, is a reminder of the traditional desire for a large meat meal.

Even during the late-17th and 18th centuries, when Christmas was out of fashion, some of this food tradition hung on. Mince pies and Christmas cake have direct links with Tudor food, while Christmas pudding stands in for plum porridge.

Mince pies in late-Tudor recipes use hot water crust pastry – like that used for pork pies – and contain minced meat as well as the suet, dried fruit and spices that we are used to. Gradually over time the amount of meat in the recipes diminished and the amount of fruit increased. Victorian recipes vary, some have as much as 50 per cent meat and others have none at all. In the 1840s new technology brought inexpensive baking tins onto the market, which meant that pies could now be made of any type of pastry as the tins supported the pies in the oven. Shortcrust pastry became the usual one.

Christmas cake was once served on the twelfth day of Christmas under the name of Twelfth Night cake. Made light with yeast rather than eggs, it still contained all the ingredients you would expect to find in a modern Christmas

CHRISTMAS DINNER MENU

Ox tails	Boiled onions
Cold Ox tongue	Turnips
Roast turkey	Gravy
Forcemeat balls	Orange jelly
French fried potatoes	Damson
Brussels sprouts	blancmange
Leeks	Christmas pudding
Braised red cabbage	Brandy butter

Bread, herbs and an egg waiting to go into the stuffing.

The fat and pork for the forcemeat balls first had to be pounded to a paste. Not having a pestle and mortar, I made do with a rolling pin.

MAKING MINCEMEAT

INGREDIENTS

2 lb (1 kg) sirloin beef (boiled)

2 lb (1 kg) suet

8 large apples

6 lb (2.72 kg) currants

A two-penny loaf (small loaf)
  – grated

Mixed spice (nutmeg, cinnamon,
  cloves, ginger and coriander)
  to taste

A little pepper and salt

2 lb (1 kg) sugar

Grated peel of an orange and a
  lemon (perhaps 2 of each)

Juice from 6 oranges and
  2 lemons

Diced candied peel (optional)

1 pint (56.83 cl) brandy

1 pint (56.83 cl) port

**MAKES ENOUGH MINCEMEAT
FOR 16–20 LARGE MINCEPIES**

Diced candied peel is a
traditional ingredient for
mincement.

One of my small guilty pleasures of the festive season is a good old-fashioned mince pie. Of course, mince pies should really be referred to as mincemeat pies because traditionally they would have contained some form of meat. However, the mid- to late-Victorian period was experiencing something of a revolution in the composition of this festive dish, and as I scoured our collection of Victorian cookery books for some recipes – or receipts – I was surprised to see that mixes without meat were beginning to gain favour with some of the upper echelons of society.

However, I selected my recipe from the book that most amused me. John Murray, the publisher of Abermarle Street, London, bought the copyright for New Systems of Domestic Cookery *from Mrs Rundell in 1821 and I was to use his 1853 edition of her work,* Modern Domestic Cookery.

What I found so humorous about this book was the curious anonymity of its editors. The text and content were improved by 'A Lady' but with, as it says in the preface, 'the further advantage of being thoroughly revised by a professional gentleman of great repute'.

METHOD

Don't worry about needing a 'mincer' for the meat. Traditionally, mincing meat was simply chopping it as fine as you could get it. Do this to the beef, apples and suet. According to the original recipe, the mix required 4½ lb (2 kg) of suet but, in an age when we're slightly less physically challenged, half of that quantity is acceptable.

Place all of the ingredients in a large mixing bowl and work in well together with the hands. *Modern Domestic Cookery* recommends that the mix is put into jars, with lids tightly secured, and left for a number of days, maybe even weeks, before it is used. My tip here would be to accelerate this process by placing the mincemeat in a saucepan and letting it sit on a very low heat for a couple of hours. This way it really breaks down and becomes more paste-like and pliable.

I found that the quantities recommended in this particular recipe made an enormous number of pies, so you may want to reduce the quantities of the ingredients.

Use the pastry of your choice – I'm a big fan of short-crust pastry (which uses half fat to flour). For example, rub 4 oz (113 g) of butter or margarine into 8 oz (225 g) of flour until it resembles fine breadcrumbs. Add a little water to make a stiff paste, knead it, and then roll it out.

cake, including the marzipan covering and snowy white icing. Victorian recipes are almost indistinguishable from modern ones.

Christmas pudding has undergone a few more changes. The earliest references are to plum porridge rather than plum pudding. It began as a beef stew thickened with wheat grains and breadcrumbs and flavoured with a dash of spice and a small handful of raisins. Soon the meat element was reduced to the use of a little beef stock to moisten a dish of dried fruit, spices, suet, breadcrumbs and flour, and cooked rather like Moroccan cous cous. Finally, it was steamed in a cloth rather than thickened in a pan; it lost all the meatiness apart from a little suet, and became the Christmas pudding that we are all familiar with.

Making the Christmas pudding – while stirring the ingredients remember to make a wish!

While some elements of a Victorian Christmas meal had links with the past, some other parts were new. For instance, Brussels sprouts were not widely available in Britain until around the late 1880s. Roasting potatoes was also a new idea; they were usually boiled or mashed. Potatoes themselves only entered the British diet slowly, and long after our Irish neighbours had become dependent on them. Indeed their prominence in Ireland made people in the southern parts of Britain reluctant to adopt the potato. However, by the end of Victoria's reign, they had become common in all walks of British life.

Rather than boiling or roasting potatoes for our Christmas dinner, I chose to use another new method of cooking them – deep fat frying. In her book, Eliza Acton describes this recipe as 'an admirable way of dressing potatoes, very common on the continent, but less so in England than it deserves to be'.

Our Christmas dinner also had a range of other dishes – cold meats, jellies and blancmanges – that helped to fill the table without having to cook everything all at once. Jellies and blancmanges were popular at Victorian parties as they look good, and are light and clean tasting, clearing the palate between courses of richer food.

Pinning the ox tongue to a board with skewers helps it to keep its shape as it cools.

CHRISTMAS PUDDING

INGREDIENTS

2 lb (1 kg) of pre-soaked fruit
   and nuts

1 lb (450 g) of fresh breadcrumbs

5 oz (100 g) plain flour

1 tsp ground ginger

1 tsp ground cinnamon

Grated rind of one lemon

8 oz (225 g) soft brown sugar

2 eggs (beaten)

Juice of a lemon

A little milk or alcohol to mix

A Christmas pudding is a very rich steamed pudding. It is part of an important and very British way of cooking that popped up, seemingly from nowhere, around the year 1600. No other country has a tradition of these filling, hot sweet dishes. There are none in recipe books before 1600, but immediately afterwards they are everywhere, in a huge variety of flavours and textures. Quite how they came about is a mystery, but from then on they have been a major element in British cookery. Spotted Dick is a very plain plum (meaning dried fruit) pudding, and treacle sponge another. Jam roly-poly, Bedfordshire clangers, Devonshire pudding and Clouty dumplings, the list goes on and on.

Older recipes often include ground almonds and rosewater as flavourings, others use candied orange peel and sweet wine. Flour (and sometimes breadcrumbs) with a little fat of some kind, wetted with anything you fancy and maybe an egg can also be used. Once you know the principles you can invent to your heart's content.

At Christmas we put the richest and best ingredients into our pudding in such profusion that there is hardly any room for the flour and suet that forms its base.

METHOD

Blanching the almonds before they go into the pudding.

Which fruit and nuts you use are up to you. Choose things that you actually like. If fair-trade dried mango and apricots are your thing, then use them. If you hate cooked raisins, then leave them out. The better the quality of the fruit and nuts you choose the better tasting your pudding will be. Enjoy the shopping, poke around and find the best and juiciest stuff.

Assemble your dried fruit and nuts and get rid of any stalks or pips and cut up anything very large such as whole figs or dates.

Mix all the fruit together and put it to soak. The aim is to soften the fruit to make it juicier, to bring out and blend the flavours. Alcohol is, of course, the traditional thing to soak your fruit in. Once again, choose something that you like. Whisky, brandy, wine, sherry, port, beer and cider, they all work. If you don't want alcohol then apple juice or cold black tea works very well too. Leave your fruit to soak overnight.

Next mix all the other ingredients together (keeping back 28 g/1 oz of flour). Get everyone in the family to have a stir and make a wish as they do so.

The finished Christmas pudding wrapped in a tea towel and ready for the pot.

Now put a very large pan of water on to boil or prepare your steamer, or pressure cooker, whichever you have.

Take a clean tea towel, run it under the tap and wring it out firmly. Spread the damp cloth out on your work surface and sprinkle some flour over it. Spread the flour around with your hand so that it covers the cloth leaving no gaps. Dollop the Christmas pudding mixture onto the middle of the tea towel. Gather up the edges around the mixture and tie up into a round bundle.

Boiled to perfection, the pudding must be allowed to drain dry and cool.

When the water is boiling vigorously (or your steamer is steaming) drop the bundle in. If you are boiling your pudding in an ordinary pan it will need about eight hours to fully cook. Make sure that when you top up the water in the pan that you do so with boiling water from the kettle. If you are using a steamer, the same time will be needed. A pressure cooker will be much quicker; follow the manufacturer's guidelines (but usually an hour at full pressure will do it).

Once cooked, your pudding must be allowed to drain dry and will then keep for months – even till next year if stored somewhere dry (not in the fridge).

On Christmas Day the pudding will need to be re-heated. Pans of boiling water for an hour or two, the steamer, pressure cooker or microwave can all be pressed into service here.

CHRISTMAS DAY

 A Victorian Christmas dinner is familiar to us all and includes a roasted bird, a Christmas pudding and Christmas crackers; as many of the good things as we can eat and as many family and friends as we can gather together. Some things, however, were a little different. The bird was open roasted before the fire rather than baked in the oven and the potatoes were not usually roasted, but boiled. Sausages and stuffing, however, would then, as now, accompany the turkey and brandy sauce was served with the pudding.

Oh what fun. We had a really good day. I put the range into overdrive first thing and it did me proud – everything cooked to perfection with the exception of the forcemeat balls, which I left in the oven a bit too long. I was especially pleased with the turkey. I am so used to roasting in front of wood fires, but have never done it with coal before. Open roasting is always so much more interesting, flavourwise, than oven roasting. I think it a great shame that most people in modern Britain never get the opportunity to taste the real thing.

I dropped the grate down into its lowest position and pulled the burning coals forward against the bars, replenishing from the back of the grate and only pulling the coal to the front when it was burning well, so as to keep the temperature even.

The bottle jack oven needed a little more attention than I had hoped, needing rewinding every ten minutes or so. If I had been using the old wood technology I would have had to tend the roast about the same amount, so I wouldn't say that the Victorian bottle jack was an enormous improvement. The shield around the meat, though, proved very useful, keeping not only the heat but also the grease of the roasting contained.

Tom, Paul, Andy, Hillary and Rupert all came to dinner. Rupert brought us a bottle of his homemade mulberry wine. It was delicious, and very typically Victorian. Imported wine from grapes was expensive, so home-made fruit wines were much more common than in modern Britain. Andy brought his flute along so we had music as well. Later we all played shadowbuff. This turned out to be surprisingly good fun. We were all a little tipsy by then. What with Hillary wearing a chamber pot on her head and Peter with a bucket on his, dignity flew out the window, and what might have seemed odd in the cold light of day was, in fact, a great deal of fun.

Decking the halls with boughs of holly.

Preparing pink rabbit blancmange and orange jelly for the Christmas dinner.

OVERLEAF *The Victorian Christmas meal was enjoyed by everyone, as can be seen by the empty plates.*

CHAPTER THREE

IT'S ALL ABOUT
THE BREEDING

Animal Husbandry

 Animal husbandry is the term given to raising or breeding livestock. It is first thought to have started at the end of the Pleistocene period (*c.*12,000 years ago) as our ancestors began to change from a hunter-gatherer lifestyle to having a more direct involvement in food production (essentially farming). Reasons often cited for this shift are climate change, resource stress, population expansion and migration. Certainly throughout history animal husbandry has been linked in some way to human's social evolution.

In Britain there had been some attempts to improve domestic livestock, but it was in the 18th century that major developments in animal husbandry began. Prior to this period, animals were reportedly often underweight and prone to disease and many had to be culled during winter due to a shortage of feed. However, breed improvers such as Robert Bakewell, the Colling brothers, and John Ellman developed breeding practices that started to change this, and the way that animals were reared and farmed in Britain.

The Pioneering Breeders

Much of Robert Bakewell's fame comes from the attention paid to him by publicists such as Arthur Young; however, other breeders were experimenting with animal husbandry. Two such breeders were the Colling brothers, who were students of Bakewell. They continued his work on their farms, developed his methods and became famous for their improvements to the shorthorn breed of cattle. Using Bakewell's techniques they improved the Durham cow, producing a shorthorn that was good for both milk and beef and which rapidly became more fashionable than Bakewell's longhorn. Not only did Charles Colling become the first breeder to receive more than 100 guineas for a shorthorn cow, but he also made 1,000 guineas when, on his retirement, he sold his prized bull, Comet. Today, shorthorns have been bred into two blood lines: a beef shorthorn and a dairy shorthorn.

John Ellman is another livestock improver whose work exists in the shadow of Robert Bakewell. He had a farm at Glynde in East Sussex and, in the late 18th century, decided to do to the tall, wiry and lean South Down sheep, what Bakewell had done to the Leicester breed. He managed to breed the South Down sheep so

ROBERT BAKEWELL

Robert Bakewell is the most well-known breed improver of the 18th century, and is often referred to as 'the father of animal husbandry'. After a period of travelling in Europe he began to work for his father on his tenant farm in Dishley. Whilst farming, Bakewell started to experiment (*c*.1745) with the mating strategies of his animals – focusing largely on a process which became known as 'breeding in and in'. In 1760, when his father died, Bakewell took over the running of the farm.

Robert Bakewell.

Up until this time animals had been largely left to their own devices when it came to breeding, with males and females occupying the same fields. However, 'breeding in and in' meant that the sexes were separated and only animals with certain characteristics were selected to breed with one another. By breeding animals that were closely related (essentially inbreeding), Bakewell was able to control the ways in which they developed and was able to create a distinct 'breed' of animal. In reducing the genetic diversity, he succeeded in creating uniformity and consistency. He also selected traits that he wished to exploit, such as the size of the animal. Importantly, Bakewell kept detailed breeding records and emphasized their value to the wider animal husbandry community.

He started experimenting with old Lincolnshire sheep, crossing them with the best Leicestershire or Ryeland sheep, resulting in a breed called the new Leicester. The sheep he created had an improved meat quantity and, as the *New York Times* commented on 17 May 1885, Bakewell was a man who 'saw that the day was near when meat would be more valued in the ox than draught or in the sheep than wool'. Bakewell started hiring out his rams, a process he popularized, in 1755 for 16 shillings (about 75p) each and later formed the Dishley Society to try to protect his new breed of sheep. After 1789 his rams were being hired out for 6,000 guineas a season (around £450,000).

Bakewell's sheep rearing was the most successful of his experiments, despite reports that once the sheep had passed a certain age (around two years) his methods produced a very fatty meat only fit for the poor. However, he also experimented with horses, playing his part in breeding the modern shire horse, and cattle, with which he was less successful. The principles he used for sheep when applied to his new longhorn cattle, created a bovine breed that, while being larger, was poor for milking and produced an excessively fatty meat. Sadly both of his sheep and cattle breeds no longer exist. The closest sheep breed to Bakewell's new Leicester existing today is the Border Leicester.

It is sometimes suggested that his 'in and in' method came from the world of race-horse breeding. Although the practice was similar to horse breeding, his use of closely related animals reflects more the world of bird breeding. Moreover, Bakewell told Arthur Young that he was influenced by his experience of pigeon fanciers and cock breeders. Modern-day methods of line breeding are a development of 'in and in' breeding, but they use animals that aren't directly related and employ the technique of outcrossing (bringing in an animal from outside the breed) to increase genetic diversity.

Bakewell also worked on improving the wider elements of farming: field drainage and irrigation, grass cultivation, manure and housing for livestock.

that it had a better quality of wool and produced more mutton. He won several prizes at agricultural livestock shows with his sheep and was very open about his breeding techniques. By all accounts he was a decent man with a generous heart, especially as an employer providing fair living conditions and a school for his labourers' children. His work was continued by Jonas Webb in Cambridgeshire. The effect John Ellman had on his sheep is still evident today.

They say 'the proof of the pudding is in the eating' and the average weights in pounds of sheep, cows, lambs and calves sold at Smithfield market in 1795 are more than double the 1710 figures. This shows the success that livestock improvers had on producing breeds that yielded more meat per animal. Bakewell may not have been the best livestock improver but he was certainly very good at publicizing the idea. Since the 18th century, animal husbandry has been constantly refined and improved with results such as a continuation in increased milk production year on year. Some of this is down to breeding and some of this is down to other developments in agriculture and technology.

Change for the Better

On our Victorian farm we can see the results of these improvements in livestock. We have two shorthorn cows (Forget-me-knot and Iris), a Gloucestershire Old Spot pig (Princess), a shire horse (Clumper), ten Shropshire sheep and one Shropshire ram (Fred). The Colling brothers improved the shorthorn cow.

Bakewell may not have been the best livestock improver but he was certainly very good at publicizing the idea.

Bakewell is thought to have been interested in pig improvement although no record exists of this, but he did have a hand in breeding horses that eventually led to the shire horse. Improvements in the sheep of the Long Mynd in Shropshire, Cannock Chase in Staffordshire, and Morfe Common on the borders of Shropshire, Staffordshire and Worcestershire began in the early 19th century following the developments pioneered by Bakewell and John Ellman. These improvements resulted in the Shropshire breed of sheep whose development was heavily influenced by two local farmers, George Adney and Samuel Miere. Then, in 1883, the Shropshire Sheep Breeders' Association produced and published a flock book that listed all their sheep and the prizes that they won at shows. This enabled purchasers in Britain and abroad to be able to identify reputable breeders.

Writers in the early Victorian period remarked on the extent of the physical change of animals since the mid-18th century, although these improvements

continued to be made throughout the 19th century and beyond. The Victorian period brought new technologies such as meat freezing, transport infrastructures (the railways), and a greater and more demanding population largely focused in urban centres. This all helped facilitate an even greater need for meat production and, therefore, a greater need for advancements in animal husbandry. However, the new technologies also created a world market, which ultimately lowered the price of domestic meat by at least a quarter in the last third of the 19th century.

Much of the agricultural practice on our farm is influenced by the writings in Henry Stephen's *Book of the Farm* (fourth edition). In it, it is written: 'Mixed husbandry is in ordinary circumstances the safest, because, should his stock be much lowered in value, the farmer has the grain to depend upon; and should the grain give a small return, the stock may yield a profit.'

This circumstance of relying on animals for profit would not be possible without the improvements made to livestock and those improvements would have been difficult without advances in agriculture. All of which helped fuel the industrial revolution while simultaneously being boosted by the progression of industry.

Illustration of a Shropshire ram as featured in Henry Stephen's **Book of the Farm**.

Pigs

Once our pig sties were fully formed it was time to fulfil their function and send in the pigs. The museum was only too happy to lend us three young Tamworth pigs and Judith Sims, the President of the Gloucestershire Old Spot Pig Breeder's Club, lent us Princess – a pregnant Gloucestershire Old Spot sow. 'Princess' is her matriarchal line name so all her daughters will be called Princess too. According to the British Pig Association 'the breed currently has four male and fifteen female lines'.

Princess arrives at the farm accompanied by Richard Lutwych.

The Gloucestershire Old Spot pig is affectionately known as the orchard pig and folklore maintains that the spots on their bodies are bruises from falling apples. They are a very hardy pig and a generally laid-back breed. They are the

oldest spotted pedigree in the world and are thought to originate from the Berkeley Vale on the southern shores of the River Severn – a cross between the original Gloucestershire Pig and the unimproved Berkshire. The majority of traditional native breeds have less than five hundred sows although the Old Spot is the largest numerically of the British breeds. Old Spot pigs are a breed that produce very good-quality meat (the best according to their breeders!).

Tamworth pigs are the oldest pure breed of pig in Britain and are thought to be descended from the old English forest pig. This is because, in the late 18th century when other breeds were being improved, the Tamworth was considered unfashionable and left alone. Subsequently, the Tamworth has the longest snout of the present-day domestic breeds.

PIGS, PAST AND PRESENT

The five genera and nine species of pig live on every continent of the world (except Antarctica). Originally forest-dwelling animals, they were initially believed to have been domesticated in the East and Far East, although evidence is

The Tamworth pigs with their characteristically long snouts.

Manure

Our sizeable muck heap steaming away. Manure steams because it generates heat as it decomposes.

There was a time when I thought the word 'manure' was a polite way of saying animal poo. However, I now realize, as with most aspects of this farm, there is an entire science behind the term manure. Strictly speaking, today the term manure is used to refer to organic matter that is used as a fertilizer (usually animal excrement or green crops), but in the past it has been used as a blanket term for fertilizers including chemicals. (Mills were often put to use grinding bones – including the bones of lowly soldiers who were killed on the battlefield – to use as bone manure.)

The main purpose of manure is to put nitrogen back into the soil which is the essential ingredient needed for the cultivation of white crops such as wheat and barley. Prior to the Norfolk four-course rotation (see page 23) farmers were heavily reliant on manure to replenish the nitrogen levels in the soil, but it is nowhere near as effective at fixing nitrogen in the earth as legumes such as clover which get their nitrogen from the air. However, manure isn't just put on fields – it can also be used to force plants and vegetables in a cold frame (see page 51). It is not unknown for very large dung piles to spontaneously combust, and they are very hard to extinguish and, unsurprisingly, they foul the air for a considerable radius.

During our time on the farm we have generated quite a sizeable muck heap, made up from the soiled bedding of Iris and Forget-me-not, our two Shorthorn cows that we over-wintered in our cow shed, and the bedding of our pigs, Princess, our Gloucestershire Old Spot and the three Tamworths. Ideally, a muck heap should be turned and be allowed to break down until it is ready to be spread on the fields or in the garden. We have also produced quite a good green manure from the leaves and stems that we cut off of our mangle-wurzels. This can be ploughed back into the soil and will also replenish the nitrogen levels.

The only problem with working on the farm shovelling manure every day is that you get used to it. I remember when the pigs arrived and I went to muck them out for the first time. The stench of ammonia was overpowering but now I don't bat an eyelid. However, we had a visitor the other day and he commented on the smell and Alex and I looked at each other knowing full well that neither of us notices it anymore unless, of course, we find ourselves in polite society and then we step back and think, 'Yes, we smell bad'.

Mucking out the pigs: a daily chore that was a joy to undertake.

emerging for other areas of independent domestication, such as central Europe, Northern India and South East Asia.

While rooting around in the grass, the pigs enjoy having their backs scratched.

In the early 19th century in Britain, pigs were to an extent the second class citizens of the farmyard, but as the century wore on pig keeping emerged from the shadows and again became a specialist aspect of farming in its own right. Pigs were very important to cottagers because, apart from being a source of cheap meat, they were a way of repaying social and monetary debts. In addition, as industrial towns expanded, pigs were kept in and around the slum dwellings that developed. They were slaughtered by their owners until the 1860s, after which time it became illegal to slaughter animals other than in a place designed for that purpose.

Pigs are akin to humans (we are known as long pigs). They have similar internal organs to us, although their sweat glands are relatively ineffective so therefore they seek relief from the heat through water and mud – which also acts as a sun-block. They are very intelligent animals with, I think, soulful eyes; however, they are prone to depression. Whenever we let our pigs out (and we often did), they would come and see what we were doing in Glebe meadow and sometimes try to help out.

IT'S ALL ABOUT THE BREEDING

CATTLE

Towards the end of October, having acquired our flock of Shropshire sheep, it was time to think about what cattle we would need for the year. A bovine concern was a key element in a system of mixed farming and, in preparation, we had cleaned out our cattle shed and found it to have four regular-sized stalls and a cow and calf stall.

Obviously, we didn't want to over-burden ourselves and find ourselves dedicating a disproportionate amount of time to cattle farming, so our objectives were modest. Certainly, later in the year we would be requiring milk for our dairy ambitions. It was also a target of mine to successfully deliver and rear a calf, as I was aware that this was a major source of income to low-scale tenant farmers of the late 19th century.

Shorthorns enjoying the grass in the upper meadow.

Cattle farming in the Victorian period had undergone something of a mini-revolution. Whilst much of the pioneering work in selective breeding had taken

place in the late 18th and early 19th centuries, it was left to the Victorians to refine the resultant breeds and to adopt an approach to dairy and beef production on a mass, factory-styled system.

A key aspect to the 'factory farming' of cows was the over-wintering of animals in cow barns, tethering them to stalls where they would be fed, watered and mucked out.

Improved fodder crops and storage meant that cows could be fed a diet as rich and nutritious during winter as they would expect during the late spring and summer months. Furthermore, sheltered from the winter winds, rain, sleet and snow, the animals wouldn't needlessly expend fat and 'stock' reserves just trying to keep warm. This was important to beef farmers as they needed to keep a bullock in a continually improving condition in preparation for market. If a beast is allowed to get lean and perhaps even run down, it will take a greater investment of foodstuffs to bring it back up to an acceptable size for slaughter. The same rules apply to dairy cows. They need to be kept in a constant condition of excellent health for both abundant milk production and for the welfare and safe deliverance of calves.

One of the other benefits of over-wintering was the accumulation throughout the winter months of cow manure. Everyday, twice-a-day, Peter and I were responsible for mucking out the cow shed and, in a very short period of time, an

Forget-me-knot was a sociable beast and really quite friendly.

THE SHORTHORN

On the basis that they were both good for milk and beef, we decided to opt for the Shorthorn breed. During the Victorian period, these were by far and away the most widespread and numerous of the cow breeds, and played a significant part in the development of the livestock industry in Britain. Furthermore, vast numbers of Shorthorns were exported around the world during the late 19th century and, as a consequence, they were to earn British farmers a good deal of money.

The breed originated from County Durham in north-east England, and is often referred to as the 'Durham Breed' or 'Teeswater Cattle'. It is thought that they are a descendent of the aboriginal cattle of north-eastern England, but their popularity grew out of the work conducted by the Colling brothers in the Valley of the Tees in the early 19th century. Charles and Robert Colling are said to have very quickly developed a superior breed directing themselves to the improvement of the cattle where they were most defective. A large, high-standing cow that was a good milker but slow to mature was, through the breeding practices of the Colling brothers, turned into a breed that was wider in the rib, shorter in the leg, slightly smaller, heavier in flesh and speedy in growth – especially in the accumulation of flesh and fat.

Henry Stephens, author of *The Book of the Farm* and mentor to me throughout the year, was keen to put the success of the Colling brothers down to what Robert Bakewell termed 'in and in breeding' – the breeding of closely related animals which possessed desirable features. This practice Stephens describes as 'an uncertain agent, which, according to the manner in which it is directed, is possessed of great power for good or evil' (see also pages 110–11). Stephens was quick to rebuff claims that the Colling brothers had injected fresh blood into their mix and imported specimens from their Dutch and Danish counterparts. However, it would seem that his faith was misplaced. More recent DNA testing of the shorthorn breed demonstrates that it shares a common origin with cows from across the English Channel and North Sea, and it was therefore likely that the Colling Shorthorn is a product of cross breeding.

Nonetheless, the Shorthorn is a marvellous cow and probably the last of the great 'dual-purpose' cows. As milkers, they can be expected to produce 700–1,000 gallons (3,180–4,545 litres) per year (not far off what you might expect from a modern Friesian) and crossed with a Herefordshire bull, they could produce fine beef. They can adapt extremely well to a range of climates, soil and terrain and have a good temperament to boot.

The model Shorthorn cow as featured in Henry Stephen's Book of the Farm.

Our two Shorthorns – Forget-me-not, left, a three-year-old in calf, with two-year-old Iris by her side.

enormous dung heap started to grow in our stack yard. Given twelve months to breakdown, this would be ideal for spreading on the fields over the course of the next winter.

Forget-me-not and Iris

Our cows arrived in early November ready to spend the winter in our freshly cleaned cow shed. Forget-me-not was a three-year-old cow in calf and due to give birth in May. She was stalled alongside Iris who was one year her junior and without calf. They both settled in very quickly, enjoying the snugness and shelter of our cow shed, but with even just two cows, Peter and I realized we were to have our hands full. Morning and evening they would need feeding and mucking out. Each day each cow would need at least three buckets of water, three wads of hay, two buckets-full of sliced roots and half a bucket of milled oats. This was a big commitment, but in a very short period of time, Peter and I both grew to enjoy our role as stock-men. The care and dedication that these graceful beasts require can have a calming effect on one's soul and we would often find ourselves engrossed in conversations about how many buckets of water each had taken and how they preferred the barley straw to the clover hay.

Forget-me-not's calf.

SHROPSHIRE SHEEP

*What every farmer knows is that sheep are the only creation on God's earth that are
looking for the quickest way to die.*

*You can do everything right and lose the lot or get everything wrong and come out
smelling of roses.*

RICHARD SPENCER, sheep farmer and one of our key advisors

 Certainly, we couldn't have picked a more appropriate breed of sheep
to begin our flock. The Shropshire – or 'Shropshire down' as it is sometimes known – probably reached its peak in population in the late 19th
century and, better still, it was as local as a sheep can get!

Improvements in the breeding of livestock were a feature of farming during
the Agricultural Revolution. Sheep that were, to a certain extent, indigenous to a
region would be developed to produce more and better meat, to mature earlier and
to yield a better fleece.

The local sheep of the Staffordshire and Shropshire areas were hardy, good
wool sheep and had their origins in the hills of the Long Mynd in Shropshire
(a mere twenty-minute walk from our farm) and Cannock Chase in Staffordshire.

This breed was subjected to improvement during the first half of the 1800s,
and the key exponents of this programme of breeding were George Adney and
Samuel Miere. Adney believed in what Robert Bakewell termed 'in and in'
breeding. This came down to running the best rams with ewes with the most
desirable features from within the breed and, on occasions, the same blood line.

Miere was more an advocate of introducing blood from outside species. Thus,
the Shropshire was crossed with the Southdown to rid the former of its horns. To
make the breed more docile and better suited to the enclosed pastures of
Shropshire's river valleys, the blood of the 'Leicester' – famously developed by
Robert Bakewell – was introduced.

Either way, the resultant sheep were enormously popular and considered at
the time to be adaptable to a range of different terrains and soils. Their popularity
was confirmed by their increasing presence at agricultural shows. The Royal
Agricultural Society – founded in 1838 – held annual shows at county towns and,
although from the outset the Shropshire did not have a class of its own, it competed

Fleece of wool rolled up.

VICTORIAN FARM

well in the 'Shortwools' classes. In fact, it impressed the judges so much that by the Canterbury meeting of 1860 the Shropshire Downs were given their own class.

In the 1884 show at Shrewsbury, 875 Shropshires were exhibited – more than twice the number of all the other breeds put together – marking the breed out as one of the most popular of its day. It was seen as a sheep capable of producing high- quality meat and wool.

Shropshire sheep: a versatile breed, good examples of which are said to be clear of wool in the face and legs.

FLOCK BOOKS

Although records of the pedigree of certain rams had been maintained since the early 1850s, it wasn't until 1883 that the breeders' association put together a 'flock book' to record the names and breeding of certain animals and any prizes that they had won. This makes the Shropshire Sheep Breeders' Association the oldest flock book society in the country.

Flock books enabled buyers to be sure of the reputation of breeders and the pedigree of rams. For the Shropshire breed of sheep, the flock book aided an already flourishing home market but also stimulated interest from abroad. Between 1880 and 1900, 253 registered rams were exported, and from 1900 to 1920 as many as 6,700 rams crossed the seven seas to establish flocks in New Zealand, Australia, the USA and to other destinations around the world.

However, by the 1920s, the 'Golden Age' for the Shropshire sheep was over, and for various reasons they fell out of favour with sheep farmers around the British Isles. The First World War had disrupted shipping and the export market suffered badly. Furthermore, successive Foot and Mouth outbreaks in the 1920s and 1930s dealt a severe blow to the fortunes of many Shropshire breeders.

It was about this time, too, that the division between the woolly-faced and the clean-faced sheep began. Interestingly, the woolly-faced sheep – developed for the American export market – was not proving popular with home breeders.

Richard Spencer getting to grips with Fred, our Shropshire ram. Throughout the year, Richard proved to be an invaluable source of advice.

Monday 22nd October

Our consignment of Shropshire ewes arrived early in the morning. We had decided to start the sheep off in the Upper Glebe Meadow. Our plan was to 'flush' the ewes. We've all heard of Flushing Meadows – the site of the US Open tennis tournament – and the place name essentially relates to an area of rich pasture that sheep can be turned out on two to three weeks before mating. Flushing can affect fertility in two different ways. Firstly, it increases the ovary activity to result in more 'heat' periods and, secondly, it can cause multiple ovulations that can lead to twins or triplets.

Essentially the ewe should be gaining weight up to the point when they are run with the ram and should maintain condition throughout the period that the ram stays with them. So, we would begin the sheep in the Upper Glebe Meadow for a couple of weeks and then, in November, when they were due to run with the ram, bring them down into the Lower Glebe meadow where they would be closer at hand.

Things didn't quite go to plan though. As they were being lead down the lane to our farm, one of them bolted and jumped a wall into a neighbouring garden. Peter and I sped in after the escapee sheep whilst Richard Spencer and Sue Farquhar – our sheep gurus for the year – held the others in the lane.

Peter and I tip-toed through the garden of the adjoining property – hoping not to get seen – and clambered into the small wood behind where we suspected the ewe had fled. We reached the top edge of the wood only to catch sight of the sheep in the adjacent field running around as if startled. We figured that something must have triggered this behaviour and that it was highly likely that our sheep had disturbed our neighbour's flock. So early on in the proceedings, it was highly unlikely that we would recognise our sheep from the many different varieties of breeds that seemed to constitute the flock in this field.

So, back to the Upper Glebe with our ewes and already one down, we were feeling a bit deflated. It was imperative that we retrieved our sheep so that we could run her with the ram when he arrived in early November but, of course, it was now very much in the hands of the local farmer as to when he could make time to weed out our errant sheep.

Thus, members of the flock book society took steps to confirm the true attributes of the Shropshire breed as 'naturally clean soft black faces and legs'.

During the year, I frequently canvassed the opinions of Shropshire breeders and found this debate alive and well with some favouring a woolly face and others the clean face. My own personal opinion very much favours the clean face, for the main reason that they appeared to be much cleverer than their woolly-faced sisters!

The breed probably reached its lowest ebb in 1973 with only 402 breeding ewes registered. With the help of the Rare Breeds Society, there has been a steady improvement in the numbers since, and by 1992 there were 1,844 breeding ewes. We were hoping we could play our part in the revival of this once-popular sheep and add to the swelling flock book a significant number of our own sheep. This would depend, however, on how well we listened to our sheep advisors, as well as vigilance, dedication and, if Richard Spencer's words of advice are to ring true, a good deal of luck!

OVERLEAF *During the winter months our Shropshires became bolder and bolder, often waiting alongside the feed trough ready for their twice daily meals.*

THE POULTRY YARD

Although poultry are fed upon every farm, and it therefore might be expected that we should give a detailed account of the various breeds and their respective management, yet we, upon reflection, thought that it would only uselessly swell the work, as every housewife is so well acquainted with the means of rearing them, that, upon that subject, we could teach little that is not generally known; and as to the history of the different sorts, and their peculiar habits, we must leave to naturalists, for we doubt whether our farmers wives would read it.

British Husbandry for the Society for the Diffusion of Useful Knowledge

 The poultry yard was traditionally the responsibility of the farmer's wife, and throughout the Victorian period little happened to change that. Poultry was the last area of farming to be modernized and the last area to come under a largely male management. *The Book of the Farm* by Henry Stephens talks hesitantly about the potential for improvement, but has little in the way of ideas for how to do so.

The ducks keeping warm in the poultry shed (above), and (right) taking a walk around the farmyard.

Feeding the turkeys who had strayed into the meadow.

Chickens, ducks, geese and turkeys lived in and around the farmyard. They had a hen house or poultry shed to keep them warm and safe at night and the occasional handful of grain to supplement whatever they could pick up for themselves. For many farmers' wives that was largely it. For those with the time and skill there were things you could do to improve their egg laying and the size of the birds for the table.

A dust bath of sand, wood ashes and sulphur in a corner of the yard allowed the birds to keep themselves free from parasites. A little raw onion now and then was felt to cure most diseases. Chickens were also known to do much better if they got a mixture of green foodstuffs, meal or grain, a little salt and were allowed to peck at bones now and then. Grubs and worms from the dung heap completed the balanced diet. Charcoal was often recommended for health in turkeys.

For ducks, the very finest diet was slugs. Ducks, especially young ducks, are truly fantastic at controlling slugs in a garden or field of young turnips. They hunt them out and wolf them down with gusto.

Cleanliness in the poultry shed was of course important to prevent disease and encourage good laying. As well as being mucked out regularly – the manure is powerful stuff on the vegetable garden – poultry sheds were white-washed annually to sterilize them. Keeping the shed in good repair also helped to keep rats and foxes out. Rats can kill as many chickens as a fox, or indeed the neighbour's dog.

The surplus eggs from our chickens began to be a useful source of ready cash and barter power.

If you want the birds to lay well and be successful at rearing chicks when you wish them to, you also need to provide comfortable nests for them. Hopefully they will then lay in the nests and not dot their eggs around the hedgerows.

LAMBING

Fred the ram had left the meadow and ten pregnant Shropshire ewes remained. They are a breed of sheep notorious for having twins, so we could have potentially turned ten sheep into thirty. Neither Alex nor I had done this before and it was an exciting yet nerve-racking experience. We visited Richard Spencer's farm (the gentleman who lent us the ewes) for a crash course in lambing. We delivered a healthy lamb each and also learnt how to persuade a ewe to 'adopt' a lamb. In addition, I removed a still-born lamb from a ewe's womb. It was a fast-paced, emotional day, which I found life assuring as well as confidence inspiring. However, you still wonder, ' will I be able to do it?'.

Alex outside the Shepherd's hut. Inside, there is a table, two benches, some cupboards, and at the far end a little bed with a dog cage underneath.

In preparation for our lambing saga we borrowed a Shepherd's hut from the home farm so that we could have a base in the field and be close to the flock if we needed to be. Essentially it is like a mini-caravan that is horse drawn, with an orange under-carriage and blue wheels. Inside there is a little pot-bellied stove that warms the hut and enables us to heat water to wash our hands between aiding each ewe, and also to make the essential teas and coffees. The hut is designed for one man to live in while tending the sheep but we often sat in there, played chess and read our Shropshire sheep flock books published in 1901.

We also cleared out two bays of our cart shed that opens out into Glebe meadow where our sheep were, moved the sheep feeder into it and hurdled off the front and sides. We laid a good, thick covering of straw on the floor and started feeding the sheep in the shed. This got them used to going in there and, as the due date drew nearer (put your ram in on Guy Fawke's Day/5 November and by April Fool's Day, you have lambs), we began to shut the sheep in at night. I have been told by sheep farmers that it is the rain that kills lambs. If they are caught in the rain just after birth, and before they have had a decent dose of colostrum (their mother's milk), they will die. (We did have one lamb that escaped from the hurdles and got caught in the snow – we fed it colostrum and kept it warm but it died after a few days.) We also kept our eye on the flock to watch for signs of imminent lambs. The vulva becomes pink and swollen and the ewe's udders drop prior to birth. Also, ewes will tend to separate from the flock and we noticed that their breathing became quite rapid and shallow.

To our great relief our first two lambs were delivered without incident. Shropshire sheep are renowned for having twins.

Lambing: March–April

... For about a fortnight, we had been out in the fields checking for signs; the udders drop, the sheep retires to a corner and separates itself from the flock and as it starts to get contractions the head is pointed upwards to the sky.

Fortunately we had been given a masterclass in lambing by Richard Spencer, one of our Shropshire sheep gurus for the year. Less than five minutes after arriving at Richard's farm for what we thought would be a leisurely afternoon's tutorial, Peter had his hand up a ewe's backside and was feeling around for the front feet of an extremely big lamb.

With sheep, it is all about 'presentation' – the position of the lamb as it passes from the womb into the pelvic passage. If it is coming front feet first with its head facing forwards, things should go okay. However, if the head is tucked down between the forelegs or doubled back along its spine, problems can occur and the shepherd has to try to rearrange the position of the lamb's body. Breach births, where the lamb effectively bridges the gap between the pelvic bones are perhaps the worse.

It was almost to the hour of putting Fred to the ewes on 5 November that we saw our first lamb, and not very long after that his twin sister arrived, on 1 April. As we were there, we assisted with the birth of these lambs; however, several of the sheep had no complications and just dropped their lambs all by themselves either in the night or during the day. Although, one Sunday I went to check the sheep and there was a ewe with a lamb's head hanging out of her rear end. However, its tongue was swollen which is a sure sign that the lamb needed assistance right away. I leapt over the hurdle and swiftly put the ewe on her side. Then feeling with my fingers I located the first foot and pulled it out and found the second, and in one smooth movement I extracted the lamb from the ewe. I then rubbed it vigorously with straw to start circulation, removed the birth sac from its face, and pinched its ear so that it gasped and began breathing. I then presented it to the ewe although, out of the corner of my eye, I was aware that something had gone horribly wrong.

She had turned herself inside out and her uterus was now on the outside. This usually happens prior to birth and only some of it comes out. These sheep will often have recurring problems and a trip to the butcher may be in order, but those whose womb comes out post-birth rarely repeat the feat with later pregnancies. It sounds horrid and it is. The biggest problem is infection due to contamination from mucky straw or other detritus that litters a lambing pen. Thankfully this happened when I was there and I was able to keep her upright, keep the uterus clean, and wait for the vet, who gave her three injections: one to numb the pain while she stuffed (literally) the womb back in, one dose of antibiotics, and one to close her up. The vet then popped a box stitch in her vagina which Alex and I removed a week later. I'm happy to report that there have been no further complications. Although we did nickname the lamb Odd-head because, for a while, she had quite a swollen head.

CARING FOR THE LAMBS

It is advisable to keep newborns in the pen for about forty-eight hours. However, we kept Odd-head and her mother in for a week, and some of the others for quite a while too, because we had a bout of really grotty weather, including snow. During this quarantine period it gave us the opportunity to clean the sheep's hoofs and cut its nails (one of the smelliest jobs). The ewe and her offspring are then marked up for future identification. We used raddle (red ochre powder mixed with oil) and daubed the ewes with letters in the order that they gave birth; so the first ewe was marked AB and her firstborn was marked A and the other one B (we put the marks on the right for boys and on the left for girls). The next ewe (who also had twins) was CD, and so on. If they just had one lamb they only had a single letter. We got up to P, which equates to sixteen lambs or 160 per cent. The average rate for Shropshires is 170 per cent (although Q did pass away).

Once they were marked and their feet sorted, we moved them from our farmyard to Ovenal – the field next to the one in which we sowed our wheat crop. It is a distance of about 760 yd (700 m). To move the ewes, we picked up their lambs by the front legs in one hand and dragged them away from the ewe, at the same time mimicking the lambs' bleat. By dragging them (it need only be the hind legs and the tail) you leave a scent trail for the ewe to follow; the bleat is emotional blackmail, but once they've got the idea the ewe will come. With some of the ewes it was like being at Crufts, with the sheep trotting by your side.

If I was a sheep, ovine heaven would be Ovenal, with its lush grass, its ha-has for the lambs to play on, its daffodils and its slightly undulating terrain. With Acton Scott Hall in the background, smoke coming from the chimney, the golden glow from the late-afternoon sun and the lambs playing in the flowers while their mothers grazed, it truly was a picture of spring.

A lamb enjoys its mother's milk (above). One of the ewes with her lamb back in the field (left).

133

Farrowing the Pig

When I was ten my parents won a piglet in a raffle which they promptly sold to a group of hungry looking Germans; that is the closest bond I have had with a pig until now. Therefore, it was only natural that I was apprehensive about farrowing a sow (helping her to give birth). We had been told Princess's due date based on when she went to the boar (the gestation period for a pig is three months, three weeks, three days), and we were told to look out for the signs.

These are 'bagging up', which is a swelling of the teats, milk lactating when the udder is squeezed, and nesting. We were also told that she was usually two days late and sure enough two days after she was due her swollen udders started to yield milk when squeezed. This is the most reliable sign of an imminent birth as the piglets will arrive within twelve hours of this happening. However, I had no idea what nesting was going to look like. In my mind I saw her just moving her bedding around in her sty but, in reality, as I was mucking her out she started gathering straw, hay, grass and twigs in her mouth and depositing them in her sty.

Princess is a good mother and her piglets soon learnt who is in control in the sty.

It was a truly heart-melting moment. It was then that I knew that I was in for a long night so I gathered some provisions and made my way to the sty. When I got there she had already started giving birth. I got into the sty with her but only because my clothes already smelled of her, and after a couple of months of prolonged back scratches (which she comes up to me and asks for with a certain noise) we were close friends. However, as Richard Spencer says, if a sow takes a dislike to you she can and will kill you.

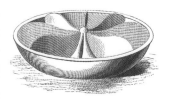

Ring pigs' trough.

The piglets produce a chemical that lets the sow know that it is time for them to come, and they came thick and fast. As they popped out I cleaned them off and moved them round to the teats (once they have settled on a teat they always return). I also cut their umbilical cords with my thumb nail because they are over 1 ft (30 cm) long and the piglets can get tangled up – but I was careful not to cut too close to the body (5 in/13 cm is good) as one can rip out their innards. We had a couple of stillborns. I tried everything I could think of, including blowing into their noses with straw, but there was no saving them.

Eight piglets survived in the end and began to grow very quickly, and soon became quite inquisitive and boisterous. However, Princess is a good mum and has them under control; she has them all 'pooing' in a single corner of the sty so the bedding stays clean, she feeds them milk but only when she wants to and will alert them to this fact by lying down and emitting a continual series of grunts. We let them out every day and, like their mum, the piglets love a good scratch and a roll in the mud. I will miss them.

The piglets at a couple of months old – they seemed to grow at an amazing rate.

THE HEAVY HORSES

There is scarcely a country, town or city scene from the Victorian age that isn't complete without a horse of some description. Up until the advent of the internal combustion engine, the horse, and particularly the 'heavy' horse, undertook the bulk of so many jobs in rural, urban and industrial life. It would have been impossible to farm competitively in the late-Victorian period without the help of horses. From the movement of bulk goods ('carting') to the working of engines and the pulling of heavy farm machinery, the horse was central to the economic survival of the farm.

Thus there would be a direct chain of command from landlord, to bailiff, to wagoner, to ploughman and finally to groom and stable boy with the welfare of the farm's team of working horses of the utmost importance amongst the responsibilities of this hierarchy.

Essentially, the modern heavy horse can trace its origins back to the medieval warhorse and perhaps as far back as the Norman Invasion of 1066, by virtue of the fact that it is undoubtedly a distant cousin of the French 'Percheron'. A large and powerful warhorse was a prize asset for any aspiring Knight of the royal court, and it would need to be strong enough to carry not only the rider and his weapons but also the heavy plate armour and chain mail that was a feature of warfare during the 13th to 16th centuries. So important was the size and strength of the medieval warhorse that Henry VIII passed laws banning the breeding of smaller horses.

However, technological developments in later medieval warfare made the heavy horse obsolete. Although strong, it could be slow and cumbersome, and certainly by the time of the English Civil War, both Cavaliers and Roundheads favoured lighter, faster and more manoeuvrable cavalry horses.

Just when it seemed that the heavy horse had had its day, developments in the harnessing and yoking of draught beasts meant that it could make a sideways movement and find a new role in the fields and farms of the British landscape.

On the continent, horses had for some time been used in heavy farm work, but in England, farmers seemed to have resisted the move from oxen to horse for that much longer. Traditions and customs always die hard – especially in the rural hinterlands – and it may well have been the English passion for good roast beef that keep so many oxen teams in work despite the improved pulling powers of the

Smiler, a part broken-in Swedish Ardennes belonging to Mr Acton, who became a friend for Clumper.

heavy horse. As late as the 1920s, oxen were still being used in Sussex to plough the heavy clay soils of the Weald and I have seen early 20th-century silent movie footage of a horse, paired with an ox, pulling a dray loaded with hay.

By late November, Clumper and I had developed a good working relationship.

British Breeds

There are considered to be three native breeds of heavy horse in the British Isles, with the 'Shire' horse being perhaps the most famous and most numerous. It is thought to be a descendent of the 'Black Horse' – a large heavy horse recorded in the mid-17th century in the Midlands – and the term 'Shire' denotes that it comes from the shires of central England. Although today the most popular colour for a Shire is black, 'greys' (actually white in colour when they get older) and bays (brown to the lay man) are acceptable. The 'Clydesdale', the Shire's Scottish cousin, is similar in height but with a slightly lighter conformation and springiness of step. They are traditionally dark brown or bay in colour with a white stripe on the face and white legs to just over the knees and hocks. Finally, the Suffolk Punch has perhaps the longest history and was described quite accurately in the 15th century in John Campden's *Britannica*. Although shorter, it was a stockier horse,

LOOKING AFTER THE HORSES

 We have two horses on the farm: Clumper, a shire horse, who was leant to us by Brian Davis and is an ex-rescue horse from the RSPCA, and Smiler, a Swedish Ardennes, who is owned by the Actons. Clumper was brought in to work on the farm with us but we keep him in the field with Smiler because horses get very depressed if they are on their own. This doesn't mean that they have to be with another horse, they can be with a donkey. At the home farm, Captain, the retired Percheron, hangs out with Dusty the donkey – one of the most charismatic animals you will ever meet.

Over the winter months, when there's not sufficient grass, we feed the horses hay and oats (especially when they have to work as oats get a horse really fired up). However, they do like their treats such as parsnips, apples and pears, and if you ever need to bribe Clumper to do some work – peppermints. For this reason I made a batch of peppermint crèmes.

Mostly the horses stayed outside but, inevitably, when they had been in the stable we had to do the mucking out.

We leave the horses out all year round, although they do have shelter in the field. However, if it is particularly miserable we will bring Clumper into the stable over at the home farm to give him a feed and brush. He is not a fan of enclosed spaces so it took a while for him to get used to it (he certainly will not go into the low-roofed stable in our farmyard) but the home farm stable is a large, grand, airy building with a high-vaulted ceiling. We don't brush him very often because he is a working horse but, in spring, when his coat is moulting he is in need of a good brush. Also for May Day we thought it would be nice to give him a make-over for our celebrations of the end of winter and new life on the farm. One thing you can say for all the animals on the farm is that they each have a personality, and working with them as we do means that we form quite close bonds with them. It is the one thing that I am really going to miss more than anything else.

The horses having a feed in the home farm stable.

always in 'chesnut' (without the 't') and with an excellent temperament. Bred especially for the flat open and often wetter expanses of East Anglia, their lower legs lack the silky feathering so characteristic of both the Shire and the Clydesdale.

As was the case with so many other breeds of livestock, it was in the 18th century that close attention was paid to the specialist breeding of horses to accentuate and develop desirable features. With horses, it wasn't necessarily about developing a breed that grew larger and fattened quicker; it was about desirable characteristics, temperament and ease of movement.

The first documentary evidence for this programme of breeding appears in the late 18th century when the lineages of certain horses began to be recorded. In all of the three breeds, there were popular stallions of great renown that could command quite a fee for their 'siring' abilities. It wasn't, however, until 1877 and 1878 that the Clydesdale, Suffolk and English cart horse (later to be called the 'shire horse') societies were founded and comprehensive stud books were embarked upon.

The decline of Britain's heavy horses is irrefutably linked to the introduction of the internal combustion engine to virtually all walks of daily life. Numbers of working horses were at their peak before the First World War, with 2.6 million employed in trade and agriculture. Both wars in the early part of the 20th century spurred on the developments in engineering, and with the crisis of rationing, thousands of beasts were slaughtered. The lowest ebb for all three breeds came in the 1960s and 1970s and, if it hadn't been for a few dedicated and passionate breeders, sponsorship from some of Britain's breweries, and help from the Rare Breeds Survival Trust, it is unlikely that what was once the back-bone of Britain's rural and urban industries would have survived to this day.

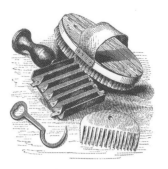

Horse grooming items as featured in Henry Stephens' Book of the Farm.

Lead reins, croppers, a tug chain and back chains hung up and ready to use.

OVERLEAF *A Shire/Cob cross takes a well-earned snack after pulling the coal barge, while a Clydesdale waits to pull away our coal-laden tip cart.*

Post-and-rail Fence

Having cleaned out the Glebe farmyard buildings, stock-proofed the fields, and built a stunning set of pigsties, we started the new year with a full compliment of animals, cows, sheep, pigs, horses, ducks, turkeys and chickens. Absolutely brilliant, but it rapidly became apparent that we needed a way of controlling our stock. The obvious answer was to reinstate a post-and-rail fence that would divide the stack yard, where we kept our mangel-wurzel tump and dung pile, from our farmyard, where we pottered with machinery and processed fodder. A divide between these two areas would also enable us to let the pigs run around while we had other animals in the farm yard (a pig's sociable and curious traits can scare other animals such as horses and cows).

We enlisted the help of Dr Damien Goodburn, who is an archaeologist and ancient woodwork specialist, and has both the historical knowledge and the practical experience needed for a project such as this. We could have built the post-and-rail fence out of elm, larch or pine, but he advised that oak would be preferable because Victorians didn't treat the wood with preservatives as we would today, and oak has the best properties for survival underground. Therefore, the first step was to find ourselves an oak tree in Mr Acton's woods.

Sharpening a bill hook with a stone.

Into the Woods

'Tree shopping' was harder than I thought it would be, as many factors had to be taken into consideration. We didn't want to take the mightiest oak in the forest but equally we didn't want its weedy sibling. Our tree needed to be about 1 ft (30 cm) in diameter with a near circular circumference (I'm glad you asked that question and no, surprisingly, most trees are not circular), and it needed to be reasonably straight with no knots and a good 9 ft (2.7 m) until the first big branches. Furthermore, it couldn't be too tall, and we needed an obvious gap into which we could fell it. A bit like looking in a haystack for a piece of hay (that has to be pointy at one end, with a hole at the other, and made of metal).

Once we had located our tree, a maiden oak (which means that it had grown from an acorn that had fallen from another tree in this planted and managed woodland), we started preparations for felling. Our safety was paramount. It is

OPPOSITE *Cutting out the 'gob' using a felling axe – this was an extremely strenuous job.*

Making the initial cut of the 'gob' with the cross-cut saw.

Damien Goodburn persuading the tree to fall.

important to have clear escape routes which are at 120 degrees from the direction of felling; so if the tree is falling to the north, the escape routes will be to the south west and the south east. One must not go behind the tree as it can fall in the opposite direction and it may also kick out backwards when it is felled.

We started felling the tree by removing the buttresses at its base with a felling axe. This reduces the amount of timber that we would have to saw through and makes the tree easier to fell. We then took the two-man cross-cut saw and began cutting in from the direction that we were going to fell the tree. This cut needs to be parallel to the horizontal (a tough feat if the tree is on a pronounced slope as we found out) as it will determine the direction that the tree falls. With the felling axe we began chopping at an angle towards this parallel cut from above to form the 'gob' which resembles an open mouth that doesn't quite reach half way through the tree. We then cut in with the cross-cut saw (again parallel to the ground) from the other side towards the 'gob' and about 1 in (2.5 cm) above the level of the base of the 'gob'. At this point you have to be ready to run, stopping sawing at regular intervals and listening to the tree. When one hears that tell-tale cracking it is time to remove the saw and make use of the escape routes as the tree is starting to fall.

Our tree almost fell in the direction we intended and only got caught up a little bit in the branches of another tree. Our initial cut to form the base of the 'gob' was a few degrees off horizontal, emphasizing how important it is to get this right. However, with the use of splitting wedges, levers, brute strength, and a smattering of colourful language we managed to persuade the tree to fall completely over. I feel it is important to emphasize that the tree we felled was utilized completely – it was grown to be used as timber, by removing it we opened up the canopy to allow light in and help other plants grow, and the stump that was left behind (which protrudes further from the ground than stumps left by modern tree fellers who have chain saws at their disposal) was still alive and it will grow into another tree.

REMOVAL AND PROCESSING

Once the tree was down, the next step was to process it. We cut off the branches with an axe, which is a technique known as 'snedding', and with our cross-cut saw we cut the remaining trunk of the tree into sections selecting the best 8 ft (2.5 m) straight length to be made into our main post. To remove these parts of the tree we had to call on the services of our trusty 17 hands (178 cm) shire horse, Clumper. The process of dragging logs out of a forest and to the saw pits and mills is known as 'tushing'. Mr Acton had given us a metal swingle tree to which we

Preparing our felled oak for transport.

Clumper pulls a section of the tree – an action known as 'tushing'.

145

attached a tushing chain, which has a loop on the swingle tree end and a hook on the log end. The chain gets wrapped around the fatter end of the log and attached to itself and Clumper is harnessed to the swingle tree.

We had reservations about Clumper's ability to adapt to this kind of work but, once again, he proved to us why horses were still the engines of farming well into the 20th century. Prior to the work we brought him into the forest a few times so that he could get used to the new surroundings and the strange smells and noises. If he was a working forestry horse he would have had horse shoes with metal studs on to give him grip on the oft-slippery woodland tracks.

Once Clumper had moved the processed sections of oak tree up to the saw pit area we started work on transforming our best straight 8 ft (2.5 m) log into our main post-and-rail gate post upon which we intended to hang our 10 ft (3 m) farm gate. Firstly the log needs to be cleaned, often a job for a young child (or an archaeologist-come-apprentice woodsman), to get rid of all the grit and dirt that has covered the log's surface during transportation because this will quickly damage sharpened saw teeth and axe heads.

In the saw pit. Notice the pit dogs and the wooden wedges.

We then dogged the log in place to cleave off two sides. 'Dogging' is the term given to securing logs prior to processing them so that they don't move. Dogs look like large iron staples (around a foot in length) that are hammered into the log and the beam that the log is resting on. There is a popular belief that the use of dogs in the saw pit gave rise to the terms 'top dog' and 'underdog'. Maybe these terms were taken to the urban areas with the population migration of the 19th century.

Anyway, to cleave off the first two sides we made regular (every 8–12 in/ 20–30 cm) vertical wedges in the wood with the axe to the depth that we wished to cleave. We then cleaved the wood between the wedges with the axe, which was best done by standing on the log. Having not grown up on Bondi beach nor owned a skateboard, standing on a log whilst swinging an axe proved very hard indeed.

Once we were happy with the sides which we had cleft we moved the log on top of the saw pit and began to mark it up. This is a simple process of securely placing a string covered in chalk or charcoal (depending on the colour of the wood – light for dark and dark for light) over the imaginary line you wish to saw. The line is then 'snapped' by gripping it between thumb and forefinger, raising it

A selection of the carpentry tools we used. Carpenters of the time were involved with the management and harvesting of the woodland as well as the fine processing of the wood.

up vertically several inches (which can be monitored by your saw partner), and letting go. This leaves a visible line on the wood along which you can saw. We made two lines on the top, then with a plumb bob we drew the lines on the ends of the log before turning it over and snapping another two lines on the other side. This allows both the person on top of the log and the person in the saw pit to be able to see the line which they should be sawing.

A pit saw is different from a cross-cut saw. A cross-cut saw has triangular teeth, it curves with the fattest section in the middle, and it cuts in both directions. The pit saw has hooked teeth (like a circular saw), it tapers towards the end that is facing down, and it only cuts on the down stroke. For novices like me, it is best to make a notch with an axe at the end of the line before beginning to cut with the pit saw. It is a very physical process as you use a lot more than just your arms. However, it wasn't as hard as I imagined largely, because we hammered a wooden wedge into the cut behind the saw which stopped the wood from biting the saw. In addition, we had sharpened the saw teeth as well as sanding and oiling the surface of the saw. Throughout the process we continued to apply oil to help the saw glide through the wood. Surprisingly, one of the hardest aspects of pit sawing was the concentration involved. We had to keep the saw dead centre on the line and if it veered off we needed to correct it by twisting the saw on the down stroke into the error. As I was in the bottom of the pit, I expected to be covered in saw dust, but most of the detritus fell in front of the saw and onto the ground.

Making the Rails

With the remainder of the oak I cleft some rails for the fence. This was different from the cleaving we did for the two rough-cut sides of the main post. Rather than

Mortice holes for our cleft rails. Victorian farm carpentry was functional with a rustic look derived from cost of time, material and labour.

cutting off sections I just split the entire log using iron-splitting wedges. I would start the split with the axe, driving it into the end of the log with a sledge hammer, and follow the split with the wedges banging them in at regular intervals. As long as the grain was straight and the piece of timber was fairly knot-free, the split was straight. We also used this method to split a couple of quarter logs for fence posts. Splitting is less effort than sawing but it wastes wood and it is harder to split straight through a twisted grain than it is to saw.

When we had processed our wood it was a simple task of cutting mortises for the rails to sit in, and sinking the posts into the 2 ft (60 cm) holes that I had dug in our farmyard – the soil matrix was mainly clay, making digging tight post holes fairly easy. We then sunk the posts with the rails in place (most farm carpentry was fairly rough so the rails didn't need to be too firm in their mortise holes as long as they couldn't fall out), and packed the posts with the backfill of the holes so that they were solid. Our final action was to hang the pedestrian gate that Alex and I had made, and a 8 ft (2.5 m) farm gate that the estate carpenter had made some years previously. I must thank Mr Herbertson, the home farm blacksmith, who made the hinges and pintels that held the gates in place. The final test was to let out the pigs and cows and sure enough our post-and-rail fence kept them separate.

The post-and-rail fence works wonders at keeping our animals apart and allowing us to control our stock.

The Dairy

Milk, cream, butter and cheese were all important farm produce in the Victorian period. The agricultural depression of the 1880s made them even more important to the farming economy. When grain prices plummeted, those who could turn to dairy farming were in a far better financial position than the rest of the farming community. While many of the smaller holdings were being driven out of business, those who could successfully supply the towns with milk, cream, butter and cheese could still make a living from very small patches of land. By 1880 the smallest viable arable farm was around 50 acres – any less meant penury. But in Shropshire and southern Cheshire half of all farms were still smaller than this at the outbreak of the First World War, many still surviving, and feeding their families on tiny 5-acre holdings. The difference was cheese. Good-quality cheese was able to hold its price throughout the period. Cheese making didn't require heavy investment and pasture didn't need to be the highest-quality land. Good cheese was a matter of skill not capital, and as such formed a lifeline for the small independent farmer.

New Markets for Milk

The biggest change in dairy farming that occurred during the Victorian period was the rise in the raw milk trade. The railway lines that were now criss-crossing the countryside made it possible for farmers living near one of the innumerable halts, stations and sidings to transport raw milk to their ever-growing number of customers in the towns while it was still fresh. Before the railways, cows had to be near the customers for the milk to be fresh. Small dairy herds therefore were kept in a variety of yards and cavernous cellars in town to supply low-quality (due to conditions) fresh milk. The country cow keeper had to process their milk into butter and cheese for it to make the journey to market in good condition.

Enterprising farmers with a bit of spare capital were quick to take up the new opportunities that the improved transport offered. There was money to be made from raw milk sales, so long as you had a big enough herd to offset the railways' prices and negotiate a good deal with the town dairies.

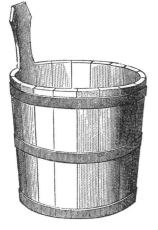

Milk pail.

Much of the advice to farmers about dairying centred on this new modern, profitable section of the market, and it was here that men became pre-eminent first. Traditionally, all dairy work had been women's work, and the sale of the produce had often been viewed as the wife's money. But during the Victorian period there was a definite shift towards male-run dairies, especially in the raw milk market. With bigger and bigger herds, male cowhands alongside all the other care of the cattle were doing more and more of the actual milking. When cows

Milking was often done in the field twice a day.

IT'S ALL ABOUT THE BREEDING

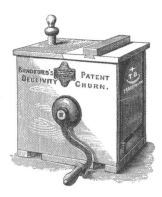

Box churn.

had been mostly out in the fields, there had not been a huge amount of labour associated with keeping cattle, but now that they were kept in the yard over long periods, fed prepared feed and their dung carefully gathered each day, a full-time labour force devoted to the care of the herd was necessary. It made economic sense, therefore, for this same workforce, which was mostly male, to take over the milking as well.

This does not mean that no women milked anymore. Thomas Hardy records in his novels the large groups of milking girls employed on some farms to go out into the fields twice a day to milk. But it is noticeable that such women are milking outside. The cows are not being kept in a yard. Where farmers moved over to keeping cattle in the yard and cowhouse in order to preserve their manure to fertilize the fields, then an indoor (male-staffed) milking parlour soon became convenient. Small farms, however, were different. If you didn't have the capital or the land for large herds then the raw milk market wasn't usually an option. A small farm with a small to medium herd was better off sticking to tradition.

Butter remained a useful source of income for the small dairy farmer but it was cheese that could pay the rent. Hard cheeses keep very well indeed so no matter how remote the farm, how bad the transport links, a good cheese would arrive at its final market in top condition. The price that a cheese fetched was based upon the quality of the cheese and did not suffer from the same economies of scale that many other agricultural products did. The most sensible economic option for a farmer, therefore, was to ensure high quality. The most skilled sector of the workforce as far as cheese making went was still likely to be his wife. Thus on small farms up and down the country dairying remained a fairly traditional,

Butter and soft cheese, which was made in the dairy.

low-investment and female world. Some new practices, however, penetrated even the smallest and most traditional dairies.

As well as changes in transport and farming methods, the Victorian period was also one of changing tastes. This had a much bigger impact on the small cheese maker than all the many new gadgets that were emerging for dairy use. First and foremost, the Victorian urban housewife wanted Cheddar cheese. In the 18th century, stilton had been the king of cheese, but now people were coming to think that it was indigestible and too strongly flavoured. The Victorian palate favoured mild flavours. This was an age in which 'blandness' in food far from being a bad thing was something that all the medical men recommended. Cheeses, too, were supposed to be large. Enormous rounds were thought to keep better and be better flavoured. Partly the size reflected herd sizes – lots of milk all at once gave people the option to make much larger cheeses than before and many did so out of pride for their new improved herds. But at market it was the large rounds that got the best price pound for pound. Urban customers also liked to know what they were getting; they wanted predictability and a degree of standardization. Local customers got to know the local producers and buy the unique flavour that they prefer, but in huge towns and cities that sort of relationship was more difficult.

Even very modest dairies run by the farmer's own wife were therefore making the most of new-fangled thermometers and cast-iron cheese presses to produce the sort of cheese that sold well, even if they could not afford the latest steam-jacketed vats that the larger modernized dairies were investing in.

A large round of cheese in the cast-iron press. How long and how hard you press the cheese will affect the flavour.

Cheese Making

Cheese is milk that has been separated into a solid (the curd) and a liquid (the whey). The whey is discarded and you eat the curd. There are many ways to separate the milk. If you simply leave it long enough it will separate by itself. A pint of milk of dubious age that has gone off is cheese if you just pour away the whey and eat the curd. It's not a great-tasting cheese, but it is edible. A range of acids such as lemon juice and vinegar will also cause milk to separate, and can, if handled carefully, make a reasonable tasting cheese. However, the yield will be low. The best cheese comes from milk that has been separated by rennet – the natural enzymes found in a calf's stomach.

The quality of the milk is of course crucial if you are to make a good cheese. The best comes from healthy, relaxed (yes, stress levels make a difference) cows that are fed a varied and nutritious diet. Fresh summer grass is always preferable to concentrates, hay or silage. The properties of the milk vary from breed to breed, and indeed between individuals within the same herd.

MAKING CHEESE ON THE FARM

Essentially, cheese making is very, very simple. Making delicious cheese is rather more of a challenge.

We poured 20 gallons (90 litres) of milk into the wooden vat – half from the previous day's milking and half from that morning's milking. We then filled three large, clean enamelled jugs with near-boiling water and carefully lowered them into the milk. We needed to bring the milk up to 85°F (29°C).

The marvellous steam-jacketed vats that were available to Victorian dairyman with money to invest could do this with the turn of a tap, allowing hot water to pass all around the mass of milk between the double walls of the vat – rather like a giant bath-shaped radiator. We did it the older and much cheaper way.

When the water in the jugs cooled, we refilled them and popped them back in until gradually the temperature had reached 85°F (29°C) on our trusty thermometer.

Next we stirred in our rennet. I made this from a calf's stomach about a month before cheesemaking proper began. Having given the stomach a really good clean and removed all the unnecessary membranes, veins, fat and so forth, I salted it thoroughly and hung it up to dry. A piece of the cured calf's stomach about 1 x 2 in (2.5 x 5 cm) soaked overnight in warm water gave us enough rennet to separate the 20 gallons (90 litres) of milk. We put the lid on the vat to keep the warmth in and left it to set.

About 40 minutes later the magic had happened and the whole vat was full of junket – a jelly-like substance that some people like to eat at this stage. To make cheese, the next thing to do was to cut the curd and begin releasing the whey.

We used two rather wonderful curd knives, one with the blades set horizontally and one with them set vertically, to very gently and slowly reduce the curd to evenly sized cubes. This can be done with an ordinary

Warming the milk the old-fashioned way using enamel jugs with near-boiling water.

RIGHT *Cutting the curd with a curd knife, so as to achieve evenly sized cubes. Katherine, my daughter, came to help.*

knife or with your fingers, but the Victorians valued the new precision of tools such as curd knives, and with very large volumes – ten times that of ours – they are something of a necessity.

The lid went back on the vat once the curd was cut for twenty minutes.

The 'cheddaring' process starts at this point. In order to make a long-keeping cheese with a cheddar texture you need to raise the acidity level of the curd by gently heating it within the whey.

In a steam-jacketed vat this would be a simple matter of letting more hot water into the jacket of the vat and monitoring the temperature. Without such a convenience, we used the older traditional method of carefully removing a portion of the whey, heating it in the copper, and returning hot whey to the vat.

We were aiming for 100°F (37.7°C), and keeping it at that temperature for at least half an hour or until the curd was sufficiently 'cooked'. It took a little over an hour each time to raise the temperature enough, and any amount of running back and forth with hot whey.

Draining off the whey came next. We didn't waste it, but put it aside to feed to the pigs.

The curd was then piled up at one end of the vat, covered in a cloth, and the lid returned to place. Over the next twenty minutes the curd fused into one mass and the gentle weight of one lump of curd on top of another pressed a little more whey out.

Turning and stacking the curd happened a further three times at twenty-minute intervals. Each time

'Cheddaring' – drawing off some the whey.

RIGHT *Milling the curd.*

taking care that pressure was evenly distributed and that we conserved as much of the heat as possible.

Now the curd was ready to be milled salted and put in the press. A curd mill, much like the mills that the boys use to prepare the animal fodder, was a great advancement on crumbling the curd by hand and ensured a really even texture.

About 7 oz (198 g) of salt went into the curd and was carefully mixed through before we packed it into the cloth lined cheese mould, or 'hoop'.

Our press was a simple model, but highly effective – probably the first piece of modern dairying equipment that a small farmer would have invested in. The older methods, using stone weights, work, but it's hard to reach the very high pressures needed for large Victorian sized rounds and still be able to lift the stones easily. This cast-iron model just requires turning the screw, and allows you to see exactly what pressure you are applying on the gauge.

Each cheese gets eight days in the press, being turned over and the cloths changed daily before being put on the shelf to mature. You still have to look them over every day turning them regularly to prevent one side drying out while the other becomes over damp. Any sign of mould is carefully cleaned, off and the atmosphere in the room is monitored, as this can affect the flavour. Not too hot, not too cold, not too dry and not too damp. *Et voila* … cheese. It takes about three months to bring a large round of cheddar to perfection.

Packing the curd.

Wrapping the pressed cheese.

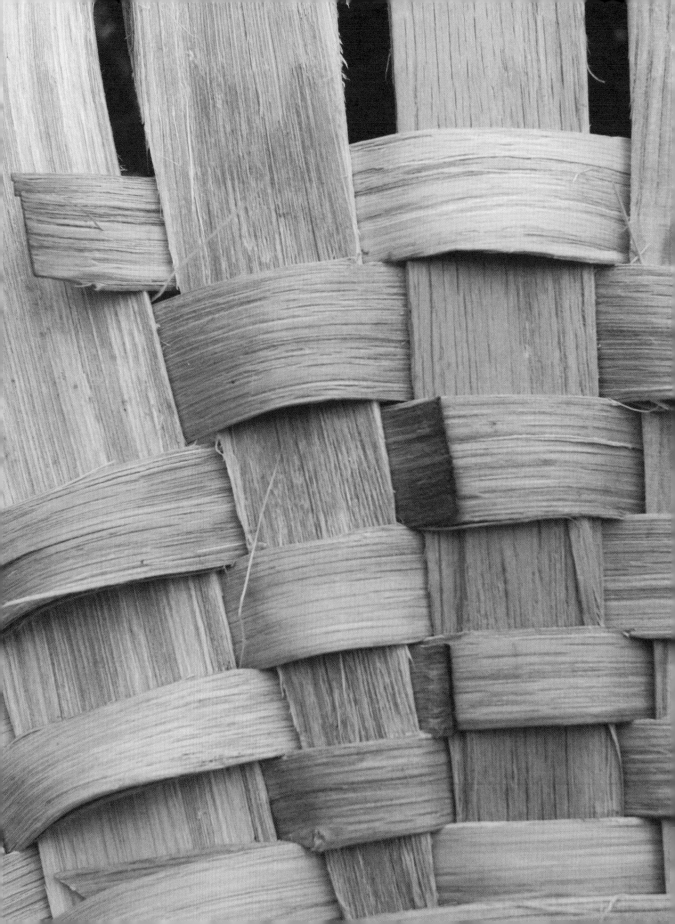

CHAPTER FOUR

Arts and Crafts

RURAL CRAFTS, TRADES AND COTTAGE INDUSTRIES

In an age when anything and everything that we consume, use, cherish or discard can be sourced from the four corners of the world and delivered to our doorstep, it is difficult to comprehend a society in which all essential everyday items were fashioned and purchased within a few miles of where they spent the rest of their lives.

This, however, was the situation in rural Britain in the early to mid-Victorian period. Wheat grown just a stone's throw from the village centre would ultimately find its way, via the miller's grindstones and the baker's oven, onto the table of the very labourer who had worked so tirelessly to bring in the harvest. The plough that set about turning the land over for the next year's crop would have been forged in the blacksmith's workshop and would be pulled by horses whose raw power was harnessed by the skill and craftsmanship of the local saddler.

Except in instances of extreme specialist goods – perhaps a rare book, a fine cloth or an exotic spice – most of the material requirements of rural communities

The tools belonging to stonemason and all-round crafts guru, Paul Arrowsmith. Paul was an enormous help throughout our year on the farm.

in the British Isles could be sourced, if not within the confines of their own parish, at the local market town – at worst, a day's return journey away.

This had undoubtedly been the case for centuries and, as communities grew, so too did a stable and enduring economy founded on reciprocal exchange, doorstep transactions, bartering, shared labour, co-operation and mutual support. Skills were passed from father to son to grandson, and generations of families would be forever associated with a particular craft or specialism. Seven-year apprenticeships (five spent under the tutorage of a local master and two spent refining skills in a placement in a neighbouring village or town) in the case of many of the more common trades – blacksmith, cartwright or thatcher – are testament not only to the long-term outlook of the rural craft industry but also to the value placed in developing and honing a skill to the point of artistry.

With it, this level of interdependence would have undoubtedly brought a scale of social interaction unfamiliar to many of the rural communities of today. The prevailing fortunes of family groups, the conduct of infamous characters, scandal, mishaps and achievements would all have been gossiped over in the queue for a fresh loaf or the posse of farm hands loitering in the blacksmith's yard.

TRENDS OF THE PERIOD 1850–1900

Events, however, on the global scene were conspiring against the craftsman of late-Victorian Britain. The smooth running of village life had been dependent on a raft of craftsmen and women whose positions were held in some degree of regard yet with the many changes that were taking place in the increasingly industrial landscape, the almost privileged status of the village artisan was under threat.

The decline of rural crafts and skills can be put down to a number of factors. Firstly, the economic changes in agriculture of the late 1870s and early 1880s had caused a migration of people away from the rural scene and into the towns and cities where more secure and better paid employment could be found in the growing industries and factories. Put simply, there were less people and less demand.

Mass-manufacture, however, was probably the greatest contributor to the demise of village workshops. Factories could produce goods in bulk and at much lower costs. Furthermore, increasing transport links both internally (the developing network of railways in Britain) and externally (more reliable and quicker shipping routes) meant that products could be delivered to the buyer irrespective of location.

Of course, awareness of the latest products and innovations did not simply come about through word of mouth. Large-scale manufacturers set about publishing brochures for their products, and a feature of the later Victorian era is a growing commercialism within which advertising and 'sales' were to play a key role.

A local butcher gave us a masterclass in how to joint and preserve our slaughtered Tamworth pig.

The rural craftsman, though a master of his art, simply could not compete with the business savvy and retail expertize of the growing number of vendors who acted as middlemen in the trade of imported goods. Village and town stores could stock many of the requirements – both commodity and luxury – for the rural farming and labouring classes. For many British rural crafts, the writing was on the wall. When cartwheels could be bought off-the-shelf from a manufacturer in the USA, shipped and delivered to a farm in rural England at a cheaper cost than could be offered by the local wheelwright, what chance did he stand? Equally, shoe

A page from, The Country Gentleman's Catalogue, *1894. Wrought iron hurdles and gates and galvanized wire fencing signalled the end of the traditional hedger's craft.*

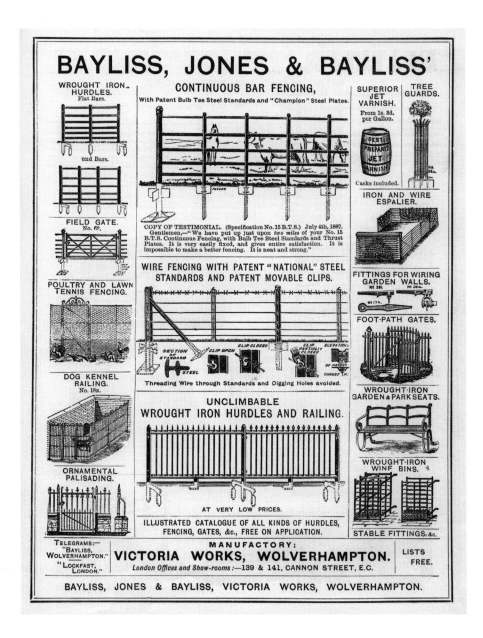

and bootmakers, for years stalwarts of the village scene, were finding themselves less and less able to compete with the mass-produced boots of Northampton's growing shoe and boot industry. Forged iron gate hurdles, which were more durable and competitively priced, began to affect the fortunes of the hurdle maker, whose beautifully hand-crafted gate and wattle hurdles had for centuries been the blessing of the British sheep farming industry. There is scarcely a rural craft or cottage industry that was not affected by the events taking place in the wider world of the late 19th and early 20th centuries. By the end of the First World War, when the skilled rural labour force had been dealt perhaps its final blow, the rural skills base and the crafts that had been passed from generation to generation for hundreds of years were rapidly diminishing.

LOSS OF REGIONAL PERSONALITY AND CHARACTER

Of course, the process of change was slow in many areas, and many craftsmen invariably adapted. Many blacksmiths would begin to understand the increasingly mechanical nature of British agriculture and could diversify, using ancient skills to patch up factory-bought replacement parts. The village shoemaker could even look to stock some of the latest fashions and move towards mending and repairs.

WHAT IS CRAFTSMANSHIP?

'Craftsmanship' is, perhaps, a clumsy term by the standards of modern gender equalities and tends to distort the fact that a great many women were instrumental in some of the major cottage industries. It also ignores the unrecorded 'craft' of domestic life – from rearing, feeding and emotionally developing the next generation, cleaning and cooking and the entirely women-dominated unwritten support, care and welfare structures that existed in rural communities.

However, there should, perhaps, be an emphasis on the material – the 'artefact' for want of a better word. William Morris (1834–1896), the famed poet, writer, craftsman, designer and socialist – a man who mastered over a dozen crafts in his own lifetime – drew attention to what he felt was the very essence of craftsmanship. Morris was at his most prolific in the second half of the 19th century and reacted strongly against the mass-produced goods that were beginning, in his later days,

to overwhelm locally crafted products. Accused by many as being over-sentimental and romantic, he argued for the superiority of dedicated handicrafts over the meaningless machine-processed commodities of the factory floor.

A key difference between the machine operative and the village craftsman is that the latter is invariably both the 'designer' and maker of the product. Craftsmanship is very much the skill of making something with one's own hands and being able, whimsically, to alter the shape and form of the artefact in question, to impart individuality.

It is the unbroken line of communication between the eye and the hand; the corollary through which concept takes form that marks out a 'craft'. Unlike the chain of individuals upon which factory production is dependent – designer, creator, producer, operative and distributor – the craftsman or woman can claim both authorship and artistry over their work.

For many, the route away from poverty depended on finding new skills, new audiences and taking on different work.

In the long term, therefore, it was perhaps the crafts rather than the craftsmen that suffered. Another significant and often unheralded impact that industrialization and mass-manufacture was to have on rural England was the weakening of regional character – or 'regionality'.

Today's 'global village' has its origins in the Victorian age when the world was undoubtedly becoming a smaller place. Underneath the uniformity of national road signs, the like-for-like retail parks and pan-Atlantic decor and furnishings of our houses, the regional character and personality of our provincial towns is more difficult to discern. The situation, however, would have been very different in the early years of Queen Victoria's reign.

When manufacture was local, local people would have used local materials to make implements, tools and buildings that met with local needs and suited local conditions. The geology, terrain, soil, topology and ecology would all have determined the design and materials used in the making of day-to-day artefacts. One of the best and most often quoted examples of this is in the making of bill hooks, which famously differ not only from county to county but also from town to town. Bill hooks are tools used predominantly in skills where 'small' wood requires a degree of manipulation – such as hedging, thatching, and basket and hurdle making. In different regions, though, different species of shrub, bush and tree grow on differing terrains and thus a bill hook designed to work with wetland species such as willow and alder will be fashioned very differently from one designed to work with downland species such as hazel and ash.

We had a number of bill hooks provided with the farm when we arrived, and I found that for much of the work I was undertaking a particular shape was proving most versatile. It had a fairly straight-edged blade culminating in an almost hatchet-like end rather than the characteristic 'hook'. I took the opportunity to

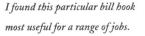

I found this particular bill hook most useful for a range of jobs.

enquire of a local farmer whether this was indeed a regional design of a bill hook. He looked at me quizzically and retorted, 'That's a 'bromock', not a 'bill hook'!'. I've since researched the shape of the 'bromock' I've been using and, while it is not similar to the traditional Shropshire type, it is very similar to what is called the 'Knighton' type from Knighton in South Shropshire – less than 20 miles away.

This incident highlights that, not only were regional characteristics in design and material important, but so too was the terminology used. One need only spend a short while with thatchers from all over the UK to realize that a plethora of different terms are used to describe the same tools and techniques.

In many types of implement, tool or machinery, the regional differences became celebrated and almost accentuated. Carts are another good example of where regional conditions determined the shape and design. In hilly country with steep slopes and narrow hollow ways, the carts would be smaller and the 'lock' of the front wheels would need to be tight to negotiate sharp twists and turns. On flatter terrain with large open expanses of fields the carts could afford to be larger and with a wider turning circle.

Owen Jones, basket maker, and a total 'whizz-kid' with all things wood-related, made us an extremely durable 'spale' basket from split oak.

The very essences of this regionalism came under threat in the latter part of Victoria's reign as factory-made goods became more widely available. Today, thankfully, there are a growing number of areas where regional differences are being considered important in the conservation of local and historic landscapes. For example, the National and Landmark Trusts are beginning to recognize the importance of their thatched buildings being thatched in a traditional and regional style. Dry stone walling and hedging are also skills that are currently being rediscovered with one eye on regional differences.

Key and Peripheral Rural Crafts Network

Craftspeople throughout the villages of rural Britain in the 19th century would have been fundamentally dependent on each other, and a network of individuals locked together enabled communities to survive. As the title of Paul Stamper's book says: *The Farmer Feeds Us All (A Short History of Shropshire Agriculture)*, so I shall start with the farmer who would have worked tirelessly to bring in the harvest. Perhaps the most important of all harvests would have been with wheat sold to the miller who may or may not have, at some point, to call on the millwright to reset the grindstones on the mill. The baker would acquire the ground flour from the miller, and his craft would be to turn this raw product into a wholesome golden loaf to sell on to the rest of the village. Barley was another of the farmer's crops that would have found its way to either a local brewer or families who had time to brew their own – from which barrels of beer would be produced.

The wood-working craft that the brewer was perhaps most reliant upon would have been that of the local cooper.

Much of the farmer's time, however, would be dedicated to the sowing and harvesting of a wide range of crops for animal fodder. So the farmer, too, would have provided meat for the village population.

SADLER AND FARRIER The by-products from slaughtered livestock would have provided the raw materials for a great many industries of the time. In particular, the saddler would have been one of the most important people within any village, as his skill in making the belts, straps, collars and saddles would have served to harness the raw power of heavy horses, ponies and donkeys. The wagoner, as head horseman of the farm, would have taken pride in his horse tack, and well-made, good-fitting tack made his job all the more easier. Of course, to get the leather to a condition where it could be used by the saddler, boot and shoemaker, it would have been worked extensively by the tanner and currier – both crafts involved in the preparation of raw cow-hide into supple leather. Tanning and currying would be done in large centres, such as Walsall, and brought in by village shoemakers.

The horses of the community would have depended on a range of craftsmen – not just the saddler, wagoner and farmer. First and foremost, they would have needed shoeing, and the farrier would have been one of the busiest men of the village as horse shoes were removed, feet trimmed and shoes nailed back on. Should, due to wear, another set of horse shoes need making, the farrier might call upon the services of the blacksmith to knock them into shape. Although coal was increasingly working its way into the forges of rural Britain, there was still a market for charcoal, and the charcoal burner's produce was still much in demand for smithy work along with a range of other crafts.

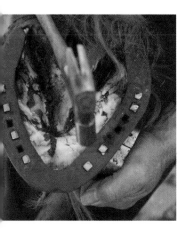

A team of hard-working horses would need constant attention paid to their feet by the village farrier.

BLACKSMITH The blacksmith's work was linked to many of the other crafts in and around the village and he had to be able to work with a variety of artefacts and implements. He would have to make and repair ploughs and harrows, forge gate hinges and pintles, make tools such as hoes, spades and shovels, fix cooking utensils, repair iron fittings on horse tack, ring pigs – the list is endless. In fact, there are so many requirements of the blacksmith that it may well have been the case that some blacksmiths would have specialized in certain jobs.

In particular, the blacksmith would have worked closely with both the cartwright and the wheelwright. The former would have needed any number of iron fittings to bolt together and fasten many of the constituent parts of the cart, while the latter would have needed the iron 'tyres' that were heated up and dropped on to the ready made cart wheels.

We were fortunate enough
to have a highly skilled
wheelwright on our doorstep.

Carts were versatile vehicles used for moving a range of goods around the farm. Stones might be shifted around for the stonemason and dry-stone waller, or bricks brought from the kiln of the brickmaker to the building site of the brick-layer. The traditional role of the cart was at harvest time. The stooks of wheat would be brought back to the stack yard and a giant rick would be made and thatched by the local thatcher. His skill would depend heavily on the quality of the spars – thatching pegs – made by the spar maker who would work closely with the hedge layer and brusher as he thinned out the recent years' growth of hazel from the many hedges throughout the landscape.

In later Victorian times, a different set of skills was needed – those of the engineer and mechanic.

HEARTH AND HOME Inside the cottage a whole range of crafts would be needed to facilitate the running of a family home. The bowl turner, potter and basket-maker would have provided many of the day-to-day receptacles for the provision and storing of food for specific jobs. Even implements that you and I today take for granted, such as the broom, would have been made by a local or travelling broom squire or beesom maker from the birch wood collected in the local copses.

At the very end of the day, the labouring family might sit down to a fish supper, caught by the local fisherman in nets made by the local net maker. The vehicle that enabled him to traverse the upper reaches of the faster-flowing rivers to lay his nets was the coracle and the makers of these prehistoric crafts – coracle builders – endured until well into the 20th century. Finally, as grandfather rose from the table, he might be obliged to call upon the services of the local walking stick maker to aid him as he clambered up the cottage staircase – installed by the village carpenter - to his bed.

CRICKET

The origins of cricket are somewhat unclear, but in the Victorian period the game became an established sport. Indeed, cricket remained largely unchanged from the days of W. G. Grace (1848–1914) until the modifications of the game in the late 1960s and early 1970s. As with many sports of an international stature, the Victorians played a major part in popularizing them, and it is partly because of this that it was proposed that we should have a cricket match on the farm.

For a cricket match one needs a bat – so I went to manufacturers, Gray-Nicolls, and met Alex Hohenkerk to see if he could replicate an 1870s-style bat for me. Gray-Nicolls started making cricket bats in 1876, and have been making them ever since. Before going to the factory I was quite ignorant about the processes that go into making a quality cricket bat and I was amazed to find out how it is done.

I understand that Gray-Nicolls is the only British cricket bat manufacturer who grow most of their own willow. The rules of cricket state that the blade of the

MAKING A CRICKET BAT

SPLITTING ROUNDS *Once the willow has been harvested the bark is removed. It is then cut into roundels and separated into splits (each of which will form a single cricket bat).*

CUTTING CLEFTS *The wood is then cut into a cleft. At this stage, the craftsman decides which area of the cleft will become the face of the bat. It is vital that the face should be free from blemishes and knots as these may impair preformance.*

SEASONING *Willow is a soft fibrous reed which in its natural state is very moist. In order to produce a bat of good performance and weight it is necessary to dry the clefts. To do this they are placed in a custom-built kiln in which the temperature is monitored and maintained at approximately*

room temperature. The willow remains within the kiln for approximately six weeks. Once the cleft has been dried, it is pressed at approximately 2,000 lb (900 kg) per square inch. This produces the drive and durability that is essential for good performance.

FITTING THE HANDLE *Once the blades are ready to use, they have a handle fitted. The handle is made out of layers of cane and rubber and is glued into position, although the notch cut for the handle to be slotted into is so precise that it is an effort to remove it even before the glue is applied. Once these 'blank' cricket bats have been created they go to the craftsmen who then shape them using planes, draw knives and spoke shaves.*

bat has to be made out of wood. Willow is the traditional wood used for the blade of a cricket bat; it is flexible and grows well in boggy conditions such as river banks. This means that the willow is not grown all in one place but is planted in various plots across the counties. Each tree that Gray-Nicolls harvest is replaced.

Most country crafts have been eroded over time with the advent of mass production, mechanization, and new materials. However, these cricket bats are still made by hand, and with the evolution of the game, each craftsman now makes several main families (or styles). Measurements are made by a skilled eye, incisions by a skilled hand, and if a player wants an alteration they need only bring the bat in and a tiny stamp on the base will tell them who initially made the bat.

A cricket bat for us represents a bridge between Victorian leisure and country crafts and, due to the popularity of the game in the 19th century, if a Victorian farmer had willow on his land and the necessary skills he may well have turned his hand to making a few bats to supplement his income.

Before playing with the bat we had to knock it in. This takes about five or six hours and can be done with a cricket ball in a sock hitting the surface to compress the fibres of the willow. However, W. G. Grace used to give it to a boy in the practice nets because he wouldn't be able to hit it as hard as 'The Old Man'.

We decided that we needed some practise before our cricket match on the farm, and to get used to our new bat.

HEDGING

Some of the greatest and most striking icons of the British countryside are our hedgerows. Hedging in this country is at least over a thousand years old with documentary evidence dating back to AD 800 (Anglo-Saxon), but archaeological evidence indicates hedge usage in Roman Britain (AD 43–410), and one could argue a case for hedges prior to this date. The development of the sort of hedgerows we know now began in the 13th century, when there was an initial systematic planting of hedges with the first enclosure movement. However, the creation of hedgerows for enclosure was most prevalent in the 18th and 19th centuries when it is estimated that 200,000 miles (322,000 km) of hedges were planted prior to the slump in farming of the 1870s.

Hedges are common in the lowlands of Britain and they act as a protective barrier to stock-proof a field (or a garden) as well as providing the animals with a form of shelter from the wind and rain. They are also a haven for insects, wildlife, small game, wild plants, fruits and berries. Hedges, which commonly consist of hawthorn, blackthorn or holly, not only provide food for humans (if you can beat the birds to the berries), they are also a source of fuel. When a hedge is trimmed, the off-cuts can be gathered up into bundles, known as faggots, which are used in the lighting of fires – especially bread ovens. In the medieval period, the legal right of commoners was recognized, known as 'hedgebot', to gather fuel and winter feed for animals.

Laying a hedge was a very skilled country craft, so much so that it is said that one could tell exactly who laid the hedge by studying the nuances of the technique used. Each region and county has different styles of hedges, such as Somerset and Derbyshire, although there is an overlap and blending of styles. These styles will often reflect the function of the hedge (for instance, is it a barrier for sheep or for cattle?), as well as the local landscape (is the hedge on a hill?).

When a stem of a young plant is partially cut in order to be laid (always uphill) it is called a pleacher. A pleacher is still alive, so the hedge will continue to grow and thicken becoming a stronger barrier. On the Acton Scott estate there is a line of large oak trees which were once laid in a hedgerow when they were young plants which is evident from the characteristic sideways 's' bend of the lower trunk. The pleacher is then bent over from the vertical to become more horizontal (or laid)

Mr Acton, with a hedging hook or 'slasher', about to teach me about hedging.

but it will have to be laid either close to the left- or right-hand side to the next plant in the hedgerow. If all the pleachers are laid to the same side (e.g. the right-hand side) this is known as single brushed and the scrubby top-growth will face one side of the hedge, but if alternate pleachers are laid to different sides across the midline (i.e. left, right, left, right, etc.) this is known as double-brushed and the top-growth will be present on both sides of the hedge. The angle of the pleacher to the ground depends on the hedge's purpose and local practice. The hedge may then be pinned with stakes and secured with binders made from hazel, willow, briar or clematis. Once a hedge is laid it will be several years before it needs to be laid again; however, it will need to be brushed or trimmed back, which was a job that could earn a tenant farmer some extra money.

However, in the 20th century (especially after the Second World War) as farming became more mechanized, many hedges were ripped out because small fields were more difficult to cultivate than larger consolidated fields. Hedgerows are now protected and, despite their decline, it is thought that there are still over half-a-million miles of hedgerows in England today.

Giving hedging a go and finding that it is not as easy as it looks.

Coppicing

Coppicing woodland is a practice that dates back thousands of years but no greater was the demand for good coppiced timber than in the Victorian period. As well as providing the appropriate material for the most ancient of jobs – such as wattle and daub work, thatching and firewood, it was also being used for more modern and period-specific jobs such as rake, chair, tool handle and gate-hurdle making.

A 'copse' refers to any woodland area where certain trees have been cut from an early age. From the severed stump a number of new shoots will sprout. Left to grow for one to two years they will grow to something resembling a good finger-thickness. Left for ten to twenty years they could be anywhere between the thickness of the arm, from wrist to shoulder. Thus, the woodman could manage the copse in such a way as to provide thin hazel wands for wattle work and thicker timbers such as rafters for roofing.

Deciduous trees provide the best species for coppicing. Oak, ash, hazel, willow and chestnut are amongst the most regular varieties, and within any copse a number of the ash and oak trees will be allowed to grow to their full extent so that a reasonable canopy can develop. This will shield the shorter coppiced 'stools' from the sun, encouraging straight and rapid growth as the plants climb up to the light. As time rolls on, continuous management of a stool will see it grow to quite some width, capable of providing vast quantities of timber in a range of sizes.

Many large estates in the Victorian period would have had coppiced woodlands with staff dedicated to their upkeep. Check out any local Ordnance Survey map and, in all but the most extreme areas of Britain, the chances are that there will be a handful of copses to pick out and explore. Acton Scott has a couple of coppiced woodlands and I could see no problem sourcing the wood we'd need for the various jobs we had lined up on the farm.

The coppicing kit is comprised of a number of must-have tools. I always find that a good bow saw is probably the most important to have on board and a bill hook useful for a number of jobs. Otherwise, a hedging hook can help to clear dense undergrowth – in particular brambles – so that you can get in a clean cut.

Depending on the uses for the material, much of it would be processed on the forest floor. Coppiced wood for charcoal burning, wattle hurdles and bodging

The leftover coppiced wands from a wattle hedge were used to make a bean tepee in the walled garden.

could there and then be processed. Some of the materials themselves were used to make the devices, such as brakes, lathes and huts, required for the 'bodger's camp'.

However, it was common in the 19th century on large estates for timber to be hauled back to a workshop or covered area for some of the more complex items to be made – such as gate-hurdles. Remember, the best time of the year to be out coppicing is unfortunately when the weather is at its most cold and miserable, and for some of the more intricate carpentry a covered area, at least, is a must.

Because of the nature of coppiced wood, it is manageable entirely by hand tools, and this is why I'm a big fan. I don't want to have to go lugging about vast power tools to source and process tree trunks for 'carpenter's' timber when I can work with the wood to do the same job.

A steam-powered saw-bench enables larger timbers to be cut on the forest floor.

Hurdles

Ancient sheep farming relied upon transhumance – the seasonal movement of livestock, and the people who tend them, between lowlands and uplands. During the summer the sheep would be lead up onto the hillside or mountain pastures to graze and then brought back when the weather turns in late autumn and fed on the lowland and valley pastures.

Gradually, as the population grew and the demand for wool and mutton increased, sheep farming became more intensified. By the mid-Victorian period, the enclosure of much open and common land and the sowing of fodder crops in crop rotations created a greater need to pen sheep and control their movement. Hurdles, both wattle and gate, could be used to fulfil this purpose and make a moveable fence within which to pen your sheep.

Out in the fields, sheep might be penned on clover or root crops, but this wouldn't just be for feeding purposes. Their manure would serve as a vital fertilizer for the next crop anticipated in the cycle, and skilful arrangement of hurdle pens could result in an evenly distributed dressing of sheep droppings. Judicial use of hurdles can also allow the shepherd to get closer to his flock for examination purposes. Funnelled into a hurdle pen in the yard, the sheep are much easier to get

A four-rail gate hurdle made from locally sourced ash.

among to inspect for root rot, pregnancy and general condition. During the lambing months, they also serve as temporary protection for ewes and lambs in those critical moments after birth. The other demand for hurdles was at the large rural sheep fairs where flocks would converge to be bargained for and auctioned.

The art of hurdle-making was yet another rural craft under threat. By the late 19th century, mass production of iron hurdles was in full swing and they represented a cheap and more enduring alternative. Photographs from the 1890s taken at a sheep fair in Craven Arms – a local town that grew up round a railway station – show hundreds, if not thousands, of sheep penned in with iron hurdles.

Barbed wire and wiring netting were also gaining popularity among farmers who needed a cheap and speedy method with which to pen off parts of fields and pastures to restrict sheep movement. The writing was on the wall for hurdle makers and, very soon, the skills to speedily erect robust wooden hurdles would be confined to a handful of rural craft skills 'revivalists' and hobbyists.

Of the two types of hurdle – gate and wattle, I had made several of the latter but had never plucked up the courage to take on the far more attractive of the two – the gate hurdle. We had managed to borrow eight hurdles from the Working Farm Museum, but this would barely cover our needs. We would require at least another four if we were to create a secure and spacious lambing pen in our cart shed and have some left over to pen off any newly born lamb with its mother.

A wattle fence was made to bridge a gap in one of our hedgerows. Note the 'Beetle' – a large mallet, made from a single piece of ash, to bang in the stakes.

Ash was used for the stakes while hazel sourced from the local hedgerows was used for the weave.

MAKING A GATE HURDLE

TOOLS NEEDED

Bill hook (or hatchet axe)

Bow saw (or H-frame saw)

Froe

Mallet

Chisel (¾ in/2 cm-wide blade)

Brace with ¾ in (2 cm) bit

Draw knife

Claw hammer and nails

Hand drill and nail-sized bits

Pencil

MATERIALS FOR A FOUR-RAIL HURDLE

One 3½ ft (106 cm) pole –
    max. diameter of 3 in/75 mm

Four 6¼ ft (190 cm) rails –
    max. diameter of 2 in/50 mm

Nails: selection of 2½ in
    and 3 in (65 and 75mm)

It is well worth trying to make a batch of gate hurdles because singles are not of great use! Start by making one slowly, paying special care and attention to get the difficult bits right and then make a batch of, say, four or six.

If you are to successfully and safely make gate hurdles, it is absolutely imperative to have your tools as sharp as possible. Gate hurdle making involves working with wood in a very flexible way, but the enjoyment can be taken out of the whole process if you are working with blunt tools. You will also need to make a number of 'devices': an A-frame cleaving brake, a shaving horse, a morticing brake and a chopping block.

Certainly the brakes are easy enough to make and a chopping block shouldn't be hard to come by. A shaving horse, however, is a rather more complicated piece of wood-working equipment and although, because of its versatility, a must-have for any serious craftsman, a flexible work bench can be used to do the same job.

It is extremely important to get good coppiced timber of chestnut, ash, hazel, oak or willow. This kind of wood was a lot easier to come by in the Victorian period but it is worth taking the time to get suitably straight and knot-free wood so as to make the job easier.

INSTRUCTIONS FOR A FOUR-RAIL HURDLE

First, take the 3 in- (75 mm-) thick pole and cleave for the end posts. Bang the froe in at the ends at the middle point of the wood, fix the pole in the cleaving brake and apply downward pressure to the froe. If the split appears to dive down, simply flip the pole over (so that the froe handle is on its other side) and apply pressure down.

Strip the bark with your bill hook. Mark up on each thick pole where the four

Splitting an ash pole with a froe on an A-frame cleaning brake.

The share-horse in action, left; clamping a rail and using a draw knife to shape the tenon at the end. And, above, pointing the end poles with a bill hook on the chopping block.

mortices will go. Drill two holes as the top and bottom of the mortice and cut out the rest with your chisel and mallet. Point the tip (the thinner end of the pole) of each end post on a chopping block with a bill hook.

The four 2 in- (50 mm-) thick rails will also need cleaving and bark stripping. With the draw knife, tidy up the body of the rails and shape the tenons at each end. It is important, when you look down the line of the rail for straightness, that the two tenons are on the same alignment. My tip here is to make the mortice holes as close as you can in size to the shape of your end bone and knuckle of your thumb and in this way you have an easy gauge for the tenon ends as you're shaving them down. Make sure you shave down the length of the tenon to the width of the end post otherwise you will run the risk, as you are hammering it in, of splitting the post.

Gently bang the tenons into the mortices. Nail top and bottom. I strongly advise pilot drilling holes for the nails at the ends of the rails. I re-used Victorian period cut-iron nails, and if I hadn't drilled pilot holes, I would almost certainly have split the wood.

Drilling the mortice holes, with brace and bit, on the mortice brake.

Make sure the hurdle is sitting square before you add the upright and diagonal braces. These are prepared in much the same way as the rails but can be sawn to length after they have been nailed on. Don't go over the top when nailing the hurdle together. Top and bottom for end posts, upright and diagonal braces with every other or alternate fastenings for the middle rails should suffice. The hurdle will be sturdy enough and if for some reason you need to undertake a few running repairs, they're easier to take apart! Stack the finished article on a flat surface and weigh it down for at least three weeks so that it doesn't distort as it dries out.

Gently coaxing the end poles onto the rail with a mallet.

BASKET-MAKING

Owen Jones came to the farmyard to show us how to make a basket out of riven oak that was typical of this area in the 19th century. I could only run in and out and watch now and again as I had so much else to do, which was a real shame. Craft skills like this are both subtle and beautiful. This is what technology is all about: the understanding and deft manipulation of materials from the world around you. Who would think that a piece of timber could be rendered so flexible? It reminded me of preparing flax to be woven into linen cloth. The cooking of the oak had broken down all the connecting tissues leaving a set of long fibres that he split apart into thin flat ribbons. The weaving of the basket made absolute sense. He had made the tree into a textile – oak cloth.

Skills and knowledge like this takes years to master. Anyone who has been on a basket-making course knows that you can make lopsided vague shapes that hold together as long as you don't use them for

The second thing to do was to boil the oak billets for several hours in order to soften them.

much. But the leap from that to taking a tree and making something strong, beautiful and very functional is a huge one that requires a great amount of practise. Owen's hands said it all: strong, precise and responsive to the idiosyncracies of each piece of wood.

Owen kindly let me have a go at some of the easiest bits of the operation. I managed not to muck it

ABOVE *While the oak cooked, Owen made the top of the basket by bending a hazel rod around a former and splicing the ends together.*

LEFT *First, Owen split the oak logs into manageable billets.*

LEFT *Once cooked, using a sharp knife to get started and then just the skill of his hands, Owen tore thin flexible strips from the billets of oak.*

Owen showed me how to work the oak in firmly.

up, and it was good to feel the texture of the oak as it moved in the hands.

Once finished, the whole basket was incredibly strong. Owen turned it upside down, put it on the ground and told me to stand on it. Having seen how soft and flexible the riven oak strips were I was a bit reluctant, but woven up it was more than strong enough to take my weight. It actually bounced a little as I shifted my weight.

The best thing about the basket, however, is the way that it fits the body using it. All the angles, sizes and curves fit very comfortably against your body. I can carry some serious weight in it by balancing it on one hip – loads that I would not be able to manage at all in, say, carrier bags. It spreads the load properly and holds it close to the body, not stressing the back. Factory produced items seldom have that sensitivity towards the user. Their shapes are often more determined by what is easy for machines to produce or easy to pack and stack. But having things around you that sit well with your shape or fit the hand makes life so much easier. These things work with you and become unthinking extensions of yourself; there's a 'rightness' that is both efficient and pleasing.

Owen mentioned that he has taken baskets like this in for repair that he knows to be fifty years old. This really impressed me, too. Making things to last, reusing them over and over again, repairing things when they wear, and getting them back into use is the true ecological approach. Taking your used carrier bags to the 'recycling' bin at the supermarket is such a very poor alternative.

LEFT *With the main ribs in place, the thinner oak laths were woven in. Each strip was carefully knocked into place tightly.*

RIGHT *The finished basket is not only strong but also beautiful.*

A Woman's Place

The role of women in Victorian Britain was not single and clear cut, but one of ambiguity and difference. Florence Nightingale, in her autobiography, describes the torment of endless empty social obligations. Never having fifteen minutes to herself, never being free to concentrate or work upon anything, but always required to be at everyone's beck and call for mind-numbing social commitments. Yet Victorian Britain was full of women for whom fifteen minutes away from endless uninterrupted work was a blessed relief.

Some women found that their traditional employment opportunities were being taken away, while, for others, doors were opening throughout the century. Nursing, teaching and, later on, university places and professional positions, were beginning to open up to women. Many industrial types of work, mining and agriculture were at the same time increasingly turning women away. Brand new industries offered different opportunities and education was slowly becoming more accessible for most. Social pressures both encouraged women to stay out of the paid workplace and demanded that they should re-enter it so as not to be a financial burden upon the poor rate.

Our Victorian ancestors were learning new ways of living and different ways of thinking.

As the century progressed, men were seen to be providers who held a corrupt world at bay, and women as moral guardians who provided the base and strength that allowed their menfolk to achieve. It gave both men and women a variety of roles to play. For women it sanctioned roles as givers of charity, upholders of religion, teachers of the young, nurses to the sick, controller of the family finances, providers of physical comfort, arbiters of taste and aesthetics and bearers of children.

Domestic Contribution

Historians have long characterized the Victorian period as one in which many (especially middle-class) women retreated, with active encouragement from their menfolk, from the outside world of paid work, back into the home and domesticity. But this view can lead us into a misogynistic way of looking at the evidence.

Throughout the Victorian period, women do unpaid work within the household. Wages become increasingly (not exclusively) a male phenomenon. But the 'retreat' of women into the home is a phrase that is loaded with value judgements. It implies that the cut and thrust and hardship of life are in the paid workplace, that the domestic space was one of idleness and a lesser contribution. Yet there is no doubt that the widespread adoption of coal as our major fuel and energy source significantly increased the amount of work needed to keep a home and family clean and fed. In towns, especially, the domestic burden was rising.

Perhaps one could say with equal justification, therefore, that men 'retreated' from the domestic space to work in factories where the hours were shorter and the work less heavy than that done by their stalwart wives. Some people at the time thought so. The magazine, *Punch*, for example, published a cartoon, shortly after the legal reduction of factory hours, showing a man at a table enjoying his supper while his wife was scrubbing the floor with the caption '16 hours so far and I ain't finished yet'. Social mores required women not to mention the housework they did, yet, even for middle-class women with a servant to help, the sheer volume of work to be done meant that they worked very hard. We have perhaps been fooled by their polite reticence into imagining that they were idle. It is pure prejudice to see this hard-working domestic contribution as somehow lesser and intellectually poor. It required brains, skill and ingenuity to run a Victorian household.

A large portion of my time on the farm was spent working alone indoors.

*Much of a woman's work
on a farm was based around
supporting the men.*

RURAL LIFE FOR WOMEN

On the farm, different factors defined the roles that men and women could play. Work roles had a longer history of a male–female divide than the newer jobs of the towns and cities. Pollution was less extreme. The rhythms of nature, too, exerted a stronger pull. Yet the notion of women as homemakers was embraced by both sexes.

It is often noted that here, too, women were becoming less involved in the practical farming than they had been before, and that they were increasingly confined to the domestic sphere. Few farmers, however, could afford the luxury of keeping their home life and business life entirely separate. Even among the large well-off farming families, who could afford sufficient staff to do all the manual labour, most relied upon wives for some supervisory role.

The Housewife's Friend and Family Help, for example, published in Leeds is a book clearly aimed at married women. Its main thrust is cookery, with a little household medicine and instructions for making artificial flowers. The female readership was clearly expected to take their domestic role seriously. And yet there is also a 'farmer's department' section, with handy hints for 'hands-on' farmers' wives, such as how to raise a shepherd's dog, how much seed is needed to plough an acre, and cures for diseases in livestock. The smaller the farm the more likely that wives and daughters would be called on for agricultural work. Cheese making and poultry care, especially, remained in female hands on such farms.

The Family Save All, published in 1861, gives numerous helpful hints and advice on poultry care, pig fattening, gardening and simple dairying. It's only other mention of farming being, 'General precautions against fires in farms etc.'. This, too, was a book aimed at married women and it clearly expects its readers to have a productive agricultural role. What we now call domestic work was also part of the work of the farm. Laundering cheesecloths, feeding staff, making pigswill and bottle-feeding lambs in the kitchen are all domestic as well as agricultural tasks.

Elizabeth Armstrong worked on a farm in Cumberland at the end of our period. She described her day in M. Bragg's *Speak for England* as beginning at 6.00 a.m. with the milking. She then cooked breakfast, cleaned the dairy, washed up, prepared vegetables, looked after the pigs, took the men in the fields their lunch, and milked again in the evening; she also had a range of field work to do.

Those who work together, often play together.

> *Whatever season was on, I had to help with it. Pick potatoes and help with the harvest … you were on call whenever the men decided they wanted a bit of help, and maybe to go and help move some sheep out of a field … help if the cows were calving or anything that was on a farm … you had to start on your housework as well after you got in, whereas the men were finished once they got their horses groomed and fed.*

On some farms men were taking over work, such as milking, that had traditionally been done by women particularly, on the largest farms. Machines took over some other traditional female jobs. A reaper binder meant no work binding the sheaves, just as it meant less work for men to cut the corn. Agricultural roles for women declined fastest in those areas that concentrated on arable farming and large-scale commercial production, and hung on longest where livestock were the mainstay. Small farms continued to be run along traditional work/gender split lines while the new, larger farms adopted new working practices. After all, traditional farming systems had been developed when most holdings were small and a family unit provided the most efficient method of working them. The new holdings were larger than they had been and new systems were needed to provide the economy of scale that they demanded. Agricultural work was changing: less labour was needed, and especially less female labour, but female labour was still required.

The census of 1871 records 24,000 female farmers in their own right and 187,000 wives of farmers working on their husbands' farms, and a further 92,000 daughters and other female relatives also at work on farms owned by relatives. In 1891 'agriculture', as defined by the census, still employed 16 per cent of all employed women. The amount of casual female labour is almost impossible to calculate, and the work done by family members on an ad hoc basis that didn't make it on to the census returns can only be guessed at.

OVERLEAF Domestic and agricultural work often overlapped. Boiling up the coppers could be for the laundry, dairy or preparing food for livestock.

CLOTHING

Clothes matter to us. We may like to pretend that they are trivial, but the truth is that we all mind very much indeed. Everyone knows that if you don't dress appropriately at a job interview you are unlikely to get the job. Clothes are how we declare our allegiances to a particular social group. In Britain, a person's clothes can indicate the sort of music someone listens to, religious beliefs, or whether he or she sees themselves as a rebel or someone who fits in. The way people dress can mark out how successful they are, or defy the usual norms for an alternative code. Many of us use clothes to advertise that we belong to certain sub-groups. Football fans, punks or bikers, for example, take pride in displaying their allegiances. Of course, the messages we wish to send can be varied in different circumstances. Clothing plays a role in social history, and provides a wonderful insight into people. Victorian clothing can tell us many things about the Victorians.

VICTORIAN CLOTHES

There were a number of things I wanted to know before I decided what I should wear for my year on the farm. The date, of course, was foremost; fashion in

My somewhat basic Victorian sewing kit, including a pretty pin cushion.

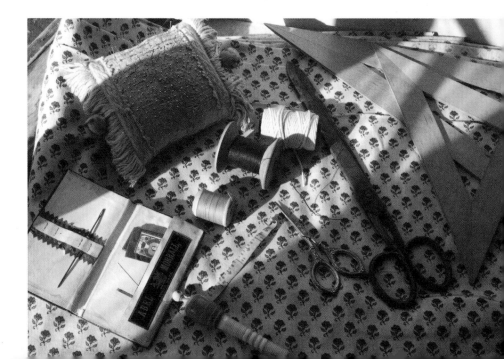

Victorian Britain was constantly changing. How wealthy/poor we would be so that I would know what I could have afforded, and where our farm was located were also important factors. Although mass-produced clothing, which offered the same clothes to everyone in the country, was beginning to take hold, there were still regional differences, especially in the countryside. Then I needed to think how a woman in her mid-forties, living and working on a small Shropshire farm might have thought about herself and her clothing. Would she have been fashionable? Would she have felt pressure to conform, and if so to what particular standards? What fabrics could she get? Who would be making the clothes? What messages would she be trying to convey through the way she dressed?

I wouldn't be able to send any of these messages if the clothing wasn't made in a Victorian fashion. Just getting the general look isn't good enough; all that tells you about are modern methods and taste. In an experiment like this, I wanted to know how the real thing felt and how it coped with the lifestyle. The clothes had to be Victorian and not just 'dressing up'. Making such clothes is a real challenge and absolutely fascinating. As *Cassell's Household Guide* points out:

Luca Costigliolo came to give me some expert advice on Victorian dressmaking.

The best way to learn dressmaking is to begin by turning old dresses. In unpicking you will see how they have been made. You then turn them and make them up the same way. If you have an obliging person in the house to work for you, and you assist her, you will learn still more; and it is also possible to get practise by volunteering to help friends who make dresses at home … It is a good plan to have a dress occasionally thoroughly well made for you, as it will prove a guide for home use.

I took a pattern from the *Englishwoman's Domestic Magazine*, which was edited by the Beetons. Its main selling point was the quality of the patterns that each edition carried. These included embroidery, knitting, crochet, lace and dressmaking patterns. Printed paper patterns for use at home were becoming very popular, and allowed many more untrained people to make at home the more complicated and fashionable dresses.

Previously, most home making had been restricted to underclothes and unfitted clothing. All fitted garments had traditionally been made by trained, professional male tailors, or (but only from the 18th century) professional dressmakers. Full-sized paper patterns took some of the fear out of cutting complicated shapes and allowed hard-working amateurs to achieve a reasonable fit.

Many a woman used this new knowledge to reduce her dressmaking bills (or have more dresses for the same budget). Others went on to use home experience as a way of learning the trade. A young woman who could make dresses could command higher wages as a servant, could hire herself out to help other women,

or could even set herself up in business as an independent dressmaker if she was lucky.

Before making anything, however, I carefully read as many sets of Victorian instructions on dressmaking as I could. I was also lucky enough to get the opportunity to have a really good look at several original dresses of ordinary and working women from this date. It soon became clear that Victorian methods differed quite significantly from those taught on modern dressmaking courses. This is why so many theatrical, film and television costumes don't always look totally convincing. If you use modern methods, the finished garment will hang differently on the body.

CORSETS

As everyone knows, Victorian women wore corsets. The more fashion conscious the woman, the more likely she was to use those corsets to significantly alter her body shape. Did anyone go without corsets? Well, if they did, they were in for a rough ride. Even in workhouses, corsets were the norm. The overseers of the poor would provide them – of the cheapest kind of course – if a woman didn't have any. To go uncorseted was to have no self-control. Immorality was thought to be sure to follow. A tight corset not only was thought to keep a woman neat and attractive, but also to act as a physical moral reminder. Loose women were, well, loose. A 'neat' waist – meaning a small-constrained waist – is often mentioned along with cleanliness as being indicative of an honest and decent woman.

The issue in Victorian Britain was not whether you wore a corset, but how tightly you laced it. In his book *The Complete Dress and Cloak Cutter* 1877, Charles Hecklinger asserts that as a result of many years of experience he can say with confidence that the 'proportionate' size of a woman is a waist of 10 in (25.4 cm) less than her bust measurement. His patterns for the average woman are all based upon a 34-in (87-cm) bust, a 24-in (61-cm) waist and a 36-in (92-cm) hip. When he talks about large sizes, he bases his measurements on a 42-in (107-cm) bust and a 34-in (87-cm) waist. My own bust is 34 in (87 cm), but my natural waist is 29 in (74 cm). I would have to squeeze in my waist by 5 in (13 cm)

RUTH'S DIARY

Dressmaking: March

To my delight, Luca arrived today to get me started on making myself a summer dress. He and I have worked together in the past on 16th- and 17th-century clothing, but Victorian clothing is fairly new to me.

He was reasonably happy with my brown winter dress – I had cut it half an inch too low at the back waist of the bodice, though. But my corset cutting really hasn't cut the mustard, according to Luca – not enough shaping under the bust apparently. Although it can be a bit disheartening to have your efforts criticized, Luca really knows his stuff, and frankly I am very grateful for his comments. Under his guidance my summer dress will really be the bees knees.

The sewing machine is a nightmare, however. 16th-century clothing was all handsewn, of course, and that is where my expertize lies. I have never got to grips with the machines. Modern electric machines give me the willies – they run away from you. Two minutes to sew and two hours to unpick it all again. I would rather spend the two hours sewing it properly by hand in the first place.

OPPOSITE *This Victorian treadle machine doesn't run away quite so much but it's hard to get the hang of. It reminds me of learning to drive.*

Strips of whalebone sewn inside a Victorian bodice.

to be 'proportionate'. This 'proportionate' figure, however, was normal and not what Victorians called tight-laced. Tight-lacing would require me to loose 10 in (25.4 cm) from my waist.

While most tight-lacing occurred in unmarried wealthy girls, there were a few women from other walks of life whose vanity (or low self-esteem, depending on your viewpoint) pushed them to join in the torture. We have accounts of servant girls with 18-in (45-cm) waists. A farmer's wife on a tiny Shropshire farm, with no servant to help her, was unlikely to lace her corsets tightly, but none the less a small degree of constriction from the corset would certainly have been socially expected. This state of affairs did not go uncriticized. Many doctors railed against the health implications of tight- lacing and a few eccentric individuals were beginning to question whether corsets should be worn at all.

THE RAG TRADE

Historians acknowledge that the textile industry (along with iron) acted as a spur to the industrial revolution. Certainly, textiles were important and the invention of the Spinning Jenny (1764) – a machine that span thread or yarn many times faster than could be done by hand – kick-started a new era in textile production, a mainstay of the British economy. British textiles came to clothe most of the world.

Like the cloth itself, British-made clothing also began to move well beyond our national boundaries. New technology went hand-in-hand with new working practices and new ways of selling, which resulted in a huge clothing export trade. The British style of dress began to appear all over the world – the three-piece suit in particular. There had been a small trade in loose-fitting, ready-made clothing before Victoria's reign. Sewing machines and new cutting systems allowed clothes to be made more quickly and cheaply. With a new larger market at home and abroad it became economically viable to develop a system of standard sizes. Large batches of standardized garments could be made – and buyers found – without time and labour-consuming fittings.

It is easy to think that the revolution in the rag trade was the result of technology. The sewing machine often gets the credit, but just as important was the organization of the trade and its marketing. If you look at surviving Victorian clothing you cannot help but notice how much handsewing it contains. Nor was this mass production all about factories. A huge proportion of the clothing was made at home by outworkers.

This vast increase in the output of cheap clothing came at a price. Henry Mayhew's interviews with the poor give testament to the many destitute and desperate women who took pre-cut garments and sewed them on a piece rate basis. The employers did not have to pay for heat or light or thread. If work was slack, they paid nothing, if women were desperate for work, wages soon dropped. So low was the pay that many, probably the majority in London, were forced into prostitution for the barest survival.

Those working in workrooms were not much better off. Hours were horrendous. Twenty hours a day for weeks on end was not uncommon when work was plentiful. The overcrowding in the rooms also beggars belief. A room 12 ft (3.6 m) square (about the size of most people's living rooms) could form the working space for ten women, sewing machines and all. Women within these establishments were rarely allowed to learn the whole trade (which might have allowed them to branch out on their own), but rather each person did a separate part of the process. One set sleeves, another hemmed cuffs, and so on.

Madam Elise came to public notoriety in 1863 when it was proved that one of her seamstresses died as a direct result of the working conditions. The cartoon in *Punch*, which depicted a fashionable woman looking in her mirror at the reflected image of the very woman who had died making her dress, caused a sensation, but nothing changed in the rag trade.

The nightdress that I wear is exquisitely handsewn yet appears in a Victorian clothing catalogue in 1889. It is titled 'The Cicely' and advertised as available this season for delivery anywhere within the British Isles – parcels for foreign delivery 'can be arranged'. Although it is a standardized, mass-produced item, it was nonetheless handmade. I wear it in remembrance of a woman who needed the money, worked in really difficult conditions, and never expected to be remembered.

Peter doing his best to repair his trousers. Everyone, men as well as women, could manage a simple sewing job in Victorian Britain.

PETER'S STITCH IN TIME

I have not repaired the little rips in my clothes and now I have to repair the giant gaping holes in my clothes. I remember being given my Victorian outfit by the lovely lady who made it, Sue, who worked at Blist's Hill Museum in Ironbridge. My clothes were new, clean, and most of all rip-free. As much as I wanted to get stuck into life on the farm, I also wanted to maintain the crisp and, dare I say, dapper appearance of my outfit. However, no sooner had I donned my costume and it all started to go downhill.

During the restoration of the cottage I got really dirty, I picked up a nick in my waistcoat and a hole in the seam of my trousers. Had I heeded the age-old saying: 'A stitch in time saves

nine', I may have 'nipped them in the bud' but they were only small rips. I was tired, working hard, and I had pigsties to build. Each day, working on the farm resulted in another stitch being broken. Something had to be done and no one else was going to do it. I had to get my needle and thread, set myself some time apart, and sew up my now unsightly trousers, using a backstitch as advised by Ruth.

I think I will have to sew up my waistcoat at some point, but at the moment it acts as a reminder of all the hard work that we have put into the farm. I will fix it, but not today, although as they say: 'procrastination is the thief of time'; 'don't put off to tomorrow what you can do to day'.

PRACTICAL NEEDLEWORK

Decorative needlework was a Victorian woman's leisure activity. It was an opportunity to be creative and a way to personalize a home. Women's magazines abound with ideas and patterns for just about every type of small decorative object from greetings cards to lace curtains, pin cushions to fire screens. Many of these patterns presume that the readers are very skilled indeed. This is one of the quicker and easier patterns, 'do-able' in a couple of evenings.

An illustration of the leaf design from The Englishwoman's Domestic Magazine.

Appliquéd Cushion

The somewhat brief, original instructions came from *The Englishwoman's Domestic Magazine* (Vol. 2). Very simply, this pattern calls for you to cut out some leaf shapes from fabric, lightly glue them in place on a cushion cover, sew them on, and then finish with a little embroidery for a stem and some veining on the leaves. Alternatively, you can use braid to form the stem and veins.

You will need a plain-coloured cushion cover and some fabric for the leaves. If you don't have any suitable fabric at home and you can't buy any fabric that grabs your fancy, then look in your local charity shop. They will have any number of clothes in almost every colour and texture you can think of, and all for very little money. Choose something that doesn't fray too much – it will make your life easier.

INSTRUCTIONS

MATERIALS

Plain-coloured cushion cover

Fabric for leaves

Glue (PVA adhesive)

Tailor's chalk

Embroidery needle

Embroidery thread/cotton (various colours)

Braid (optional)

Trace or draw the leaf shape from the design or, if you prefer, draw your own. Keep the shape simple so that it will be easy to sew around.

Next, using a piece of tailor's chalk, mark the line that the stem will take across the surface of the cushion. You could copy the line in the book or just meander across in a way that pleases you.

Lightly glue your cut-out leaves onto the cushion cover wherever you want them. This is just to hold them in place while you sew them down.

You can hand- or machine-sew around each leaf, or you can sew a piece of braid or tape around the edges.

If you wish to hand-sew the leaves, choose a fairly thick thread in a strong colour. Something slippery rather than hairy would be best. Buttonhole stitch is both decorative and good at controlling the raw edges of your leaves. A series of small crosses can look good, and featherstitch can be fun. Whichever you choose, take care to stitch fairly close together so that the leaves are firmly attached and won't catch against zips and buttons when the cushion is in use.

If you prefer to machine-sew the leaves in place, use a wide zigzag or embroidery stitch, which will cover the raw edge. Machine-sewn appliqué usually looks best in a contrasting colour.

The braid option can be really striking although a little fiddly if you are after a neat rather than rustic look. When you are choosing a tape or braid, check that it bends around corners easily without distorting too much. You will need to tack the braid in place before you start sewing it down.

Once the leaves are sewn in place, add the stem and the veins on the leaves. Again, you have a choice of whether to hand or machine-embroider, or to sew on a piece of tape or braid.

The Victorian aesthetic was for neatness and order, and while sewing machines were available when this pattern was originally drawn up, they could only do a single straight stitch. Therefore, the women who made this pattern up at home in the 19th century most likely hand-stitched the leaves on neatly with many tiny stitches and carefully attached lengths of 'passementary' braid with invisible stitches.

I made Peter some braces for Christmas. It took me a couple of weeks, snatching an hour a night upstairs by oil lamplight. When I brought them down to wrap up, I discovered that the colours didn't match. I hadn't noticed in the lamplight, but one side had been in dark green and the other in dark blue!

The Cobbler and Cordwainer

Before the project was due to start, I began to think about my footwear. Of all the items of clothing I was going to need, boots were going to be the most important. But where on earth was I going to find a pair of Victorian farm labourer's boots? Fortunately for me, my brother, Thomas, had recently taken up shoe and boot-making as a hobby/part-time job, and we quickly set about poring over old photographs of Victorian farm labourers and farmers to try and work out what styles were employed and how the boots were put together. Finally, we found some size 11 'lasts' – foot-shape moulds around which the shoe is built – and Tom set about designing some patterns.

Traditionally, a cobbler is someone who repairs boots and shoes, and the correct term for someone who makes footwear is, in fact, a 'cordwainer'. The term comes from the Spanish word 'cordovan', used to describe a soft reddish leather produced in Spain and popular for shoemaking. For centuries, the cordwainer had been a central character of the rural scene providing for all of the community's footwear needs. They would also be called upon to make other leather accessories: gaiters for hedgers and ploughmen, and knee-pads for thatchers.

The boots my brother, Thomas, made for me. They are heavy, but exremely hard-wearing.

As with so many of the cottage industries of the age, though, the shoemaker's workshop was under threat from the growing industrialization of shoe production in the late 19th century. Crafts such as these often became centred on particular regions. Lace making, for example, became associated with Nottingham in the East Midlands and Buckinghamshire. Shoemaking already had a tradition in Northampton since the 15th century, but it was in the 19th century that the trade took on a more industrial scale of production with the first machine-based factory set up in 1838. The industry grew steadily throughout the late 19th century. In some areas of Northamptonshire as many as one half of all adult males and females were employed to supply an increasingly national market place. Village cordwainers simply couldn't compete, and they declined by some 50 per cent from 1870 to 1900.

The Village Revolutionary

The low-cost mass-produced shoes and boots of the Northamptonshire industry could be purchased for as little as 8 shillings a pair, while village shoemakers were

charging something in the region of 14 shillings. It is perhaps this looming threat to their livelihood that fostered in rural cordwainers a radical attitude to improving conditions for the rural poor. In 1892, Anderson Graham wrote, in *The Rural Exodus: The problem of the village and the town*, of the distinctly 'revolutionary' character of the village cobbler, 'for, lying beside his awls, his broad knives, his files and his paste-pot, is a copy of *The Rights of Man*, which is his Bible'.

Thomas Hardy, the campaigner for parliamentary reform (not the novelist), was perhaps the most famous radical shoemaker of his time. In the 1790s, as a founding member of the London Corresponding Society, he campaigned for working men to have the vote and set up links with other radical groups. Eventually, his activities got him in to trouble and it wasn't long before he found himself imprisoned in the Tower of London on a charge of high treason.

The government attempted to associate Hardy's actions with the revolutionary events afoot in France, and as a consequence an angry mob attacked his house causing his pregnant wife to flee via a back window. Hardy was ultimately found not guilty by the court and upon his release a large crowd gathered outside the Old Bailey to escort him home. He received a good deal of sympathy, not only for his politics, but also because while he had been locked in the Tower, his wife had died giving birth to their stillborn child – most likely as a cause of her hurried escape.

This photograph, from the late 19th century, depicts a team of boot and shoemakers.

ARTS AND CRAFTS

Boot-making

My brother, Thomas, acquired a hide for each pair of boots that he was to make for us. The soles came from the stiffest part of the hide and the uppers from the softest and most pliable part. The leather was soaked to soften it and beaten to close up the pores. The pattern was marked out on each hide, cut out and then stitched together or 'closed' as this process is referred to. The tongues were stitched to the uppers to stop water ingress and then the combined uppers were 'lasted'. The insoles and soles were cut out and, around the outer edge of the soles, the rims were punched with an awl. Through these holes, two waxed chords were threaded through, passed in opposite directions and pulled to right and left. As in the Victorian period, glue was used as a further bonding agent between the uppers, insoles and soles. Finally the heel was built up using leather and nailed together, toe and heel plates were fitted, and the soles were studded with hob nails.

I watched in amazement as Thomas slowly pieced together our boots and marvelled at the finished product. They felt like real boots and a work of genuine craftsmanship – all hand-cut, hand-punched and sewn. They were very heavy but certainly had the feel and appearance of a boot that was built to last. My job now was to keep them in good order. In the past, I had used the services of a local cordwainer who, every time I took a pair of virtually unmendable shoes to him, would repeatedly bawl at me, 'Shoes worth wearing are worth are repairing!'

So proud was I of my new Victorian boots that I vowed to keep them in good order and kept a keen eye on the soles to ensure that no hob nails had dropped out exposing the leather directly to the ground. I also sought out a Victorian substance for waterproofing boots, and found a combination of tallow fat, beeswax and pitch to be most effective.

Waterproofing Boots

Clockwise from the top: pitch, tallow fat and beeswax. When heated and mixed together, they are perfect for waterproofing.

I took these ingredients: four parts tallow, three parts beeswax and one part pitch and heated them on the stove in the cottage. I then mixed them together, and with an old rag, liberally applied the blend to both boots. I made sure to work it into the stitching and seams on the uppers and between the soles and the uppers to ensure minimal water ingress. It took a while to work it in to the leather but very soon I was getting a perfect sheen. I poured the remaining mix – as there was quite a lot of it – into a tub to let it cool, and now use this regularly to polish up and revitalize the leather.

All in all, both the boots and the waterproofing have turned out to work excellently. Our farm is by no stretch of the imagination located in a well-drained part of the valley, and over the course of the winter the yard and meadows have both suffered from water logging. Relentless trudging through wet, muddy yards and fields has proved a stern test for my Victorian boots but, so far, my feet have remained as dry as a bone.

Working my home-made Victorian waterproofing mix into my boots. Time-consuming, but essential.

RECIPES FOR LEFTOVERS

The wonderful book, The Family Save All, *has become the most useful of all the cookery books at the farm. It contains lots of recipes for leftovers and for using up odds and sods in the store cupboard. I find myself turning to it again and again. The recipes are, in general, simple and very quick, as well as being extremely economical.*

The second half of the book is a series of handy hints on any practical subject that a wife might need to know, such as how to estimate the weight of meat on a live pig, what to do if your clothes catch fire, how to kill slugs that are eating your vegetables, and so on.

I have used the recipe for Pheasant Hash perhaps more than any other in the book. It works equally well with leftover Christmas turkey or roast chicken. However, the wording is a little convoluted and so I have adapted it slightly.

Potted meats or sandwich spreads have, traditionally, been Britain's answer to paté; they brighten up a picnic and make great late-night snacks. While factory-made sandwich spreads were available in shops at the end of the 19th century, the good ones have always been the home-made versions.

The Family Save All *recommends potting leftover cooked beef as a means of preserving it, and indeed it does. Potted meats are sealed with a layer of fat, which, by excluding oxygen, keeps cooked meat safe for a week or so in cool temperatures.*

Potted prawns with garlic must be one of the most delicious dishes on earth, and a really good potted chicken takes some beating.

Stripping the meat off the leftover roasted bird, prior to making the stock.

The general advice when potting either meat or fish is to beat it really smooth with the butter, press very firmly into the pot and be generous with how much melted fat you pour on top – you want a good seal.

For Potted Chicken, the quality of your chicken really counts. A battery-farmed bird is never going to taste good; it will be both too wet and too insipid to be worth bothering with. Let your taste buds guide you into more ethical habits and buy something that had a decent life and a chance to develop some flavour.

Pheasant Hash

METHOD

After a roast dinner I strip the meat off the carcass, and put the carcass and any leftover gravy into a saucepan with a little water, an onion and seasoning. I leave it to simmer gently for about an hour, during which time I do the washing up and clean the kitchen. Then I take the pan off the heat, put a lid on and abandon it overnight.

When I am ready to prepare the next day's meal, I lift off the lid, scoop the cold fat off the top, and strain the liquid into a clean pan. I stir in a little flour into the liquid and then bring it up to heat. I add the leftover meat and allow it to simmer for a while until the meat has warmed through. It takes me just over half an hour. Fantastic. Tastes good, too. Serve with toast, and stuffing if there is any.

INGREDIENTS

1 leftover roasted bird

1 onion

1 pinch salt

1 pinch pepper

1 blade of mace

2 tsp flour

Toast (optional)

Potted Chicken

METHOD

Cut up the chicken as finely as you can across the grain of the meat. Now mix it in a bowl – or an electric food processor – with 1 oz (75 g) of the butter until it is completely smooth. Add the seasoning and a little more butter if it seems a bit dry. Mix thoroughly.

Press the paste firmly into a pot, making sure that there are no air gaps. Gently melt the remaining butter and pour it on top of the chicken. It should completely cover the meat to a depth of about ½ in (1 cm). Allow to cool and store somewhere cool and dry. To serve, spread thickly on bread or toast.

INGREDIENTS

Leftover roast chicken (1 chicken breast or two chicken legs

3 oz (75 g) salted butter

1 pinch ground mace

1 pinch cayenne pepper

CHAPTER FIVE

HEALTH AND HYGIENE

THE HEALTH OF THE NATION

 Medicine as a science owes a lot to developments during the 19th century. The Victorian penchant for statistical information led to a civilization that analyzed cause and effect and began regularly practicing medicine clinically, building on the foundations established by the 18th-century pioneers such as Richard Mead, William Hunter, and his brother John. However, a great deal of 19th-century medicine was born out of the necessity to deal with the problems created by the mass migrations to, and the growth of, the ever-expanding urban centres.

DISEASES

Wealth distribution, living and working conditions, and general overcrowding in the cities all had a major impact on the health of the nation. In addition, an economy in a state of flux during the 1850s and 1860s meant that little improvement of these factors was seen until the 1870s. Malnutrition and calcium-deficiency were rife, with improvements in diet not really having much effect until the end of the century, and cases of alcoholism and venereal diseases were social ills on the increase. Some of the major diseases claiming lives in the Victorian period were: typhus, typhoid, tuberculosis, diphtheria, dysentery, scarlet fever, cholera and smallpox. All of which were exacerbated by so many people living in so little space (typhus is a prime example as it is carried by body lice and, therefore, was a disease that was associated with the poor).

HOME-MADE REMEDIES

It is unsurprising that during the 19th century and beyond, home remedies and cures remained a part of rural life. When I was growing up, my parents had a Victorian cook book that had a plethora of remedies in the back, which I used to use and still do in some cases. Things like: using an ivy leaf on a cut – the rough side cleans the wound and the smooth side helps to heal it; eating an onion (raw), if one is unfortunate enough to be stung by a wasp in the throat; and my favourite – a soap and sugar poultice for drawing out a splinter.

LEGISLATION AND PIONEERS

'Cometh the hour cometh the person.' These challenges thrown up by a massive change in the domestic arrangements of society were met by pioneers of the medical profession and public health. Edwin Chadwick, a reformer of the Poor Law, started to study the relationship between health and living conditions.

An advertisement for a wide range of medical appliances.

It took ten years of lobbying but, in 1848, The Public Health Act was passed and Chadwick became the commissioner of the new Public Health Board. The Act was limited in its powers, allowing but not forcing local authorities to act, and Chadwick was not the most popular character – which in part led to the abolition of the Board in 1854 – but this Act and his actions to an extent laid some of the groundwork for John Simon's Public Health Act of 1875. This Act had more of an impact because it was compulsory, forcing local authorities to provide clean water, proper drainage, sewers, and appoint a medical officer of health.

Other factors which led to the passing of the 1875 Public Health Act were: the demonstration by John Snow and William Budd that cholera was caused by an organism that one ingested and that the outbreak of cholera in the Broad Street area of London was due to a single infected water pump; a later outbreak of cholera in 1865/6 which killed 20,000; the appointment in 1855 of Dr John Simon as chief medical adviser (who in this role made smallpox vaccination compulsory); working-class men getting the vote (1867); the Great Stink of 1858 in London (it was so bad Parliament had to be suspended); and the publication of the Frenchman Louis Pasteur's germ theory in 1861.

Pasteur's work took a while to catch on universally, but two doctors that he initially influenced were Joseph Lister and Robert Koch. Lister acted on Pasteur's work to perfect antiseptic surgery and his work must have saved countless lives (ironically one of the most vocal opponents of Lister's theories was Simpson, the pioneer of chloroform), and Koch worked on proving that germs caused disease by finding one germ that caused one particular disease. The disease he honed in on was anthrax, and the method he used to identify the organism was applied to other germs. In 1882 he found the cause of tuberculosis, and in 1883 he isolated the

Victorian apothecary set with various potions and lotions.

germ responsible for cholera. By the end of the Victorian period, germs for many diseases had been identified including diphtheria, leprosy, pneumonia, tetanus, typhoid, malaria, dysentery and plague.

The medical pioneers and innovators helped to establish the basis of what was to become the National Health Service in 1948: clean hospitals (both in the wards and in the theatres) compulsory vaccinations, understanding of germs and disease, new technologies such as the German physicist Rontgen's discovery of x-rays, and public health awareness at a Government level. Mortality rates did begin to fall in the latter half of the 19th century, from around 22 per 1000 people per five years in the mid-19th century to 17.7 at the end of the century. However, infant mortality rates showed no real signs of decreasing until the 20th century. Many of these public health milestones would have taken time to have a real effect, and it is we who have reaped the true benefits.

The harsh realities of Victorian health problems were to a large extent confined to the cities and towns, but we live on a farm. Indeed, Woods indicates

CONTRACEPTION

In 1877 the birth rate in England slowly began to fall, and continued falling until 1911. Why? Women were not dying any younger. People were not marrying any later. Marriage itself remained popular. The illegitimacy rate remained similar to before, and yet people were having fewer children.

If you look at the middle classes separately, the fall in birth rate happened even earlier, twenty years earlier than the population as a whole. The last group to follow the trend were the rural poor who were still routinely having large families in the early part of the 20th century.

Limiting the size of your family had, however, become a social norm and was actively approved of. Read any late-19th-century fiction and you will notice that people with very large families are described as 'improvident', 'imprudent' and other derogatory terms. The spacing of births also came in for comment. A child every year would 'wear out' the mother. Caring husbands would ensure that it did not happen.

There are veiled references to contraception throughout Victorian literature. Some methods of contraception had been available before Victorian times. Abstinence had always been

an option, as too had coitus interuptus, while, in Britain, evidence of condoms stretches back to Roman times. However, at the beginning of Victoria's reign a whole host of other options were becoming available to British people. In 1823, Francis Place was printing handbills describing and promoting the use of the sponge method of contraception, known previously on the continent. Richard Carlile's **Every Woman's Book** of 1828 on the same subject sold over 10,000 copies within two years. The vaginal douche or syringe method first appeared in English publications in 1834.

A variety of pessaries, including the cap, were being advertised by 1840, and the vulcanization of rubber in 1843 made both the condom and the diaphragm cap very much easier and cheaper to use.

Information about contraception was widely available to mature married people in a range of health publications. While the young and unmarried were often entirely ignorant, it seems that after the first year or two of marriage, friends and relations would quietly recommend such publications and drop a few hints about the benefits of following their advice.

in the *Journal of Historical Geography* (1982) that, from the census data of 1861, rural communities were enjoying life spans that the 'average person' wouldn't experience for another 60 years. Chadwick cited the disparities in average life expectancy between rural and urban communities in 1840 (people in the country were living about twice as long as their urban counterparts) to help his campaign for a Public Health Act, and Louis Pasteur's work highlighted the fact that there were fewer micro-organisms in mountain air than in town air. Basically, it was healthier to live in the country than it was to live in the city.

Health Fads

The Victorian age also saw many health fads. A wide range of weird and wonderful theories and cures march before our eyes. Some have passed into mainstream modern medical practice, others are still with us as 'alternative' medicine, and some have faded away entirely.

Among the many treatments making health claims were a variety of different styles of 'baths'. At home the 'warm bath', the 'cold bath' and the 'steam bath' were most common. If you could afford it, then continental spas offered a much wider range. The 'air bath', the 'dew bath' and the 'sun bath' were especially popular in the Alps, while for a range of mineral salts and muds at varying temperatures, the wealthy patient usually headed to Germany. *The Housewife's Friend* gives a succinct summary of the benefits thought to be gained from warm and cold baths.

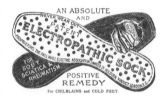

Medical items in the Victorian era often made extravagant claims regarding their efficacy.

The warm bath brings blood to the surface … it is excellent in nervous diseases, hypochondria, epilepsy, hysterics, palsy etc … the warm bath should be used three times a week. The cold bath not only preserves health, but cures disease. In most fevers not attended with active inflammation, it has a most happy effect. It lessens the burning heat of the body, moderates the thirst, abates the force of the circulation and induces sleep.

Air bathing was the practice of taking all ones clothes off and exposing ones skin to clean alpine air. Special huts were built with one wall absent so that one could be exposed without indecency. Sun bathing was much the same, but exposing one's skin to sunlight. Both were believed to act as tonics and 'detox' regimes.

For the family who couldn't afford foreign travel, in addition to warm and cold baths there was also the steam bath. Steam baths were a form of sauna, believed to be very good for lung complaints of all sorts, cases of poisoning, gall stones and gout. Household health books often give instructions on how to rig up a steam bath at home using tubs of hot water and heavy blankets. People were told to 'sweat' within them for about an hour at a time, as hot as they could bear.

PERSONAL HYGIENE

Standards of personal hygiene were of great importance in Victorian Britain. Someone who kept themselves clean was showing moral superiority over those who were dirty. It was frequently stated that washing cost nothing and that 'Cleanliness was next to Godliness'. Whenever a character in fiction was both poor and good, they were carefully described as being unusually clean and neat about their person; whenever a character rich or poor was to be seen as bad, then descriptions of dirt and slovenly dress slide in.

Of course, washing did cost something. Clean water could be hard for many people to get hold of. Heating it was even harder and did cost, AS did soap. People who were working fourteen to eighteen hours a day in order to just barely survive found that the extra couple of hours work involved in hauling many buckets of water from the stream or standpipe hard. Coal to heat the water and soap to wash with were all things that had to be rationed in most working homes. Nor is it easy

The washstand with its jug, bowl, and slop pail tucked underneath, was the nearest that most Victorians got to a 'bathroom'.

to have perfectly tidy hair when you do manual outdoor work or spot-less aprons when scrubbing floors. But none the less, cleanliness and tidiness was something to be aimed for.

Although by the end of Victoria's reign many urban middle-class homes had baths of some description, for most people washing was usually done with a jug, a basin and a flannel. The tin baths in front of the fire are not typical of working homes until the early 20th century. A jug of water, warm if you were lucky, was brought up to the bedroom. You poured some into the basin and began washing your face. You then worked your way down the body, washing each area and drying yourself before moving on to the next bit. When the water became too dirty you poured it away into the slop pail and refilled the basin with some clean water from the jug.

The early baths just extended this system a little. A large shallow pan – or bath – that was big enough to stand in allowed you to take off all your clothes at once and rinse off by pouring water from the jug all over you. Degas' painting of a woman bathing in 1883 shows the typical Victorian bath in use. Of course, taking all your clothes off can be pretty nippy in an unheated British bedroom, so washing bit by bit in a bowl remained a sensible winter option in even the wealthier homes.

Cassell's Household Guide of 1869 recommends that the face, armpits, feet, 'the groin and parts about' should be washed once a day with soap as well as water. However, the most thorough instructions for washing hair that I have found appears in *The Housewife's Friend and Family Help*:

> Wash your hair at least several times a week with soap and water, rubbing the roots and scalp well, and be careful to rinse it thoroughly in plain cold water. Then dry it with care, and if necessary, apply a little pommatom made with beef marrow, softened with a little leaf lard and just sufficiently scented to take off the greasy smell, then comb and brush it gently … Ladies in washing the hair should tie it tightly a few inches from the end, and if they do so carefully they can wash their hair just as thoroughly, and really with less tangling than men can do.

Mrs Beeton recommends borax rather than soap for the actual washing, but agrees that Pommatum, which is made from scented animal fats, is gently combed through the hair and acts as a conditioner. Bandoline was the Victorian equivalent of hair gel, to hold styles in place. Mrs Rundell suggested a jelly made from quince pips that would wash out easily and leave the hair in good condition.

The ingredients for the lip salve: lard, white wax, alkanet root and almond oil.

VICTORIAN HOUSEWORK

Keeping a farmhouse clean is no easy task in any age. Farmhouses are working spaces with people in and out all the time bringing bits of farm with them as they go.

The Victorian farmer's wife had a very wide range of chemicals and techniques at her disposal in the never-ending fight against the grime. Although by the end of the century there were branded products on the market, most women obtained the raw ingredients and mixed them, as they required them. This was much cheaper than buying brands, and allowed women a much greater degree of control.

When we think of cleaning products we tend to think of chemicals, and there were certainly plenty to choose from. Harrods in London stocked: chloride of lime, carbolic acid, ammonia, hydrogen peroxide, muriatic acid, nitric acid, camphor, and the list goes on. Some of these chemicals were very powerful, and potentially lethal if misused. Sulphuric acid certainly does take stains out of

Brick dust works wonders on our copper kettle, making it really shine.

marble, but you can give yourself some pretty nasty burns in the process. A few of these chemicals had a long history of domestic use, which at least meant that people were experienced in using them, but many were newly available to the housewife in the Victorian period. The advances in various chemical industries were producing completely new compounds and generating many waste products, which could be cheaply converted into products for sale as cleaning agents. You can see these advances as both a great boon and as a great danger. While your whites could now be whiter, your health could also suffer.

But, although one hundred and fifty years worth of advertising has told us that cleaning is about chemical products that you can buy in a bottle, cleaning is often not about chemicals at all. The physical or mechanical removal of dirt works even better. Far better to sweep your floors free of dropped food, mud and so forth than to coat the whole lot with an antiseptic spray. The Victorians employed a whole host of aids to mechanical cleaning. For example, damp tea leaves do not clean anything by themselves, but if you scatter them on the floor then dust and dirt stick to them. This makes it very much easier to sweep up the whole lot in one go, avoiding any dust flying up and helping to ensure that you are removing all of the dirt and not just a top layer. It works on carpets, too.

Charcoal powder brings out the shine on a silver ladle.

There were also a whole host of abrasive agents that make it quick and easy to remove dirt. They start with very course particles, which will shift the big stuff, and work down to the finest of powders for polishing things that scratch easily. Plain ordinary beach sand is great for things like burnt-on food or rust. You simply take a damp cloth and dip it into the sand. A thin layer of sand sticks to the damp cloth, which you can then use as a scouring pad. Brick dust is a little finer than sand. It was used for cleaning pots and pans and cooking ranges. Hart's horn powder was very fine and employed for polishing silver. If you have the right abrasive then most things can be removed with very little effort. Chalk dust is great in the bathroom, and damp newspaper is exactly the right texture to get smears off glass and gives a wonderful finish.

Eco Cleaning

Chemicals used in the home are now one of the main sources of water-borne pollution in Britain. The most polluted air in modern Britain is indoors. Anyone interested in the environment or in the health of his or her family, therefore, should have a good think about the products that they use within the home. The cocktail of bleaches, air fresheners, detergents, oven cleaners, and so on, that lurk beneath the average kitchen sink and are splashed liberally around the average home is a potent mix. Advertising implies that all are necessary for hygiene and

◉ *Take a bottle, pour in some cheap malt vinegar (about 10 fl oz/30 cl) and some cheap bottled lemon juice (about 5 fl oz/ 15 cl), and shake. Hey presto an anti-bacterial limescale removing cleaner.*

◉ *Make up one bottle for the bathroom and another for the kitchen.*

◉ *If you want a thick consistency, then a little gum Arabic (a food ingredient often used in sweets) does the job.*

social acceptance. But there are plenty of healthy, simple and cheap alternatives to be learnt from Victorian housewives.

Salt is great at killing bugs as well. Few things can live in a very salty environment. So if you have anything that needs a scrub, scatter a small handful of salt on it before you start. Scrub with a damp cloth or a dry brush and you will not only find that the abrasive power of the salt makes the scrubbing easier, but you will be killing bacteria as you go.

THE VICTORIAN LAUNDRY

Traditionally, laundry in Britain was a cold-water process using home-made alkalis to dissolve the grease and then forcing water through the fabric, between the fibres under pressure using either a wooden bat, called a battledore or beetle, or using one's own feet. It is a system that works perfectly well where there is an abundant cheap source of alkalis and abundant clean, preferably running, water. Doing the laundry has always been seen as a female job. Women soaked the laundry in lye (a solution of sodium hydroxide or potassium hydroxide in water) at home, applied any stain-removal treatments, and then took the laundry to the nearest convenient water source. The actual washing took place in the stream or river, with no need for tubs or carrying large volumes of water. Many towns provided drying grounds with public wringing posts as a convenience for the citizens near to a good washing spot. Women met up on good washing days and often clubbed together to help each other and maybe to share a jug of ale while the washing dried.

By Victorian times all this had changed in all but the most remote areas of Britain. As populations rose and became more concentrated in towns, the old system no longer worked. The alkali, which had got the grease out of our ancestor's clothes, had come largely from woodash. More mouths to feed meant more pressure to use land for food rather than woodland. More people meant more need for cooking fires, and consequently the price of firewood rose and rose. Soon it became cheaper to burn coal. London had to make the move in the late 17th century, and the rest of Britain began to follow. Canals and new pumping engines in the mines made coal cheaper still, and British homes turned more and more to the black stuff.

OPPOSITE *'Dollying' the washing: bashing it around in the water with a wooden dolly – seriously hard work.*

Wood ash is great at dissolving grease, but coal ash isn't. Those families who were now burning coal no longer had a free de-greasing agent. They had to buy soap. But soap needs hot water to work properly whereas the old wood ash alkali

Mixing up the starch.

had worked perfectly well in cold. So now families had to heat the water for the wash at home, incidentally burning more coal to do so. Cauldrons, pots and coppers long used for cooking and brewing were now pressed into service to heat water for the laundry as well. Meanwhile, the soap manufacturers expanded their businesses and became wealthy.

Probably many women were glad to be working with hot water rather than standing in freezing streams in the dead of winter, but there is no doubt that the new system brought its own hardships. Where once the flow of the stream had brought all the water you could need, now women had to carry every drop. First they had to collect the water from the stream or pump, then move it onto the fire, shift it from one tub to another several times over, and then get rid of it. No wonder that things were often not as well-rinsed as they could be. No wonder the washing often went yellow and stiff from soap residue left behind. The chemical industry rushed to the rescue with a plethora of chemicals to solve the problems. Water softeners, bleaches and optical brighteners (blue dye) were all now available and heavily advertised. And thus the modern laundry industry was born.

What Can the Victorians Do For Us?

While no one wishes to return to the drudgery that was the Victorian laundry in the modern world, there are a number of very good ideas that could be very useful

Using Victorian flat irons, heated up on the range, proved to be much easier than I had expected.

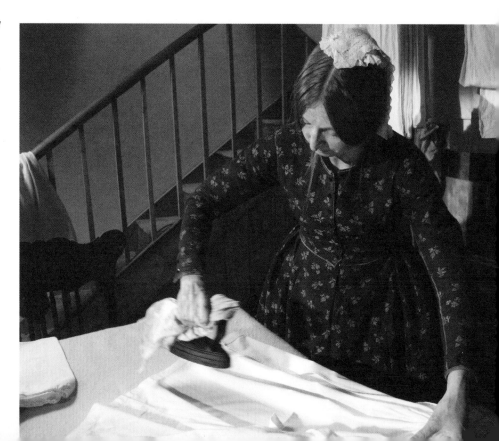

in an environmentally conscious world. The Victorian housewife and professional laundress alike were very frugal in their use of chemicals. Driven by a desire for economy they used the smallest possible amount that they could get away with.

Most of us today use far more washing powder/liquid than the manufacturers recommend, chucking in a big scoopful regardless of the size of the load or how dirty the clothes are. The recommended amounts do err on the side of generosity – the manufacturers like their profits as much as anyone. Just regularly using less will have a great impact on your pocket as well as the environment. A little soap really does go a very, very long way.

Soap, remember, is just for dissolving grease; the actual cleaning is done by your washing machine bashing the clothes around in water. It's the water being forced through the fibre that knocks the dirt out. In fact, you may want to be brave like me. When I am not living on a Victorian farm, I put no powder or liquid in my wash at all. You will be amazed at how clean everything comes out. I admit that when I first did it, I expected to have to give things a blitz now and again. Well, three and a half years on, it's all still coming out clean.

If you do cut down on your detergent use you may also come across a rather handy side effect. Softer clothes. The scratchy, stiff feeling that is described on advertisements is the result of both a reaction between soap and hard water, and from a build up of soap residues in the fibres of your washing. If you use too much powder or liquid, the rinse cycle of your machine can't get rid of it all so it sits there clogging up the fabric, irritating your skin. If you don't use any soap, there cannot be a reaction between the soap and the hard water. A couple of soap-free washes and everything begins to soften, which is great for those with sensitive skin, saves you money, and once again the environment benefits.

The Victorian laundress was also keen to use only what she needed for stain removal. The idea of adding a stain-removal product to the whole of the wash would have horrified her. You don't really need to add loads of stain remover, and the environment certainly doesn't want any extra chemicals sloshing about.

A Victorian housewife liked to be in control of everything used in her home. So, while manufacturers of patent brands were going all out to convince her that they knew best, more confident housewives still liked to have the raw ingredients of cleaning products at home. Mixing your own gives you control. You get to choose what you are happy to have around you and your family. Everyone is different, and no mass-produced product is ever going to be able to take account of everyone's allergies, intolerances or preferred smells.

KEEP IT CLEAN

A basic Victorian laundry and cleaning kit would include:

Lemon juice
Vinegar
Bicarbonate of soda
Plain soap
Borax
Washing soda
Alcohol
Ammonia for really stubborn stains

You can clean pretty much anything with the above.
Inexpensive too!

THE LAUNDRY TIMETABLE

SATURDAY EVENING

• Sort your laundry into cottons, woollens, 'coloureds' and whites. Make a special pile of the very nastiest things (Peter's shirt).
• Now check that nothing needs repairing, especially if you are about to scrub it.
• Treat all stains. Use a little milk for ink, butter for fruit stains, lemon juice for mildew, and so forth.
• Next, put everything in to soak. The delicates into cold water, the cleaner cottons into hot water, and the greasiest cottons into hot water with a dash of washing soda.

MONDAY MORNING

• 4.00 a.m. – Fill the coppers with clean water, and light their fires.
• Wipe down the dolly, washing sticks, draining slats and boards and the washing dolly.

Hot, wet and steamy work. Doing the laundry took up about one-fifth of a woman's entire working life.

• Put all the clothes that have been soaking through the wringer and lay them to one side. Empty out the dirty soaking water from all your tubs and pour away outside in your drain or soakaway and refill one of your tubs with clean cold water.
• Grate some soap into hot water.
• Ladle out the hot water into your washtub and put in the first batch of the cleanest clothes. Stir in the soap.
• Refill the copper. At this point you may need to nip out to feed the animals and the men.
• Dolly the first batch for at least 20 minutes. Wring it out and put it into the tub of clean cold water.
• Put the next batch into your hot water and dolly for 30 minutes.
• 9.00 a.m. – Perhaps you could now treat yourself to a cup of tea while you take your woollens and gently hand-wash them, squeezing rather than scrubbing them, in some warm soapy water.
• Swish your first batch around in its rinsing water, wring out and set aside. The second batch is now wrung and dropped in the same rinsing water and the washtub is emptied out and refilled from the copper. You are now ready to put the third batch through.
• Ladle more hot water into your washtub and stir in some soap. Refill your copper. Refill your rinsing tub.
• Dolly the third batch for at least 20 minutes. Wring and drop it in the rinse.
• Dolly the fourth and final – the dirtiest load – for 45–60 minutes.
• Rinse and wring the third batch and drop the very first batch into your copper to boil vigorously for 30 minutes.
• Rinse and wring the fourth batch.
• 12 noon – grab a bite to eat and make sure the men have got something to eat out in the field.

The mangle (or wringer) was a great help, although I had to watch my fingers.

• Boil in turn each batch, wringing out before dropping into the rinsing tub.
• Meanwhile rinse and wring all the woollen items.
• Refill the copper.
• Empty out the washtub and refill with clean water.
• Wring out each batch from its first rinse and drop into the second rinse.
• Empty out the first rinsing tub and refill it.
• Wring everything out from the second rinse and empty out the tub.
• A good housewife would now do a third rinse.
• Ladle the last batch of hot water into your washtub and stir in your laundry blue, taking care that it mixes well to avoid streaks. Put all your whites into the blue and stir around for 10 minutes.
• Wring everything out one last time.
• Hang washing out to dry.
• Scrub out the copper, the tubs and all other equipment, and mop the floor.
• It is now time to cook the tea and see to the animals. Happy washday.

TUESDAY

Make up a batch of starch. Dip all clothes to be starched into the gloop, wring and hang to dry.

WEDNESDAY

• If clothes are dry or at least slightly damp, heat up the irons on the range.
• Put a blanket over the kitchen table and iron everything.
• Air anything that is a little damp and put the clothes away.

My large copper takes six buckets to fill, the small one four, and the tubs use about six buckets for every rinse. By my calculations that means that each washday, with four main loads plus one for the woollens, socks etc., I need to shift 58 buckets of water. Mrs Beeton, in her instructions to the laundry maid, recommends rubbing the clothes by hand rather than dollying – slower, but better for delicate fabrics.

Grow Your Own

Manure for the Kitchen Garden

As Mr Beeton says in *Beeton's Shilling Gardener:* 'Everything that has ever been endowed with life, and all the excreta proceeding from them, are available for manure.' Garden waste, kitchen waste, cow dung, horse dung, peat, rotted turf and rotten seaweed, were all regularly used to fertilize the garden, if you could get them. Many people supplemented this, more conventional list, with sewage, nightsoil, bullock's blood, and offal from slaughterhouses, sugar bakers' scum, ground bone, hoof and horn. Any and every

Peter transporting water to the walled garden using a typically Victorian piece of equipment.

organic waste, can be pressed into service, and regularly was. Cloth, paper and cardboard, when no other further use could be found for it, also went into fertilizer. If you had the money, you could buy many of these substances pre-prepared and delivered to your door. The gardening magazines of the day carry many advertisements for such products. However, the poor tenant farmer used whatever was to hand. Since the farmland was competing for manure with the garden, it was often the household waste that fertilized the garden as the dunghill was earmarked for the fields.

Guano was the wonder-fertilizer of the day (see also page 22). But guano cost money. A prosperous farmer might think it worth his while to invest in some, but, again, the fields would get priority. There was, however, a good substitute near at hand. Guano is bird manure that has not had the nitrogen washed away by the rain. The manure from inside the hen house is much the same. A really good clean-out of the hen house twice a year yields several bucketfuls of the stuff. Obviously, not enough to make much difference on the fields, but plenty for the garden.

Our hens doing their bit for enriching the soil.

Ducks were kept in the walled garden to keep the slugs at bay.

As well as these organic fertilizers, there were also a range of mineral and chemical options. Industrial by-products such as ash, charcoal, burned clay, gas waste, lime, chalk, gypsum, copralites, marl, magnesia and ammonia were all pressed into service. Super-phosphates were on the market by 1843. All could be bought from the garden suppliers if you wished.

The Family Save All recommends soot from the chimney as a rich manure and up until the Second World War, the carts and lorries taking vegetables down to Covent Garden Market would bring back the capital's chimney soot for the fields.

Coffee grounds also receive a mention as good manure, especially for beans. The fields around Banbury still turn black in the late winter when spent grounds from the local instant coffee factory are spread upon them.

Separating out the household waste for fertilizing the garden would have been one of the day-to-day routine jobs of a farmer's wife – just like sorting the recycling today. Coal ash to go on the paths to firm them and to suppress weeds, and any food waste not destined for pigs or chickens went on the compost heap, along with any old rag no longer any use even as dish rags. All the sweepings from the floors, with and without the tealeaves used to keep the dust down, also joined the compost. Urine from the chamber pots added ammonia to the fertile mix.

PESTS

In Victorian times, slugs were (and still are) the bane of any gardener's life.

Victorian pesticides can be terrifying; just about every poisonous substance you can think of was used in a garden somewhere. The most popular poisons for garden use included arsenic for flies and rats, flowers of sulphur, 'amoniacal liquor from gas works', paraffin oil, copper sulphate, sulphuric acid, nicotine and turpentine. Homemade decoctions from poisonous plants were also popular. Black Hellebore and Foxgloves get mentioned the most often.

Unsurprisingly, most of the concoctions on this list are now banned from garden use. In creating a Victorian garden we have had to forgo most of their armoury against garden pests.

Luckily for us in our garden, many of the more dangerous options were also the more expensive options that were only ever employed in the gardens of the wealthy. It was the professional gardeners working in the walled kitchen gardens or the ornamental flower gardens of the upper classes who were most likely to suffer the health risks of frequent exposure to such poisons. The publications aimed at people like us usually recommend much cheaper homemade solutions. A few of these things still raise concerns, but that still leaves us with a reasonable set of alternatives.

OVERLEAF *Once the plants were established Ruth would often visit the walled garden to collect food for our supper. The broad beans were particularly successful.*

PESTS IN THE KITCHEN GARDEN

SLUGS *Having lost several entire crops to slugs in the past, I am very keen to use any and every method to keep their numbers down. Mr Beeton recommends fresh powdered lime. The lime needs to be sprinkled onto the soil around the tender plants every evening or, better still, '… if the ground be strewed in the evening with fresh cabbage leaves, the slugs will hide under these, and may be destroyed in the morning'.*

We have plenty of lime left over from building the pigsties, so this seems a good and economical method for us. The addition of lime to the soil has the added benefit of acting as a fertilizer.

'Gardening Illustrated' magazine recommends an even more environmentally friendly alternative. Small heaps of bran are laid around the garden in the evening. Slugs are especially fond of it, so, in the morning, each heap will be covered in slugs. A dustpan and brush is then used to sweep up both bran and slugs, which are dumped unceremoniously into a bucket of salty water. Once the slugs are dead the whole mess goes on the compost heap.

GOOSEBERRY SAWFLY *This is another pest that I have had trouble with in the past. A whole bush can be reduced to bare twigs in a couple of days. As gooseberries were such an important fruit to common working Victorian people, it is good to know that there were a number of cheap remedies.*

The 'Family Save All' suggests making a decoction of elder leaves and mixing it with household soap. First you gather a good big bunch of elder leaves, put them in a bucket and pour boiling water over them. Leave to cool overnight and then strain off the liquid. Scrape in some common laundry soap and warm up the mixture, stirring gently. Now splosh it all over your gooseberry bushes.

CARROT ROOT FLY – *Carrots form one of the winter staples in our garden, so protecting them is important. Almost every gardening book, manual and magazine mentions soot as being particularly effective. Since the various flues of the range need to be cleaned out about once a month, we have a good supply of free soot. The soot is simply spread on the soil around the carrots as they grow. Like the lime, soot acts as a fertilizer as well as deterring a whole host of pests.*

BEEKEEPING

There are few cottage industries that capture the imagination quite like beekeeping. The leisurely observance of the hive, the fascination of the bees at work, and the bountiful harvest of nature's sweetest gift, make this pastime one of the most idyllic of the rural world and one I was keen to engage with during my stay on the Victorian Farm.

From the most ancient of times through to the present day, man has developed a special relationship with the bee in order to procure one of the most sought-after delicacies of the natural world: honey. Fifteen-thousand year-old cave paintings from Valencia, Spain, depict a human figure raiding a wild beehive although by the 1st millennium BC, it is known from both archaeological evidence and iconographical depictions that mankind had mastered bee husbandry and could produce honey on quite an industrial scale.

ORIGINS OF THE VICTORIAN COTTAGE HIVE

Throughout the classical, medieval and early modern periods, beekeeping remains an integral part of man's domestication of the natural world, with honey featuring prominently in early recipe books. However, the exact process by which bees reproduced, swarmed, and built their comb remained something of a mystery to past apiarists and was, as such, shrouded in folklore and myth.

It wasn't until the late 18th century that beekeepers developed an interest in the science of beekeeping and they set about studying bees in a rigorous and methodical fashion. This led, in the 19th century, to some ground-breaking innovations that were to turn beekeeping on its head and completely revolutionize the maintenance of the colony and the extraction of honey.

In Britain it was the tradition to keep your bees in a 'skep' – a straw basket turned upside down and placed on a solid surface. A small gap would be made at the junction between basket and surface, and the bees would be free to build their comb in the skep. Skeps were lightweight, durable and extremely good – when properly sited – at protecting the colony from even the harshest British weather.

There were, however, problems with skeps that today's beekeepers would take issue with. Firstly, you can't get to the bees to inspect them, to understand them,

The swarm was successfully transferred from an apple tree to a skep.

and to check for diseases. Secondly, and perhaps more importantly, it was very difficult not to destroy the brood of the colony when extracting the honey.

Two innovations during the 19th century stand out as taking beekeeping into the modern age. Firstly, the understanding of the 'bee space', the gap between the combs of wax and honey – a distance of approximately 8 mm by today's measurements – led to the invention of removable frames. Secondly, beekeepers realized that if they could exclude the queen from a part of the hive, they could prevent her from laying eggs in the cells of the comb. The workers would continue to fill each cell with honey and would seal it with wax, but as a consequence of the queen's exclusion, certain cells would be free from larvae. The modern beehive was born, and very quickly the familiar box hive of today, with removable frames and queen excluder, was to become adopted throughout the western world.

Now, beekeepers could get up close to the bees and keep an extremely close eye on them. They could – providing they wore the right protective equipment – inspect the hive at regular intervals and, as a consequence, knowledge in how the bees operate within the hive massively increased. Action could be taken to lessen the impact of disease. Swarming – a practice that was actively encouraged in traditional skep apiculture – could be avoided or at the very least controlled.

Finally, the destruction of the brood to harvest the honey became unnecessary. A 'brood chamber' could house both the brood and the honey destined to sustain it over the winter months, while a 'super' box could be superimposed over the brood chamber. A queen excluder between the two would ensure that the honey in the latter would remain clean of eggs, larvae and pupae. The beekeeper could remove the frames from the super and extract the honey from these without affecting the wellbeing of the colony at large. Once the honey had been extracted

Brian Goodwin, local beekeeping expert, prepares to capture the swarm.

Brian and I look on as the bees steadily make their way up the sheet-covered ramp into the Victorian cottage hive.

from the frames, they could be returned with much of the comb still intact, saving the bees from the time and labour-consuming job of comb building at the beginning of the next season, allowing them to go straight into honey production.

SETTING UP A COTTAGE HIVE

Realizing that no self-respecting Victorian farmer would be without a vat of self-harvested honey, I set about finding myself a traditional Victorian cottage hive and kept an eager eye out for any swarming activity.

I found a hive in a near derelict state in one of the orchards. After cleaning out a mouse nest, tacking back together some of the boxes, and purchasing some new frames, my hive was ready to go. Location of the hive, however, was an extremely important factor to consider and I roved the estate looking for a secluded spot, free from overhanging leafage and away from any potential predators. In fact, the place where the bees chose to swarm proved ideal

ALEX'S DIARY

Beekeeping

Ouch! My first bee sting! When entering the hive, it is always a toss-up between wearing protective gloves, being that little bit clumsier and upsetting the bees, or going in with naked hands and being deft of touch. I opted for the latter and was now paying the price.

Fortunately, these bees were incredibly docile and the sting I received was due to my own stupidity – I had pressed my finger into the sting of a bee trapped between the ground and a box of frames I was replacing on the hive.

I had been examining the hive to see how honey production had been going and had fortunately got there just in time. The 'super' that I had placed on top of the brood box was nearly full of honey and in some places the bees were beginning to seal the cells with wax. With restrictions on space, there was a danger the colony would swarm. This would drastically decrease the numbers of bees in the hive and affect honey production.

I had been somewhat caught by surprise so I had to act quickly. My first job was to get in to the brood box and check for queen cells.

When they are short on space, bees will develop a queen cell with a view to swarming and finding somewhere else other than my hive for storing honey. It was a slow process, steadily lifting each frame up and inspecting both sides, but it was worthwhile as I located and destroyed three queen cells.

The second thing to do was to find another super box and frames and place it on top of the nearly full super as soon as possible. I raced back to the farmyard where I knew I had a few bits and pieces, and managed to cobble together a box and some frames. Speedily, I rushed back to the hive and added the new frames. Hopefully, this would keep them busy for another fortnight or so while I sought out yet more frames.

The good news in all of this is that my bees are doing incredibly well. The location in the walled garden was ideal, not just in that it protected the hive from severe weather and predators, but clearly there was an ample supply of flowers for the bees to work.

It wasn't long before I was extracting honey, and if I had one message to pass on, it is: 'Get bees'. The honey, freshly delivered from the frames by virtue of our Victorian honey extractor, was absolutely divine.

for the locating of their hive: the estate's walled garden. Having had virtually everyone in the parish on swarm-watch, word came from the walled garden that one had been seen hanging from the bough of an apple tree.

I called in the services of Brian Goodwyn, local bee expert, and he masterfully encouraged the swarm into a skep, set up a ramp, and persuaded the bees to take to my ramshackle cottage hive. He gave me a thorough lesson on how to check the hive, what to look out for in terms of disease and distress, and left me feeling confident that little could go wrong providing I was vigilant and always on hand to deal with any situations.

I tried to inspect the hive at least once a week – checking for any sign of disease and distress.

HEALTH AND HYGIENE

TRADITIONAL RECIPES

British food is a very cosmopolitan mix, and always has been. Many of the things that we think of as quintessentially British in fact derive from other parts of the world: fish and chips, piccalilli, ketchup and marmalade, for example. Marmalade came to us from Portugal, ketchup and piccalilli from India, while fish fried in batter is from east European Jewish cookery, and chips really are French.

Eliza Acton, in her cookery book, includes recipes as diverse as Syrian pilaw rice, Swiss mayonnaise, Viennese soufflé, Milanese risotto, chutney from Mauritius, American mint julep, Dutch beef, Venetian cakes, Jamaican coconut cheesecake, a bunch of pasta recipes, over a dozen different curry recipes, and more French cooking than you can shake a stick at. Nor is she alone. Other cookery writers include similar ranges in their collections.

I thought it would be good to try out one of the many Victorian pasta dishes that are dotted through the books. The most common by far is a macaroni cheese. The word macaroni stood for all shapes of pasta in Victorian Britain.

Butter from the dairy is plentiful on the farm, and adds flavour to any dish.

Macaroni Cheese

METHOD

INGREDIENTS

6 oz (150 g) dried macaroni

3 oz (75 g) butter

*6 oz (150 g) grated cheese
   (parmesan or cheddar or a mix
   of the two)*

4 tbsp cream

2 oz (50 g) breadcrumbs

SERVES 4

First cook your pasta. Most English cooks soaked it first for an hour before cooking. Eliza Acton, however, recommends plunging it straight into boiling water as they do in Italy. The usual macaroni on sale in British shops was very thick and so required long cooking times – up to three-quarters of an hour to become really soft. However, finer macaroni was available that needed only fifteen minutes boiling.

To make a Victorian dish, boil your pasta for twenty minutes until very tender. Drain the pasta and put a thin layer into a deep-sided dish.

Sprinkle on some of the grated cheese and dot a few small knobs of butter around. Now add another layer of pasta and again sprinkle on cheese and knobs of butter. Continue building up the layers until the dish is full.

Lastly, pour the cream over the pasta and finish off with a layer of breadcrumbs.

Bake in the oven at around 180°C, gas mark 4, for half an hour.

Pound Cake

In the 16th century, all cake was raised with yeast. Consequently, cake resembled sweet fruit bread or brioche and panetone. But, while the French and Italians stuck mostly to these traditional cake types, in Britain we, along with the Germanic nations, began to move over to raising cakes with eggs and leaving out the yeast altogether. By the Victorian period, yeast-raised cakes had become the economical version to be used only when you couldn't afford the eggs and butter. As we have plenty of eggs on the farm (despite the dog's best efforts), I have chosen to cook a pound cake, which is an egg-raised version. This recipe makes a large cake, but you can halve or quarter the ingredients for smaller versions. A pound cake is one of the easiest cakes to bake. In essence, you simply mix together one pound in weight of each of the main ingredients. I made one for Alex's birthday and it went down a treat.

Make sure the oven is pre-heated to the right temperature. The heat of the oven is of great importance, especially for large fruit cakes.

Method

Pre-heat your oven to 180°C or gas mark 4.

Beat the butter and sugar together until soft and fluffy. The more you beat it at this stage, the lighter your cake will be.

Next weigh your eggs. Most modern hen's eggs are around 2 oz (57 g) in weight, so you would need eight for the pound cake. If, however, you were to use lovely rich duck eggs or cute little bantams eggs the number of eggs would be different, so I recommend weighing them.

Stir in the eggs, flour, nutmeg and currants to your beaten butter and sugar. It is best to just gently stir the ingredients at this stage until they are all thoroughly combined.

Grease your tin – a 10-in (25-cm) diameter one would be about right (or two 8-in/20-cm long loaf tins) – and pop the cake mixture in.

Bake your cake in a moderate oven – 180°C or gas mark 4 – for around an hour.

You can test to see if it is done by sticking a knife into the cake. If when you take the knife out some mixture is stuck to it then your cake needs a little longer in the oven. If it comes out clean then the cake is done.

INGREDIENTS

1 lb (400 g) butter

1 lb (400 g) sugar

1 lb (400 g) eggs

1 lb (400 g) flour

1 lb (400 g) currants

Pinch of nutmeg

OVERLEAF *Afternoon tea in the walled garden for Alex's birthday. There was plenty of pound cake left over.*

CHAPTER SIX

MAN VERSUS MACHINE

THE ARRIVAL OF MACHINES

 In rural Victorian Britain power came from a whole range of sources and people were often in more direct contact with the various forms of power generation than we are in the 21st century. On a farm like ours, one of the primary sources of power is the horse. We are responsible for both growing food for our horses and their welfare, and in return they pull our vehicles, such as the dray and the tip cart, and our agricultural implements, such as the spike harrow and the plough. However, it's not just large pieces of equipment that can be driven by a horse; at Acton Scott home farm we have access to a horse gin, which is a device that harnesses the power of the horse and channels it to a number of small machines that would have originally been hand-powered.

A horse gear or gin enables a horse to be used as a stationary power source. Horse gins were used in mining from the 17th century onwards to hoist up coal from ever-increasing depths (as well as to lower men and equipment and operating water pumps); in 1750 an eight-horse gin was recorded hoisting 9 tons of coal an hour from a depth of 200 ft (61 m). In mining, horse gins, which started out as 'cog and rung' wooden geared mechanisms that were stationed over the entrance of the shaft and later became the 'horse driven whim gin' or whimsy that were more powerful and set aside from the shaft opening, were slowly replaced by steam. However, on the more shallow mines the horse gin continued to be used.

In farming, horse gins were initially used to power the first small threshing machines (about the size of a two-seater sofa). But, as the threshing machines grew in size, and became portable, horses were replaced by steam largely due to two main factors: firstly, steam was more relentlessly powerful and, secondly, the jarring motion of the apparatus was detrimental to the animals. However, horse gins used to power previously hand-driven barn machinery, such as chaff cutters, root slicers, and kibblers, were developed by T. W. Wedlake in Essex and marketed

Clumper took to the horse gin like a dream and it wasn't long before I could step back and let him circle on his own.

before 1850. Farms that had horse gins erected buildings to house them that were characteristically circular or pentagonal, but surviving examples are a very rare sight today. Acton Scott home farm has a gin house, but its main horse gin is uncovered outside in the farm courtyard. There is also a horse gin connected to a well to provide water for the walled garden and a portable horse gin that can be connected to the machinery that we have in our farmyard.

The main horse gin in the courtyard of Acton Scott home farm has a large cog, known as a crown wheel, that is turned by either one or two horses. Power from this crown wheel is transmitted via a pinion, gears, and shafting to a large pulley mounted on the floor of the barn. The overhead shaft above the first floor of the barn (where the fodder processing machinery is housed) is belt-driven from this pulley. For each single revolution that the horse(s) completes outside, the overhead shaft in the barn turns 52 times. Belts coming off of this shaft drive the machines. The correct running speed for each machine is achieved by using a suitable combination of pulley diameters. Crossing the belts over (twisting them) results in the machine's pulley turning in the opposite direction to the shaft pulley.

On the first floor of the threshing barn ready to use the grain kibbler.

Having powered by hand chaff cutters, root slicers, and kibblers (machines that were designed by their manufacturers to be interchangeable between hand-cranked and belt-driven) I can reliably inform you that having a horse do the work for you is far easier and labour-saving.

Muscle power of animals and people was one of the primary driving forces of 19th-century Britain, but the Victorians also utilized many other sources of power. For example, the cider mill at Acton Scott used to crush apples before they are pressed is horse-powered; however, larger mills in Victorian Britain would have been driven by wind or water, an energy source that we are looking to today to try and re-harness in the face of climate change.

They developed steam power, which was the forerunner of the internal combustion engine, and they pioneered electricity that is created by moving a copper wire through a magnetic field. One thing that electricity did for us was to remove coal from our homes and centrally locate it in a power plant. The coal is smashed to dust and burned to superheat water and drive turbines that generate electricity which is piped to our homes and used for heating and cooking. However, as we are not physically putting coal on a fire (let alone getting it from a bunker of a limited supply), we are unaware of how much we use and the only way we gauge our electricity consumption, other than vigilant monitoring of the meter, is by the monthly bill or when the fiver you put on the key card runs out.

For me, it is the Victorian period that really highlights both the problems and the solutions that we are faced with in our modern age. As a society they loved their gadgets and their labour-saving devices as, to an extent, we do now, but they were so much closer to the work involved in day-to-day processes such as cooking, cleaning and washing. They were close to the labour involved in growing food and sustaining a community and they were close to their power sources: hand power, horse power, wind power, water power (the saw mill at Powys castle is water-driven), clockwork like the bottle jack oven, candles for light, and wood and coal for heating and cooking. However, they were the society that really accelerated the development of power harnessing and world-wide communication networks.

ALEX'S DIARY

Clumper and the Horse Gin

I was seriously nervous about using Clumper on the horse gin. It wasn't the fact that he'd never worked on a gin before, or that I'd never used a gin before. It was down to the fact that we'd collectively already managed to break two pieces of equipment – the shaft to a roller and the axle on the mobile shepherd's hut – and I didn't want to make any more work for the home farm's cartwright. In fact, in both cases, the items we had broken had given way due to lack of use, wet rot and a degree of wood worm. However, I didn't want to snap one of the oak 'arms' to the horse gin as this would put out of action one of the most important pieces of kit.

Traditionally the gin would have powered – through a series of fly-wheels and belt pulleys – the oat miller, chaff cutter and root slicer located in the gallery of the main barn, and would have been used to process food stuffs for the farm's livestock over winter.

Peter and I were spending a good deal of time hand-cranking our animal feed processing machines – the daily grind! – and we were looking for a way to cut down our work load.

MIGRATION

 It would seem to many Victorians that the countryside was emptying. People were leaving – some to the towns, some to the cities, and some migrated. People were moving about as never before. In Britain, during the 1880s, despite the highest rate of immigration probably since the fall of the Roman Empire, emigration levels from Britain were so high that the total movement in and out resulted in an outflow of over one-and-a-half million people in that decade alone.

People arrived mostly from Russia, Poland, Italy and Germany. From Russia and Poland, it was mostly Jews seeking refuge from pogrom and prejudice. From Italy and Germany, it was largely people in search of work. But these people rarely settled in the countryside. Their arrival fuelled the rag trade, mining and manufacturing industry in general, just as earlier groups had added to those areas of our economy in past centuries.

The Irish navvies who built many of the canals changed rural culture as well as landscapes.

Although not strictly immigrants, since Ireland was part of the UK, the largest influx to England and Wales were the Irish. In the 1850s there were around

half a million Irish settlers, although the inward flow of the Irish tailed off in the latter part of the century. These people did make an appearance in the countryside. Not as agricultural workers but, usually, as navvies, gangs of men constructing canals and railways through the heart of rural communities, leaving behind traces of their music and culture in mainland rural life.

The largest movement of people, however, was that of people leaving. Those who left Britain went mostly to the USA, although Canada and Australia also took hundreds of thousands. Smaller trickles flowed out to the farthest reaches of the British Empire. The Irish and Scottish were more likely to emigrate; poverty at home was most extreme for them. But huge numbers of impoverished English and Welsh people went too. Few went directly from their rural homes, most trying to make a go of things in the towns and cities first. When they could find no niche there, they joined the hopefuls in search of a future elsewhere.

POPULATION GROWTH

For all this great international movement of people, the British population was growing at an unprecedented rate – from 10.6 million in England, Scotland and Wales (5 million in Ireland) in 1801 to 37 million (but down to 4.5 million in Ireland) by 1901. This newly enlarged population lived mostly in the towns and cities. In some areas, the population living in the countryside actually fell.

While the urban arres were bursting at the seams, the rural way of life was fading. Nostalgic, romantic images and ideas of the rural past floated through poetry, novels, music and art. Thomas Hardy's novels, with their beautiful descriptions of rural people and places, are filled with a sense of loss and longing. Folklorists were hurriedly collecting and recording everything they saw as about to be lost forever. Even Gertrude Jeykell's radical reinvention of the English Garden, is a peon to the sort of country gardens that she thought were disappearing fast. Lutyens' architecture did the same for rural buildings.

Packing up and moving on was something many people had to do.

People were leaving. Life in the countryside became harder and harder for many people. As agriculture became more mechanized, with more food being produced by fewer workers, rural labour demands became more seasonal. Much of the work that the machines did was the sort of work that filled in the quiet times of year. Threshing machines, for example, left labourers redundant through the coldest days of winter. The mass manufacture of tools and equipment meant less call for the traditional crafts with which rural people had traditionally supplemented their agricultural work. Cottage industries often crumbled in the face of town-based competition. The countryside was losing its industry. People increasingly had to move in search of work.

In the late 19th century, the railways meant greater movement of resources and people than ever before.

For most people this began with short hops to better-favoured local areas. The market towns had work for slightly adapted craft skills for longer than the villages. Large towns pushed up demand for food and other agricultural goods, which opened up some opportunities. For some people the move to the towns themselves began only as a temporary stopgap – a few months' work over a lean winter. But people slowly drifted away from the rural life. It was the young who moved most, and among the young, mostly the women.

Work opportunities for young women in agriculture declined faster than those for young men. Meanwhile, the demand for country-bred girls to work as domestic servants in the towns was high. In those areas with a strong manufacturing industry there was an opportunity for a level of personal independence for young women. Wage levels and the impersonal and partial supervision in a factory gave some girls something almost approaching the levels of autonomy enjoyed by men – something that society in general found very unsettling.

RURAL LIFE

Over the course of the century, the rural workforce declined from a little over 50 per cent to around 30 per cent. By modern standards there were still an awful lot of people living and working on the land. To Victorians, it was a huge and unprecedented change, one which was to have a vast impact on those left behind.

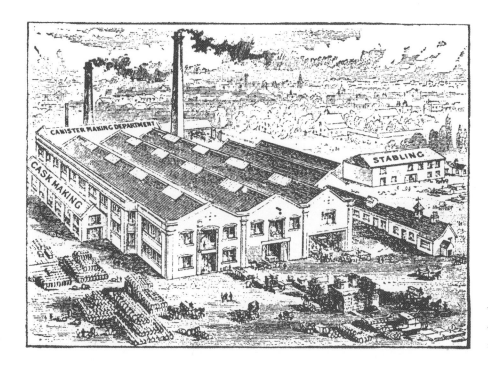

Many people were forced to leave the countryside for work in factories in urban areas.

As *The Condition of England* (1907) by C. F. G. Masterman notes: 'All the boys and girls with energy and enterprise forsake at the commencement of maturity the life of the fields for the life of the town.'

The countryside became a more male-dominated environment. Whilst in the towns and cities there were more women than men, in the villages and hamlets there were more men than women. Villages were becoming places only of agriculture. The large range of shops, workshops and small businesses of the traditional village were beginning their long-term decline. Where, at the beginning of the century, most villages could boast a list of some twenty different occupations, by the end that list had shrunk to half a dozen. The social mix was changing, too. The middle ranks of small farmers and tradespeople were either pushed back down into poverty or they left to try to maintain their position elsewhere. What remained was a much more divided population, with landowners on the one hand and landless labourers on the other.

Educationally, too, there were differences. The drive for universal primary education received more support in the urban environment – while the demand for cheap agricultural child labour remained high in rural areas. Even after the 1870 Education Act came into force, there remained exceptions to its provision for rural children. Actual, if not official, school-leaving age remained lower in the countryside well into the middle of the 20th century. Rural life was no longer the mainstay of British life and culture. The spotlight was moving elsewhere.

SHEEPSHEARING

Calendars and clocks are somewhat redundant when one is so aware of the duration of the daylight, the weather and the changing of the seasons indicated by the surrounding fabric of life such as the wild flowers in the hedgerows and the deciduous trees. Like so many activities on the farm, sheepshearing is weather-dependant so when we had a long sunny spell we decided it was time to shear (the sheep responds to the weather producing more lanolin and creating a break between the old wool and the new which has a distinctive yellow colour). The ever-decreasing monetary value of the fleece aside, one of the main reasons why we shear sheep is to protect against flies, such as the blow fly, laying their eggs in the sheep's wool. This can result in the serious condition of flystrike, a problem that is exacerbated in Acton Scott by the volume of foliage, so shearing early is advisable (one of our ewes had a few maggots under her fleece but we caught it just in time). Furthermore, around this time of year (June), you need to be more vigilant with the sheep as they will often try to scratch their fleeces, and if they get on their back, they struggle to get up again and are crushed under their own weight.

Single-piece blade shears, which are still in use today.

On a lighter note, we contacted Richard Spencer, who had leant us the 'Shropshires', and he said he would bring Keith Sessions and his son William who shear all of Richard's sheep. However, as the time to shear approached we had a spell of bad weather so Alex and I moved the ewes and their lambs (with the aid of a bucket of food) from Ovenall field, where we had put them after lambing, back to the lambing shed in the lower Glebe Meadow. Sheep need to be dry and clean before being sheared, so we kept them out of the rain and refrained from putting down new bedding that would get caught up in their fleeces. We also swept our shearing area, which was also undercover, and put down a couple of shearing boards.

Originally sheepshearing was undertaken using a large pair of wide-bladed scissors that evolved into blade shears in the late 18th and early 19th centuries. Throughout the Victorian period it was likely that farmers would have used blade shears (which are still used today – especially for shearing prize rams), however, at the end of the Victorian period, mechanized hand sets were being developed. We used the blade shears to 'de-dag' the sheep, which is a southern hemisphere term meaning to remove the wool from the rear end that has become encrusted with droppings. However, to shear the main body of the sheep we decided to use the machines.

We found a number of shearing machines on the home farm, but the one we ended up using was a hand-cranked Wolseley. This had a large cog that had a handle attached to it and a small cog that drove the hand set (a bit like a penny farthing) with a chain running around the two. For every one turn of the large cog the small cog would turn 22 times. Wolseley started developing shearing machines in 1868 when he moved to Australia, and when he moved back to the UK he started the Wolseley Sheep Shearing Machine Co. Ltd., in Birmingham in 1888 (he was later joined by Austin,, and the company branched out into cars). Much of the developments in sheepshearing come from Australia, New Zealand and America where numbers of sheep demanded new and quicker ways of shearing. Many of the hand sets in Australia were driven from a set-up similar to the gearing attached to our horse gin.

We had read about the sheepshearing machines in *The Book of the Farm* but it did not go into detail, it just acknowledged their development, so we were not sure what to expect, but it didn't take long to find out. The Wolseley hand-cranked machine is truly a full body workout due to the sheer circumference of the large

Keith shows Alex how it's done as I provide the power.

cog. When I first started using it I hit the ground running and then began to regret my enthusiasm as the task wore on because I had to maintain my pace until Keith had finished shearing the ewe. Throughout the process there is one very short respite and that is when the shearer has finished the first half of the ewe and has to reposition to do the second half. Traditionally the hand-cranking would have been undertaken in relay by boys and a clip round the earhole would be dished out if you slowed. I swapped with Keith's ten-year-old son William.

The Wolseley hand piece of 1895 and the early Lister hand sets that we found are virtually indistinguishable from the 'modern' hand sets that are used today. However, the modern hand sets do have a wider blade that requires more power, so Mr Acton and his friend Mr Greenwood adapted a bicycle to power the shearing head. We felt this really embodied Victorian engineering and ingenuity and it was certainly a lot easier than the hand crank. It is thought that you have to cycle 5–6 miles (8–9.5 km) to shear a sheep although, while Alex was being given instruction, it was a long old bike ride with quite monotonous scenery. One observation that I found quite apt was that a sheared sheep looks like a peeled orange.

When we had finished shearing, Richard showed Alex how to roll a fleece by folding in the sides and rolling towards the neck end which is then twisted and used to tie up the rolled fleece. We then put our fleeces into a traditional wool sack, which is what the speaker of the House of Lords sits on (it was introduced in the 14th century and represented the nation's prosperity as wool was a prized commodity – it is now stuffed with wool from the whole commonwealth to signify unity), and from there it can be sold. We rounded off the day with some fantastic nettle beer made by Richard's mum.

Richard rolls a fleece ready for the wool sack.

Ten freshly sheared sheep. What a difference a haircut makes.

OPPOSITE *Alex turns his hand to shearing as Keith looks on and I try out bicycle power – a lot easier!*

PLOUGHING DEVELOPMENTS

I've heard it said that farming is the oldest industry in the world and, therefore, ploughing is one of the oldest processes in the world. Through archaeological and documentary evidence, such as cave paintings, hieroglyphics and pot designs, one can map the development of the plough from a basic stick used to part the soil to the monstrous implements that are suspended behind modern tractors. However, the purpose of the plough is little changed. It is still designed to aggravate the soil and create a protective and nourishing tilth in which seeds can germinate effectively, and ploughs still have coulters (the thin blade that initially cuts the soil), shares (the wedge-shaped blade that divides the soil), and mouldboards (the shaped board that continues from the share and inverts the soil, also known as the breast).

A plough pulled by three horses, doing the same job as a modern-day tractor.

Although the key characteristics of the plough remain, much in our understanding of the dynamics of the plough – the soil conditions needed for the seeds, the materials used for their manufacture, and the ways in which we pull our ploughs – has evolved. Cattle or oxen were a popular choice of draft beast and are depicted in Egyptian paintings and models, as well as in British art. In these pictorial representations there is often one figure steering the plough while another is seen forcefully persuading the beasts on (a necessary evil with oxen).

Diagram of the soil being turned over by the plough.

Many of the advances in the intricacies of plough design took place in the 18th and 19th centuries, which is when horses began to be more widely used as the draught beast for ploughing. The first iron plough to have major commercial success was the Rotherham Swing Plough, which was patented in 1730 by Joseph Foljambe and his business partner, Disney Stanyforth. It was named after the town in which it originated and was known as the swing plough because it didn't have a depth wheel. The Rotherham plough was developed by James Small from Scotland who came up with mathematical models for the most efficient curves and angles for the plough share and the mouldboard. It has to be one of the first ploughs to be produced on a large scale in a factory and was light enough to be pulled by a pair of horses.

RANSOME'S PLOUGHS

Ransome was a firm from Ipswich famous for leading the world in the design of ploughs and other agricultural equipment. What gave them something of an edge over other manufacturers of the time was their patenting in 1785 of the 'chilling process that enabled shears to sharpen themselves as they are worked through the soil'. In principle, part of the plough share would be made of chilled steel – much harder than the rest of the share – so that as it was drawn through the ground, one side of the share would wear down quicker than the other causing the edge to sharpen and making the whole business of digging into the soil that much easier.

By 1808, again leading the way in plough design, they patented interchangeable plough parts enabling them to sell not only complete ploughs but also replacement parts should any parts break or wear down. In 1843, they launched probably one of their most famous ploughs: the Ransome's Y-L (virtually identical to the 'Newcastle', below) and so effective and popular was this type that it was in production for over a century.

Some of the features of the plough are to a certain extent timeless. The beams traditionally were made of wood and were so in some counties well into the 19th century. The 'coulter' – from the French *couteau* meaning knife – served the purpose of cutting the turf. The term 'share' to describe the triangular-shaped blade that buries into the ground and parts the earth comes from the Old English word which has a common origin with the old word for a county, a 'shire' or a division of a kingdom. The share on the plough essentially divides or shares out the earth as it moves through ground. The mouldboard, which springs from the share, carries the freshly cut turf and turns it over so that the underside of the turf is exposed to the elements and the growing plants on the surface are buried and rot down.

Along with the chilled steel share, the Ransome's Y-L has some newer features and, in particular, the land and furrow wheels were two additions that made ploughing for the amateur that much easier – certainly for me anyway! Essentially, the furrow wheel would sit in the furrow bottom against the wall of the freshly cut land and the land wheel on the land both guiding the cut of the plough. Both wheels were adjustable, and through judicial movement of the wheels to either the left or right, or even up and down, one could determine the depth and width of the furrow.

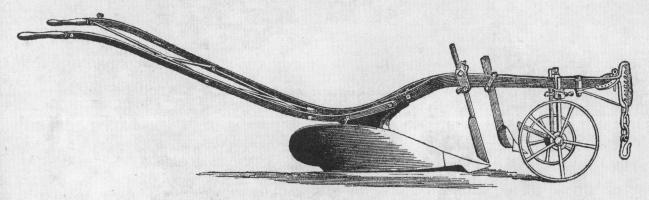

Ransome's 'Newcastle' plough.

Norfolk-born Robert Ransome is the most famous name in the world of plough mass production (see opposite). He patented a way to temper cast-iron shares with salt water in 1785 and a way to harden cast iron in 1803 to create a self-sharpening ploughshare. He was able to mass produce each part of the plough, which he named to avoid confusion when customers needed to order a replacement part, and he also standardized all the parts in 1808 so that they were interchangeable on different types of plough. Soil type and conditions will determine how much power is required to pull a plough, crop type will determine what sort of plough will be needed, and landscape will determine how one ploughs – so they varied from region to region.

Working the steam engine as it pulls the plough across the field.

Ploughing with horses took off with these plough developments, and this practice was in use well into the 20th century before finally giving way to tractors.

Steam Ploughing

In the Victorian period a form of ploughing took off that had not been seen before and was to be seldom seen again: steam ploughing. There were many innovators of the mid-19th century, but the most notable was John Fowler who strove to reduce the cost of food production having witnessed the horrors of the Irish potato famine. In 1858 he won the Royal Agricultural Society of England's prize for 'the steam cultivator which shall in the most efficient manner turn over the soil and be an economical substitute for the plough or spade' (a competition that was launched in 1854). Some steam ploughs, like one featured in Howard of Bedford's

1861 catalogue, worked using pulley systems where the steam engine was stationary in a corner of the field and a system of cables and pulleys moved the plough back and forth across the field. Fowler's steam plough employed a portable engine on one side of the field, which was made by Ransome, and encompassed a new twin drum windlass under the smoke box, made by Robert Stephenson. On the other side of the field was the anchor carriage designed by Jeremiah Head of Ransomes and made by Stephenson. The engine and anchor carriage would pull the plough back and forth as well as winding themselves along the headland.

The major advantages of steam ploughing were that it could be done in all weathers and it could tackle heavier and deeper work. However, the cost was enormous and it required large, open and relatively flat spaces to plough successfully (this is back when fields were smaller and divided by hedgerows because mechanized farming was still in its comparative infancy). Therefore, it is unsurprising that it didn't replace the conventional plough. In addition, farming suffered a depression around the 1870s, which meant that costly equipment was not used.

Despite all these innovations and improvements the actual purpose of ploughing has not changed. The ploughing process essentially creates the ideal conditions for bacterial activity. As a plough turns the soil over, the vegetable matter (maybe the remains of a previous crop, or a purposely grown green manure, or just manure) that resides on the top becomes buried and the rate of decay increases releasing nutrients into the soil. The soil that is brought to the surface is then, like a farmer's rosy cheeks, subjected to the elements. The wind, rain, frost, and maybe snow will break the soil down, aerating it and aiding drainage. This has to be one of the most vital processes that human beings undertake – every year for thousands of years they have ploughed the fields to grow food for themselves and for their animals. This is an unbroken link to the past, albeit a process that takes fewer and fewer people with the advent of new technologies.

The Fowler's steam plough was pulled between two steam engines. Here you can see the large windlass cable drum beneath one of the engines.

Having a go at steam ploughing. These ploughs can cut furrows that are half-a-mile long.

OPPOSITE *Cutting our first four furrows with the see-saw plough.*

HAYMAKING

We have many a time observed and contemplated with delight the care, intelligence, and methodical precision exhibited on well-conducted English farms in the harvesting of hay. The practice would seem to be reduced almost to the nicety of a fine art, and it is conducted with the enterprise and forethought happily characteristic of British Agriculture.

HENRY STEPHENS, *The Book of the Farm*, Fourth Edition revised and rewritten by
James Macdonald, 1888

It is difficult to comprehend just how important the hay harvest has been to the people of these isles for more than two thousand years. Cutting, drying and stacking hay for storage during the long winter months has always been fundamental to the overwintering of livestock. Herds of cattle, flocks of sheep and teams of horses and oxen could all be brought into the farmstead and survive off a diet of dried grasses, herbage and plant matter all painstakingly processed during the hot summer months.

Until the mid-19th century, this was a practice conducted entirely by hand and dates back to prehistoric times. The Romans are probably responsible for introducing the scythe – a tool synonymous with haymaking – to Britain, and this marks perhaps the first discernable innovation to a custom that was to remain very much the same for almost two thousand years.

The various parcels of 'medes' attached to grants of land in the Anglo-Saxon period and the detailed inclusion of meadowland in the Domesday record attest to the importance of the hay industry to the early medieval economy. 'Lots' or 'doles' of meadowland, most often the land closest to streams and rivers, would be shared out among the community and might provide a number of 'cuts' throughout the year.

The Hayward – a popular surname today – emerged in the later medieval period and was the individual responsible for the organization of the haymaking team and the successful bringing in of the hay. It is likely that all the available hands in and around the village would be called upon to work in the hay fields by virtue of the fact that it was such an important crop and also because speed was everything in a climate that could so quickly change from blazing sunlight and

perfect conditions to a sudden downpour and potential devastation. Thus, when the conditions were right, and when the majority of the grasses were in flower, the team would take to the meadows and work tirelessly from dawn to dusk. Fast, effective haymaking allows not only more to be cut but, the quicker the hay dries, the higher the sugar content, the better the hay.

It was important to stay on top of all of the processes at any one time − just in case freak weather conditions came about − and to share out the work so that no one process got ahead of another. Thus, each mower or scyther, who would be expected to mow something in the region of between an acre and an acre and a half per day, would set out at staggered intervals, followed by a team of haymakers. The scythers would naturally, through the action of swinging and cutting, lay the grass in 'swathes'. These would be raked out evenly across the field to dry in the sun and, after two to three hours, would be turned over. As the day wore on, the drying hay would be raked up into long narrow lines called 'windrows' which in turn, at dusk, would be forked up into cocks − piles of hay evenly spaced throughout the field.

Even on the hottest days of the year there can be a tendency for a fine dew to be left on the ground come early morning and this is the reason for building the

A 'National' mower from The Country Gentlemen's Catalogue (1894). Machines such as this marked the start of the mechanization of haymaking.

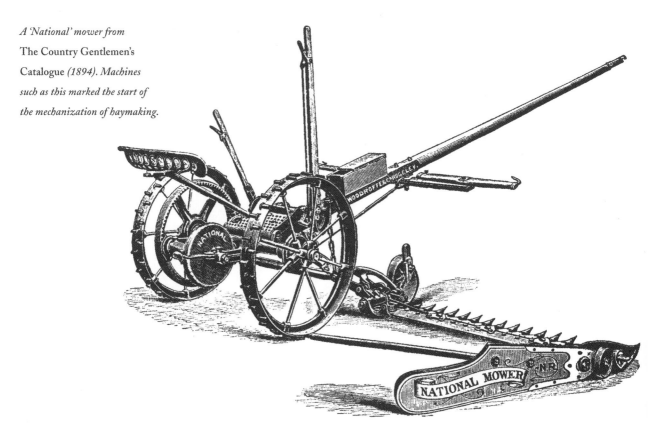

cocks – to prevent the drying hay from ground moisture. However, once the morning sun had burnt off the dew, the cocks could be broken up and raked out for another day's drying. The whole process of raking, turning, windrows and cocks would continue for perhaps two to three days until the hay was ready to be brought in.

A horse-drawn dray or sledge would be drawn up alongside each cock and the hay forked up into vast piles and carted back to the rick yard or hayloft. There is a skill in stacking hay into the vast heaps, witnessed in old photographs, of fully burdened drays and bulging haystacks and, again, the ability to move large amounts in single journeys was another guard against a sudden downpour.

With the hay brought in, the whole village could relax, safe in the knowledge that the hay harvest for another year was over.

With the hay brought in, the whole village could relax, safe in the knowledge that the hay harvest for another year was over and that the animals currently feasting themselves on the summer pastures would not go without fodder throughout the long winter months.

However, by the late 19th century this age-old tradition had gone through something of a revolution. In essence, mechanization had turned what was once a customary practice that had involved the whole community into a commercial enterprise that might involve a mere handful of people.

Mechanized Haymaking

Rural depopulation was undoubtedly a factor in the shift to mechanized haymaking but the rapid growth of horse-drawn traffic in the cities and the subsequent demand for fodder provided the commercial incentive. Hay was becoming big business and hay barges or 'stackies' transported vast quantities of hay via the network of rivers and canals to the various 'haymarkets' that have become a regular feature of so many of our industrial urban centres.

The cost of carrying hay by rail fuelled the innovation of hay pressing and weighing. Hay could be an extremely low-density but high-volume cargo and, to make it most cost-efficient, it needed to be pressed tightly but to an acceptable weight per volume. Initially, hay would be simply pressed in very much the same way a cheese or apple press might work and a 'bale' would be produced. However, standardized weights for each bale meant that very soon hay presses combined the ability to both weigh and bale the hay. Finally, by the end of the Victorian period, stationary steam-powered balers became a feature of the main hay-growing areas around the big cities.

Bamber's hay-press.

PREPARING FOR HARVESTING

 The cereal crop represents the bookends of our year on the farm. We started out by threshing the previous tenant's corn and we are going to end our year by leaving a large stack of corn for the next tenant of the farm. Prior to the 19th century, the harvesting would have been done by hand using sickles and scythes (usually with a cradle as one does not want to dislodge the grain from the ear of the corn), but at the International Exhibition of London in 1851, two American horse-drawn reaping machines were displayed (a M'Cormick's and a Hussey's). These soon developed into reaper binders like the one that we hope to use.

However, before we enter the field to start cutting the corn we have to make sure that all our equipment is up and running. The biggest repair job that I have had to undertake so far is to fix the wheel of the dray (it needed a new tyre as well as some other small repairs). I say 'I' – making, maintaining and repairing cartwheels is a very skilled job that is carried out on the home farm by the appropriately named, Mike Wright. I went to him to see if he could fix our wheel, and also to see if I could help (or at least hang around and look busy).

A cartwheel is made out of three types of wood: elm for the hub because it doesn't split, oak for the spokes because it is strong, and ash for the felloes because it is tough but flexible. The wood is seasoned before it is assembled into a cartwheel and the tyre is used to tie it all tightly together. For every foot in diameter of the wheel, the tyre circumference must be a quarter inch smaller than that of the wheel. Therefore, to put the tyre on one needs to expand it.

The repaired cartwheel fitted onto our dray and ready to bring in the cereal harvest.

We built a fire around our tyre using loosely scrunched paper, kindling and small logs stacked in a wigwam fashion until we could no longer see the tyre. We lit it and let it burn until Mike, judging its expansion by the colour of the metal, said it was ready. I had been told that it would be hot – the heat coming from the fire was intense – so we covered any exposed skin with clothes and doused our heads in water to preserve facial hair. We then knocked the fire out of the way, picked the tyre up with tongs, and placed it on the wheel. It took a little persuasion and the felloes began to flame in places – however, it went on and we evenly doused it with water to cool and shrink our new tyre onto our 'as good as new' dray wheel.

Corn Dollies

Hearing the words 'corn dollies' always made me imagine a quaint rural craft of making a child's doll out of wheat or barley straw. Telling you this lays bare my supreme ignorance of this ancient and vital pan-European ceremonial tradition. Corn dollies are a tangible manifestation of a pre-Christian ritual engrained in the pre-mechanized, pre-fertilized farming practices and beliefs.

The corn dolly can be woven into many regional designs; however, it is always made from the straws of the last sheaf of corn to be cut from a field. There are even accounts of the sheaf being left in the field uncut and woven into a dolly in situ. It was believed that the spirit that resided in the corn needed a vessel to live in and by making a corn dolly (often with a hollow centre) the spirit could live there until it was time to sow the new crop. The corn dolly would then be ploughed into the first furrow thus putting the spirit of the corn back into the soil and subsequently the new crop. This process and tradition is recorded in the poem 'John Barleycorn' by Robert Burns.

There are suggested links between the ceremony of the corn dolly and the legend that has grown up around the account of the wicker man in Julius Caesar's *The Gallic Wars*, although as farming has become mechanized the tradition of the corn dolly has waned. However, as we did not use pesticides on our wheat crop and we sowed Maris Widgeon, the long straw variety of wheat best suited for corn dollies, I decided it would be nice to make one and leave it at Acton Scott to be ploughed back into the first furrow of a new crop.

Ruth plaits some straw (above). Corn dollies are made in a wide variety of shapes and sizes (left).

Reaping and Binding

Without question, the most labour-intensive undertaking of the agricultural year was the cereal harvest. With the wheat tall in the field and the heads beginning to turn a golden yellow under the hot summer sun, it was time for landowner, farmer and labourer alike to take to the fields to begin cutting, bunching, binding and stooking. In the early editions of Henry Stephen's *Book of the Farm*, these operations are drawn out in diagrammatic form to demonstrate how most effectively a team of labourers could work in the field to speedily bring in arguably the most profitable crop of the year.

The process required extremely large teams comprised of men, women and children to work all the hours of the day. The swinging of the scythe, the bending of the back, the incessant monotony of cut, bunch, tie and stook would take its toll on the gang members. Perhaps in no other area of agriculture was innovation more desirable for both landowner and labourer. Yet, such a complex, exact and often delicate process had been, for thousands of years, beyond the reach of inventors.

Although the scythe had, for the most part, replaced the serrated-edged sickle, it was proving unbeatable – certainly in the minds of Britain's farmers – as the primary tool with which cereal crops could be harvested and at the dawn of the Victorian period, it was the tool of choice. However, by the end of the century, and before the First World War, the overwhelming majority of cereal crops in Britain were being cut, bunched and bound by horse-drawn machines leaving only the task of 'stooking' the bound sheaves in the field to the labourer.

The story of the innovation of the horse-drawn 'reaper binder' is a complex one involving reference to numerous inventors, failed prototypes, fantastical ingenuity and fierce transatlantic competition. We begin with the writings of Pliny and Palladius, classical scholars who described an imaginative implement – a cart pushed through the crop with some kind of cutting or tearing gear at the front. Presumably, the bulging seed head, freed from the plant, would drop into the cart.

So, the idea of using a machine to harvest cereals had clearly been about for sometime. It wasn't, however, until the late 18th century that the challenge was taken up by the luminaries of the emerging Agricultural Revolution who were to meet with countless failures before any practical 'working' machine was arrived at. The reports from the agricultural societies of the early 19th century were

Traditional methods for reaping cereal crops were arduous and back-breaking.

By the late 1880s, reaper binders such as this Hornsby binder had taken the place of large groups of agricultural labourers.

not good: machines with scythes attached to wheels spinning wildly devastated the maturing crop and left it trampled by the ensuing horse power. Complex and fragile contraptions would need so much tweaking and repairing that they were beyond practical use while the landscape of Britain, so varied from the 'champion' of East Anglia to the rugged terrain of the Highlands, meant that no machine could curry national favour and the concomitant financial backing.

The Great Exhibition of 1851, an international fair aimed at showcasing the latest in industrial technology and design, was to prove the turning point in the story of mechanized harvesting. Numerous reapers of both British and American design were on hand and served to boost interest nationally. Fresh impetus was given to the challenge, and by 1863 some 45 reaping and mowing machines were exhibited at the Royal Show, Worcester. The tide of opinion had turned.

The final development came in the 1870s when a mechanism for binding the wheat into sheaves was integrated with the reaper and the 'reaper binder' was born. Our 'Albion' reaper binder, made by Harrison, McGregor and Co. in Leigh, Lancashire, represented the pinnacle of the tradition (before the 'combined harvester' was to surpass all before it). The whole process was powered by the horses and this was going to be one of the toughest jobs they were to face throughout the year. We were going to need at least three, maybe four, strong horses if we were to successfully bring in our wheat crop without having to revert to the scythe and some back-breaking labour!

THRESHING

 Threshing was as basic to agriculture as agriculture was to the national economy. Year upon year this activity had been carried out by agricultural labourers throughout the long winter months through the simple technique of 'thrashing' a pile of un-threshed wheat sheaves with flails – two wooden sticks hinged together with iron loops.

The process was long and drawn-out but often provided the only source of employment for village labourers in the cold winter months. The introduction, therefore, of the threshing machine was the cause for much resentment – particularly throughout the major corn-growing areas of eastern and southern England.

When Scottish millwright, Andrew Meikle (1719–1811, from Houston Mill, near Dunbar, East Lothian), unveiled his prototype threshing machine in 1778, it was a failure. The technique employed in this early version relied on rubbing the heads of the sheaves together, but was far from effective. A new method, however, employed a 'thrashing' drum believed to have been copied from a 'scutching' machine used to beat the fibres from flax plants. Powered by a horse and later a steam engine, his rotating drum design gave better results than all other threshing machines. Meikle invented this machine in 1784. He took out a patent in 1788 and probably began manufacture a year later.

Horse-powered machines were to take much of the hard work from the labourers.

The first threshing machines were fixed in barns and crude in their construction. Small, hand-powered threshing machines were developed and, while only slightly more effective than the flail, they were still fairly exhausting and taxing on the operating labourer. Horse-powered machines were to take much of the hard work from the labourers whose job it was to then feed the machines and process the products and by-products.

However, horse power was very swiftly overtaken by steam power as the energy through which a threshing machine might be driven. The jolting motion of the threshing machine was found to be hard on the horse, which would suffer under the duress of a full day's work. By 1867 the advantages of the steam over the horse-powered thresher were so great that the judges at the Royal Show recommended that prizes for horse drawn threshing machines be discontinued.

By the later decades of the 19th century, the threshing machine had evolved into a complicated but highly efficient item of farm equipment, undertaking a number of roles traditionally carried out by hand. Not only would they beat the grain from the husks but, furthermore, they could essentially 'winnow' the wheat – cleaning it of the husk, chaff and straw – and finally depositing it in a sack, ready to be carted off to the granary.

Perhaps one of the most important developments in the history of threshing is the introduction of the portable threshing machine. This meant that instead of the often onerous investment of transporting the harvest from the field to the stack yard, the un-threshed sheaves could be built into a rick in the field. Contract firms would acquire the threshing machinery and hire it out to farms.

There can be no doubt that the invention and modifications of the threshing machine was one of the most important developments in British – and indeed, global – agriculture during the late 19th century, and as such was often the cause of much ill-feeling.

Mechanized threshing – after the initial investment of capital – was quick, easy and highly productive. Hand-threshing with flails was traditionally one of the few jobs that might tide agricultural labourers over during the long, cold winter months – a time in the farmer's calendar that was traditionally quiet. Many farm labourers realized that much of their winter earnings would be taken away by this innovative machinery.

Cooking egg and bacon sandwiches in the firebox, made Tom, the engine driver, an extremely popular man at lunchtime!

ALEX'S DIARY

Threshing: October

First thing in the morning, I had been busy over in the wheat field getting the harrows and rollers in place in anticipation of the seed drill arriving. By about half past nine, though, I heard the whistle for the steam engine go up and that was the signal to say that the engine had built up a head of steam, we were ready to start the threshing machine, and our presence was required in the stack yard.

As part of our tenancy agreement, we were to help with the day's threshing in return for a sack of threshed grain to sow in our own field. It was a real spectacle to see the threshing box come to life as the engine driver put the mechanism into gear. The belt pulley tautened and various wheels, cogs and arms sprang in to action.

It is difficult to describe the clattering, humming and whirring sounds of this intriguing piece of machinery which, coupled with the background sound of the steam engine and its occasional shrill whistle, made for quite an aural feast!

I was to be stationed at the rear end of the threshing box and while Peter pitched the full sheaves of wheat up onto the feeding platform on the very top of the box, it was my job to deal with the threshed straw as it was spat out the back. This was to be baled up later in the month and had, therefore, to be arranged into neat ricks around the stack yard.

The task was onerous and it made for a long day's work. We had a quick break for lunch when we were fed on bacon and egg sandwiches cooked on the cleaned coal shovel in the steam engine's fire box, and after a couple of mugs of warm tea, we were back to work.

Timing was everything with the task I had been assigned and it was imperative to keep on top of things. If I slackened off and spent too long dressing a straw rick to make it neat and safe, a pile of freshly threshed straw would build up beneath the threshing box and risk clogging the machine and setting everyone else back.

Also, it was important not to bend over and attempt to fork a pile of straw from the ground, while at the same time it was being spat out the top of the box.

Peter spent the day pitching the unthreshed sheaves of wheat up onto the feeding platform.

Successively bad harvests in 1828 and 1829, and the general discontent and depression after the boom years of the Napoleonic Wars, led many agricultural labourers to rise up in anger, and the threshing machine came to symbolize the focus of their angst. The Swing Riots of 1830 saw many threshing machines attacked and destroyed. Wheat ricks were burnt, and threatening letters from the mythical 'Captain Swing' were sent out to magistrates, landowners and large tenant farmers

The Swing Riots mirrored the Luddite rebellion of the industrial areas where machine-powered looms were taking much of the work from the traditional hand-loom weavers. Robert Ludd, like Captain Swing, was a fictional character created to ensure anonymity amongst the agents of riotous and rebellious activity.

Certainly, there would be no rick burning and threshing machine smashing during our stay on the Victorian Farm! We were lucky to be given the opportunity to help process the harvest from the previous year. In many cases, farmers who had newly taken up a tenancy – and who might not have any wheat of their own – might be expected to pitch in with the threshing duties in return for either cash or a measure of corn.

This we saw as our duty and we spent a couple of days helping to pitch the sheaves of laden wheat up on to the threshing platform, stacking the off-cast straw in the home farm stack yard, and running the bulging sacks of wheat grain up to the granary. In return for our hard work, we took away with us some grain to sow in our field as a winter wheat crop.

Sacks of wheat grain ready to be taken to the granary.

OVERLEAF *Our Marshall's threshing box under full steam and a long day spent in the stack yard.*

Root Crop Harvest

Roots are an essential part of the Norfolk four-course rotation – their long tap roots draw nutrients up from the subsoil allowing the top soil to rest. Furthermore they are a long-lasting fodder crop allowing live-stock (that previously may have been slaughtered) to be sustained over the winter months. Initially, one of the principal roots to be grown was the turnip. It was popularized, but not necessarily pioneered, by Viscount Charles 'Turnip' Townshend. However, the roots we were using on our farm were mangelwurzels – a fodder crop developed in the late 19th century.

Farming is a continuous cycle that has been going on for thousands of years, so to do an agricultural project for just a year will always be problematic. Our project ran from the start of September to the end of August and mangelwurzels are sown in the spring and harvested in autumn, meaning that while we could sow them, we would not be around to harvest them. In addition, we needed a cache of roots as fodder for our animals over winter. Luckily, the home farm had a large crop of mangelwurzels that they had sown earlier in the year and, in return for harvesting them, we were allowed a large amount to see us through the winter.

F. Walker's drill for sowing root crops such as mangelwurzels. Notice the spacing of the hoppers, which are much wider apart than on a grain sower.

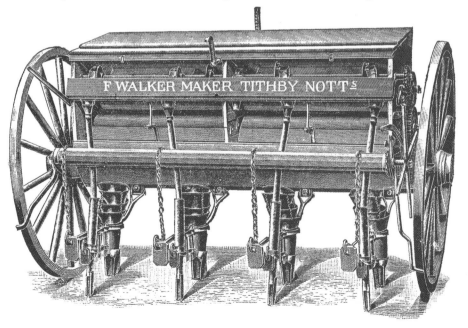

Our riven-oak basket with mangelwurzels and a root knife.

Despite one of the major characteristics of Victorian farming being mechanization, each and every one of those roots, from the smallest (about the size of a radish) to the largest (about the size of my head), had to be harvested by hand. The reason why we had to harvest even the small ones is two-fold. Firstly, waste not want not, and secondly, if they were to be exposed to the frost they will go bad and be harmful if ingested by the cattle (especially if the cows are pregnant as mouldy roots can induce a miscarriage).

To harvest the mangelwurzels we had root-knives that have a handle, a long (about 12–18 in/30–45 cm) flat or slightly convex curved blade, and a spike set at 90 degrees to the blade. The spike is designed to coax the more stubborn roots out of the ground – however, I found that most of them would come simply by pulling them. Once the root is extracted from the ground we knocked and scrapped the earth off with the knife, then we chopped the leaves off close to the top of the root. We piled the harvested roots in a line and covered them with the leaves. The leaves would protect the roots from the damaging frosts and they could be left like this until they were needed.

Alex heading to the root slicer with a barrow of roots.

Shortly after harvest we moved the roots to our farm yard and stacked them into a 'tump' and covered them with straw to act as a frost barrier. We left the leaves in the fields, to be ploughed back into the soil as a green manure putting nitrogen, the essential ingredient for white crops like wheat and barley, back into the earth.

The Victorian
Farm Year

WHAT A GREAT YEAR

ALEX'S YEAR ON THE FARM

 It will be extremely difficult to return to life as normal. Not because I'll miss the glorious Shropshire countryside, a cast of charming animals, or the daily challenge of life on a Victorian farm. But mainly because I want to do it all again … only better!

My mind boggles with all the ways in which I could improve on what we've achieved this year. I'd get my clover crop in the ground much earlier and give it a head start against the weeds. I'd have taken stock-proofing more seriously early in the year and saved ourselves needless hours of chasing sheep up hill and down dale. I'd certainly have been more vigilant of our poultry concern and not given the

During the winter months, the checking and feeding of livestock was a twice daily affair.

local fox so many free meal tickets! Mostly, I feel so much more confident with my horsemanship now, and I dream about how I could improve my ploughing, harrowing, sowing and rolling and improve productivity.

As a complete novice I was so lucky to have been loaned a horse that, in so many ways, was my tutor as well as my work mate. Clumper has become something of a friend and has battled through the year as much as I have. I will really miss him when I have to leave at the end of August.

All in all, though, I am extremely proud of our achievements from our year spent on the Victorian Farm. At times, when nothing seemed to be going our way (the weather was to prove our perennial enemy), we stuck to our tasks and pulled through with success and failure often in equal measure. The experiences I take away with me will stay with me for ever and offer me an invaluable insight into life in rural Britain over 100 years ago.

I sincerely hope our trials and tribulations will be informative and entertaining to readers of this book and viewers of the series. It seems in a day and age when we're faced with increasing food shortages and depleted natural resources, it may be of some value to look back at the past to see what we can learn to better prepare ourselves for an uncertain future.

Peter and I pit our wits against an 1897 chess puzzle, while spending a night in the shepherd's hut.

Clumper, Princess and myself discuss the virtues of the new post-and-rail fence.

PETER'S YEAR ON THE FARM

 This has been a truly amazing year and I count myself very lucky to have been given this opportunity to participate in and undertake the various activities that a Victorian farmer may have come into contact with. For me, the Victorian Farm project (the television series and the book) has been so different to my everyday life that it shall always be remembered. I have renovated a dilapidated cottage, in so doing learning the art of using lime plaster and the savagery of reclaiming bricks. Paul Arrowsmith went on to teach me stonemasonry and the subtleties of lime mortar when we built the pigsties in the worst possible conditions. They shall stand for many years to come (I hope) as a reminder of what we did here.

We constructed a post-and-rail fence (to separate our stack yard from our farmyard), which called upon the services of many different crafts and required us to source, cut down and process an oak tree. We have made cider, a simple process, and beer, a more complex process. We have used our hands to create, and heavy horses to drive the machines that reduced the amount of labour required on a farm, and we have come into contact with some of the infrastructure and machines that really altered the face of the world: the canals, the railways and steam engines used for ploughing and threshing.

Giving Princess her daily scratch as she explores the Glebe farmyard.

Our first newly born lambs on the Victorian Farm.

As Victorians we made merry playing games such as shadow buff at Christmas and dancing around on the sheep-shearing boards during our May Day celebrations. The seasons, weather and daylight have been our guides despite the irony that Victorians standardized time across the country with the railways. We have left a wheat crop for the next tenant farmer to thresh, and a respectable manure pile to use as a fertilizer on the fields generated by our animals.

And it is these animals that I shall miss the most. When you first meet them they are a horse, ten ewes, a ram, a pig, some cows and some poultry. However, after feeding them through winter, mucking them out at least once every day, helping to deliver and care for their young, giving them a good scratch and a run around the yard, seeing some of them die, and sending some of them to slaughter, they become individuals. As I go I say goodbye to Clumper, ten distinctly different ewes, Fred, Princess, Forget-me-Knot and Iris, and Mr and Mrs Turkey and the ducks, especially Punk Duck and Brave Duck.

Finally, I would just like to thank everyone who has aided us throughout our adventure on the Victorian Farm: the contributors who have shared their knowledge and skills, and the people of Acton Scott, Church Stretton, and the surrounding area that have made us so welcome.

Consulting the Family Save All *ginger beer recipe before adding the ingredients into the mix.*

RUTH'S YEAR ON THE FARM

 We are right at the end of our year now and my mind is full of questions as well as memories. Part of me is eager to jump into a couple of research projects that this year has inspired, and part of me wishes that we could carry on and do another year using the skills that we have begun to acquire.

I am, of course, going to miss our animals and the wonderful scenery of this part of Shropshire. But also the smell of a coal fire is something that I have become very fond of, and giving up cart rides will be a wrench. Those motor sport types have no idea of thrills and speed till they try cart rides in a corset. Whew, theme park rides have nothing on it.

If I had to say what has been the best and worst moments of the experience, I would have to single out coal smuts as the worst aspect of Victorian living. It really got me down, the endless black mess. Every day everything was covered in a thin slightly greasy black layer that got everywhere. Exhortations in period household manuals to dust and rub every surface and every piece of furniture daily seemed excessive, even anal, before we began the year. But now I know why they

Forget-me-not, the finest cow in all of Shropshire. I am going to miss her the most of all.

are there. With coal dust in the air, obsessive wiping down of surfaces is the only way to avoid enormous volumes of laundry, and laundry is simply too hard, tiring and time-consuming to do more than you have to. Much better to spend that extra hour or so daily cleaning away coal smuts than doubling the laundry loads.

The best and most enjoyable part of the year has been the creative aspect. Making things. I have really enjoyed learning some things from scratch and having the opportunity to practise and improve my skills in other areas. Cheese, for example. I have made a fair bit of cheese in the past, but never on this scale. Who gets a dairy and 10 gallons of milk a day to play with? It is so rewarding to have the chance to make mistakes and learn from them.

The dressmaking was very interesting; delightfully different to the Tudor work I have done before. I like pattern cutting and the intellectual challenge of sculpting in cloth. The shapes to be achieved and the different ways of solving the same problems were both fascinating. I shall never look at Victorian clothing in the same way.

As for the future, I am keener than ever to explore the links between fuel and food, how the recipes and methods are linked with the type of fuel and equipment used to make them.

I was always ready for a cup of tea – on this occasion it was Alex's birthday.

My daughter Katherine and I having a giggle. We all laughed such a lot during our year on the farm.

OVERLEAF *Harvesting the wheat crop – the culmination of a wonderful year on the Victorian Farm.*

The Year at a Glance

September

Renovating the cottage

Ploughing the field

Sowing winter wheat

Hedgerow fruit harvest

Making pickles and preserves

October

Threshing

Apple harvest

Cider making

Restoration of walled garden begins

November

Putting the ram to the sheep

Building pigsties

Processing winter fodder for livestock begins

Maintenance of heavy horse harness

December

Preparing for Christmas

Overwintering the cattle

Smoking fish and meat

Digging over the beds in the walled garden

January

Sourcing an oak tree

Making a post-and-rail fence

Gamekeeping and rabbiting with ferrets

Coppicing

Hedging

February

Start garden compost

Working the horse engine to process animal feed

Hurdle making

Waterproofing boots

Stock-proofing fields

March

Spreading manure

Spring cleaning

Farrowing the pig

Basket-making

Preparing nesting boxes for poultry

April

Lambing

Sowing herbs and vegetables in the kitchen garden

Fertilize the wheat

Sow the clover crop

Beekeeping begins – setting up the hive

May

May Day celebrations

Calving

Weeding in the walled garden

Started milking and buttermaking

Weaning piglets

JUNE

Making ginger beer

Sheepshearing

Walled garden harvest begins

Soft fruit harvest

Making cheese

JULY

Haymaking

Cricket match

Honey harvest

Repairing cartwheels

Steam ploughing – new machinery

AUGUST

Penning sheep on new pasture

Cereal harvest/Reaping and binding

Root crop harvest

Harvest Festival

FURTHER READING

Crinolines and Crimping Irons: Victorian Clothes and How They Were Cleaned and Cared For by Christina Walkley and Vanda Foster (1978), Peter Owen, ISBN 0720605008

Home Brewed Beers and Stouts 4th Edition by C. J. J. Berry (1970), The Amateur Winemaker, ISBN 900841028

Labouring Life in the Victorian Countryside by P. Horn (1987), Alan Sutton Publishing, ISBN 0862994098

Modern Cookery for Private Families by Eliza Acton (1845), modern edition (1993), Southover Press, ISBN 1870962087

Mrs Beeton's Book of Needlework by Mrs Beeton (1870), originally published by Ward Lock and Tyler; modern facsimile edition (2007), published by Bounty Books, ISBN 0753714671

Patterns of Fashion 2, Englishwomen's Dresses and their Construction c.1860–1940 by Janet Arnold (1972), Macmillan, ISBN 0333136071

Rural Life in Victorian England by G. E. Mingay (1979), Futura Publications, ISBN 0708815545

The Book of Household Management by Mrs Beeton (1861), originally published by S. O. Beeton; modern facsimile edition (1982), published by Chancellor Press, ISBN 0907486185

The Complete Book of Self Sufficiency by J. Seymour (1996), Dorling Kindersley Ltd, ISBN 0751304263

The Farmer Feeds Us All – A Short History of Shropshire Agriculture by P. Stamper (1989), Shropshire Books, ISBN 0903802430

The History of the Farmer's Tools by G. E. Fussell (1981), Orbis Publishing, ISBN 0856133590

The Mid-Victorian Generation 1846–1886 by K. Theodore Hoppen (1998), Clarendon Press, ISBN 019873199X

The Victorian Christmas Book by A. & P. Maill (1988), Treasure Press, ISBN 1850513384

The Victorian Kitchen Garden by J. Davis (1987), BBC Books, ISBN 0563204427

The Village Carpenter by W. Rose (1937), Stobart Davies, ISBN 0854420657

The Working Countryside 1862–1945 by R. Hill and P. Stamper (1993), Swan Hill Press, ISBN 1853103055

Traditional Country Craftsmen by J. Geraint Jenkins (1978), Routledge and Kegan Paul, ISBN 0710087268

Traditional Woodland Crafts: A Practical Guide by R. Tabor (1994), Batsford, ISBN 0713475005

Victorian Farming: A Sourcebook by C. A. Jewell (ed.) (1975), Barry Shurlock & Co Ltd, ISBN 0903330121.
NB This is an abridged version of the *Book of the Farm 3rd Edition* by Henry Stephens. It makes the information in Stephen's three-volume work very accessible.

Victorian Farms by R. Brigden (1986), The Crowood Press, ISBN 0946284660

A Woman's Work is Never Done – A History of Housework in the British Isles 1650–1950 by Caroline Davidson (1982), Chatto and Windus Ltd, ISBN 0701139822

INDEX

ACKNOWLEDGEMENTS

The authors would like to thank the following people:

Mr and Mrs Acton, for being a constant source of invaluable information and encouragement.

The Acton Scott Working Farm staff – in particular Merle, Mike Wright, Alan, Mr Barr, Malcolm, John, Tom – who were always on hand to offer advice and support.

Andy and Hilary who proved great friends throughout the year.

Richard, Rose and Phillip – and Sue – for instilling so much confidence in us for our debutant shepherd roles.

Judith for bravely loaning us her prize Gloucestershire Old Spot sow for the year.

Brian, Sharon, Louisa and Phil for enthusiastically being on hand for all things horse-related.

Paul Arrowsmith – a true craftsman – for tirelessly being there for all our arts and crafts needs and, also, for being a great bloke.

Marian, from the Acton Scott Gardening Club, for her helpful and handy tips in our Victorian cottage garden.

Brian Goodwin for his help and advice with our bees.

Tom and Tom – worthy pigsty builders in the most challenging weather conditions.

The people of Acton Scott and the surrounding area for making us feel so welcome.

Lastly – but far from least – David Upshal would like to thank the BBC. Commissioning Editor, Emma Willis, Head of Independent Commissioning, Richard Klein and Controller of BBC2, Roly Keating, all showed great faith and belief in the project and were instrumental in enabling it to happen.

PICTURE CREDITS

All photographs by Laura Rawlinson except for the following:

Naomi Benson: pages 11, 36, 79, 140–1, 184–5, 200, 211, 212, 214, 215
Stuart Elliott: pages 31, 44, 59, 81, 82, 83, 106, 181, 187, 188, 222, 223 236, 238, 262–3
Tom Pinfold: page 54
Felicia Rubin: pages 232, 234, 260, 261
Chris Vile: pages 225, 266, 269

Acton Archives: page 9 and endpapers
Alamy: page 111
Anova Books: pages 73, 173, 182, 183, 195, 244–5

Christmas Book – all photographs by Laura Rawlinson except for the following:
Page 1 (Introduction) copyright Mary Evans Picture Library.

Illustrations depicting Victorian life, farming methods and equipment are from *The Book of the Farm* and *The Country Gentlemen's Catalogue*.

For further information on the historic country estate of Acton Scott visit www.actonscott.com

OPPOSITE *Lion TV production crew at work.*